Learning a New Language

by María J. Cabrera-Puche, PhD

A Wiley Brand

Learning a New Language For Dummies®

Published by: **John Wiley & Sons, Inc.**, 111 River Street, Hoboken, NJ 07030-5774, www.wiley.com

Copyright © 2025 by John Wiley & Sons, Inc. All rights reserved, including rights for text and data mining and training of artificial technologies or similar technologies.

Media and software compilation copyright © 2025 by John Wiley & Sons, Inc. All rights reserved, including rights for text and data mining and training of artificial technologies or similar technologies.

Published simultaneously in Canada

For general information on our other products and services, please contact our Customer Care Department within the U.S. at 877-762-2974, outside the U.S. at 317-572-3993, or fax 317-572-4002. For technical support, please visit https://hub.wiley.com/community/support/dummies.

Wiley publishes in a variety of print and electronic formats and by print-on-demand. Some material included with standard print versions of this book may not be included in e-books or in print-on-demand. If this book refers to media that is not included in the version you purchased, you may download this material at http://booksupport.wiley.com. For more information about Wiley products, visit www.wiley.com.

Library of Congress Control Number is available from the publisher.

ISBN 978-1-394-24991-6 (pbk); ISBN 978-1-394-24992-3 (ebk); ISBN 978-1-394-24993-0 (ebk)

SKY10095103_010325

Contents at a Glance

Table of Contents

Introduction

Learning new languages has been a top goal for many people (including business leaders) during the last few years. This is especially true now that the world is witnessing and experiencing a growth in globalization and a push for more inclusion and diversity initiatives. Ultimately, it's important to remember that language rights are human rights, so speaking someone's language shows acknowledgment and respect for them and their culture.

In that context, there's a growing need to help people learn languages. This book provides an overview of what language learning entails, the factors that have an effect in the journey, the numerous benefits and advantages of learning a new language, and so much more.

About This Book

In *Learning a New Language For Dummies*, I show you what learning a new language involves and how to make it a more successful experience for you. I provide an overview of the key components in the language learning journey, the role personal differences play in the process, the importance of learning vocabulary, and the best strategies to develop and improve all your skills in the new language. I also guide you through considering your motivation(s) and goal(s) to learn a new language, and choosing the language and learning strategies that best fit your needs.

I pack this book with research-based explanations to help you understand what to focus on when learning a new language, and I highlight actual strategies you can use to achieve your learning goals. For example, I discuss the importance of both receiving appropriate language *input* (exposure to the language you're learning) and having opportunities to create *output* (using the language to communicate with other language users). So, I cover what the research states about input and output, and I give you tips and suggestions on the different ways you can apply the principles of this research to your own interactions, both when you're communicating in person and when you're using technology. I also remind you throughout this book that making errors is a natural and expected feature in language learning and development. Don't give up!

A quick note: Sidebars (shaded boxes of text in some chapters) dig into the details of a given topic, but they aren't crucial to understanding it. Feel free to read them or skip them. You can pass over the text accompanied by the Technical Stuff icon, too. The text marked with this icon contains some interesting but nonessential information about learning a new language.

One last thing: You may note that within this book, some web addresses break across two lines of text. If you're reading the book in print and want to visit one of these web pages, simply key in the web address exactly as it's noted in the text, pretending as though the line break doesn't exist. If you're reading this as an e-book, you've got it easy — just click the web address to be taken directly to the web page.

Foolish Assumptions

Here are some of my assumptions about you, dear reader, and why you're picking up this book:

>> You have some interest in finding out what learning a new language entails.

>> You want to learn a new language to communicate with other speakers of that language.

>> You're wondering about the best way to start your new language learning journey, and you aren't sure how to start or what to look for.

Icons Used in This Book

Like all *For Dummies* books, this book features icons to help you navigate the information. Here's what they mean:

REMEMBER

If you take away anything from this book, it should be the information marked with this icon.

TECHNICAL STUFF

This icon flags information that delves a little deeper than usual into the process of learning a new language.

TIP

This icon highlights especially helpful advice about what to do and how to do it as you travel through your new language learning journey.

WARNING

This icon points out situations and actions to avoid in order to progress and succeed in your language learning experience.

Beyond the Book

In addition to the material in the print or e-book you're reading right now, this product comes with some access-anywhere goodies on the web. Check out the free Cheat Sheet for info on essential input for learning a new language, strategies for learning vocabulary, tips for speaking in a new language, and more. To get this Cheat Sheet, simply go to www.dummies.com and type "*Learning a New Language For Dummies* Cheat Sheet" in the Search box.

Where to Go from Here

You don't have to read this book from cover to cover, but if you're an especially thorough person, feel free to do so! If you just want to find specific information and then get back to work on learning your new language, take a look at the table of contents or the index, and then dive into the chapter or section that interests you.

For example, if you don't know how or where to start, and need help to even decide on a new language to study, open the book up to Chapter 11 for tips on choosing a language, and then let me help you design your learning path in Chapter 12. Very soon you'll have a plan in place and be ready to start your language learning journey. Buckle up, and get ready to go!

1

Getting Started with Learning a New Language

Understand communication, its components and design features, as well as the different branches of linguistics.

Know terminology to name languages and their speakers and important components in learning a new language.

Recognize the personal features that affect language learning and assess your proficiency level as you learn an L2.

Discover the many benefits and advantages that learning a new language can offer.

IN THIS CHAPTER

» **Looking at the definition of** *language*

» **Highlighting what you need to learn a new language**

» **Understanding the components of communication**

» **Considering the functions of language**

» **Outlining the branches of linguistics**

Chapter **1**

Craving a New Language

Thinking of learning a new language? Wonderful! You're in the right place. Since you're reading this book, I'm guessing that you're pretty enthusiastic about learning a new language. If so, you already have a key ingredient for such a journey: your motivation!

In this chapter, you get an overview of the process of learning a new language. I start by defining what language is. It seems like a simple term, but *linguists* (people who study language) have pondered over how to define language for years. I also explain the importance of knowing more than one language in today's world and becoming part of the bilingual (or multilingual) team; then I dive into what communication is and discuss its components, as well as its features and functions. Finally, I briefly mention some of the disciplines that study language.

TIP

If you want to learn a language you can use with many speakers, here's a fun fact: The most spoken languages around the globe (as a native speaker and as a second language) are English, Mandarin Chinese, Hindi, Spanish, French, and Modern Standard Arabic. You can find out more about choosing a language to learn in Chapter 11.

Defining What "Language" Means

Language is a natural human ability that we acquire effortlessly by merely being exposed to it and using it to communicate with other members of our language community. Language is essential in our lives to maintain social interactions because it helps us express thoughts, ideas, desires, emotions, and culture.

Language also is a form of self-identity. Yes, that's right! The way you speak and the language you use reveal a lot about your identity and your culture. Think about it: When you hear someone talking, can you guess if they're from your area or not? Can you guess their age or gender? What about their socioeconomic status? Can you guess if they're native speakers of the language or language learners? It's not uncommon to answer yes to all or most of these questions. That's what I mean when I say that language is a form of self-identity.

TECHNICAL STUFF

Technically speaking, languages are formed by arbitrary signs (words) that are governed by certain rules (grammar). (You can read more about the arbitrariness of words in the later section "Recognizing special design features.") Despite their complexity, languages are systematic and rule-governed, so linguists are able to study them in a scientific way. Thanks to the rules that govern languages, members of a speech community produce and understand an infinite number of sentences.

Most researchers agree that humans are born already programmed to learn languages, and some structures in our brains are specialized for language processing. So, some of the work is already done for you, without any visible effort!

A FEW FUN FACTS ABOUT LANGUAGES

If you haven't decided which language you want to learn yet, you have many to choose from! According to Ethnologue (www.ethnologue.com/), which is one of the most important online sources of information about languages, there are more than 7,000 languages in the world! Here's some interesting data about these languages:

- About 90 percent of the world population speaks 700 of these languages.

- More than 50 percent of the population speaks 23 of these languages.

- Eighty-five percent of the people in the world use either Asian or European languages.

- Forty percent of these languages (more than 3,000 languages) are endangered languages (they have fewer than 1,000 users).

Gaining a Superpower by Learning a New Language

Learning new languages is an exciting and rewarding task! Bilinguals can communicate with more people than monolinguals do, and languages give you the opportunity to discover different cultures and provide broader perspectives of the world and humanity. Talk about a superpower!

And learning languages isn't as difficult as some people may think; note that you've already acquired at least one language — the one you're using now to read this book. You may only need some guidance on how to achieve your goal to learn a new one. Furthermore, you may have heard that the more languages you learn, the easier it becomes to learn a new one. So, go for it! The following sections explain what you need to learn a new language and give an overview of the benefits of language learning.

Knowing what you need up front

You need a few ingredients for a successful experience when learning a new language so that you can join the bilingual (or multilingual) superpower team sooner rather than later. (I explain all of them in detail throughout this book.) To learn a language, you need the following:

» **Strong motivation:** Learning a language should feel like a joyful act. You should feel the excitement within you, like the butterflies you feel when you see someone you're dating. You shouldn't feel pushed/obliged to learn it; you should have an intense desire to do so.

TIP

To help you find your motivation, try writing down at least five reasons why you want to learn a particular language. For example, suppose you want to learn French so you can travel around France more easily, speak with friends and family members who live there, read French literature in its original form, watch French movies without subtitles, and enjoy French restaurants even more by reading the menus in French.

» **Time and consistency:** I suggest spending at least 15 minutes on your new language every day. It's better to dedicate some time to it on a daily basis than to spend many hours working on it only once a week.

TIP

Try to connect learning a language with your daily life. For example, while your coffee is brewing, use those spare minutes to read in your new language, listen to music in the language, review flashcards, and so on. You can also change your email/phone settings to your new language, try watching TV and movies in your new language, or write your to-do list in your new language. These repetitive actions will be a huge help in your learning progress!

>> **Resources:** You need to find compelling books, dictionaries, audiovisual material, and similar resources in your target language. Being repeatedly exposed to diverse material that uses your new language will help you retain that language.

If possible, find native or proficient speakers of the language to practice with. This is a really valuable resource! You can reach out to local universities or be on the lookout for local language clubs that meet periodically; pay attention to the bulletin boards in coffee shops, libraries, and universities. You can also use online apps to find conversation partners. I share some online apps and sites you can use in Chapter 14.

>> **A feeling of relaxation:** You shouldn't feel stressed out when learning or practicing the language. You need to feel comfortable and accept the idea that making mistakes is part of the deal. In the language-learning field, we refer to that as having a *low affective filter*. You can read more about the importance of the affective filter in Chapter 7.

>> **A plan:** Consider your motivation and goals, and outline the steps you will follow to reach that goal. The clearer your plan is, the easier it will be to implement it. See Chapter 12 for details.

>> **A handle on basic vocabulary:** Building your vocabulary is especially important in the beginning of the learning process; learning words is even more important than mastering the language structure (grammar). You can start by learning everyday vocabulary, and words that are linked to your interests and hobbies. See Chapter 13 for details.

Note that you can communicate with others using just individual words. Grammatical accuracy comes with time, and it shouldn't be the focus for novice learners. Traditional classroom teaching can help a lot when it's time to polish your grammar.

Seeing the benefits of being bilingual (or multilingual) in the world

Defining bilingualism or multilingualism isn't an easy task, and consequently, measuring the number of bilinguals in the world is equally difficult. Actually, no official data about bilingualism exists. However, some researchers, such as François Grosjean, say that half or slightly more than half of the world's population is bilingual, and others, such as Colin Baker, state that the number is between 50 percent and 70 percent.

Normally the census of a country doesn't ask whether members of its population are bilingual, but the census may ask about the languages they know, which is used to calculate the number of bilingual speakers. However, we still have the difficulty of deciding what being bilingual means or what knowing a language entails. Some countries, such as Switzerland, have a more restrictive view of the definition of bilingualism than others, such as the United States. So, as you can see, obtaining reliable data about the number of bilinguals in the world isn't an easy task.

What's clear is that in some countries and on some continents (such as Asia and Africa), bilingualism/multilingualism is very common; in others (such as Europe), more than half of the population speaks at least two languages (although two of Europe's largest countries, Great Britain and France, don't have much bilingualism). The United States is one of the few developed countries where learning languages isn't a priority.

Speaking two or more languages isn't a modern feat; it has existed forever, since communities with different languages had to communicate with each other. In fact, two major causes of bilingualism are

>> **Trade and business:** For example, nowadays people use English to conduct business, but during the third and fourth centuries BCE, buyers and sellers used Greek to trade in the Mediterranean.

>> **The movement of people for political, religious, social, educational, or economic reasons:** For example, people living in regions with political or religious conflicts migrate to other countries searching for a more stable and peaceful life. Likewise, people move in search of better work or educational opportunities.

REMEMBER

Being multilingual in our diverse world is generally considered to be a great asset. Organizations such as the United Nations support multilingualism because of its benefits to the global community. Additionally, research supports the idea that multilingualism provides a wide array of benefits that range from academic to cognitive, cultural, and even economic ones. Being part of the bilingual superpower team gives you opportunities you otherwise wouldn't have. Bilingualism can open doors for you personally, academically, and professionally. You can find out more about the advantages of learning new languages in Chapter 4.

Uncovering Communication Categories, Components, and Design Features

Language is the main character in the language-learning process, but it isn't the only one. Language is the tool we need to communicate with other members of our community. Thus, communication is another main character in this language-learning play. In the following sections, I define *communication*, describe its different modes, discuss its components, and explain how these components work together to deliver the diverse functions of language.

Professor Milton Azevedo and other linguists define language as a social behavior that only humans possess and that is manifested through the creative employment of signs. These signs are arbitrary and part of an ordered system. Having an ordered system allows us to communicate with others and share our cultural expression in a wide variety of contexts.

Specifying communication categories

Communication has been defined in various ways by many linguists. In a paper published in 2017, well-known language scholar Bill VanPatten defines communication as "the expression, interpretation, and negotiation of meaning with a purpose in a given context."

In other words, communication involves people articulating ideas so that others comprehend them, and if a breakdown in communication happens, they need to negotiate the intended meaning. Language exchanges need to be purposeful and meaningful in the context where they happen.

Communication can be classified as one-way or two-way communication.

>> *One-way communication* refers to communication that doesn't require a reply. For instance, when you read an online news site, you're receiving one-way communication because you're reading and interpreting the meaning of the words, but you aren't expected to reply to the site. Another example is a reporter transmitting the news on TV. The reporter is just informing viewers, not expecting to interact with them.

>> On the other hand, *two-way communication* entails a give-and-take between the people participating in the communication. One person produces language, and the other reacts to the language produced. There may be some negotiation of meaning between the two participants in the communicative act.

ACTFL (the American Council on the Teaching of Foreign Languages; see Chapter 3) divides communication into three modes:

>> **Interpretive communication** is a one-way communication that entails understanding and deciphering messages. It can be in the form of reading (for example, the newspaper), listening (for example, to the radio) or viewing (for example, a movie).

>> **Interpersonal communication** is a two-way communication where the participants exchange information and negotiate meaning. Interpersonal communication can be done by speaking (for example, chatting with your friends) or writing (for example, sending text messages).

>> **Presentational communication** is a one-way communication where the speaker/writer delivers information to an audience, but has no expectation of receiving an answer from the audience.

TECHNICAL STUFF

When you think of communication, you may often picture interpersonal communication, where two people share information. Communication comes from the Latin *communicare*, which means "to share," "to make common," or "to inform." In fact, its root is *communis*, which means "shared by all, common, public." When you communicate, you share information and make it common knowledge. You may recognize other English words that come from the same root, such as community. Interesting, right?

We communicate for many different purposes, such as to exchange information; transmit ideas; express wishes, emotions, and feelings; describe language itself or talk about abstract concepts; have fun with language; recreate or retell the past; or even invent the future. You can find out more about the different uses of language in communication in the later section "Clarifying Various Language Functions."

Examining components of the communication chain

Figure 1-1 shows how the communication chain works and the way we communicate our ideas.

REMEMBER

In order for human communication to happen, you need to consider these main ingredients:

>> The *interlocutors,* or users (the sender/source and the receiver), are the participants in the communication. Humans and most animals can exchange their sender and receiver role at any moment in their communicative exchange.

>> The *message* is the idea, knowledge, or feeling you want to transmit, or what you receive and need to interpret.

>> The *code* is the language used to transmit messages. Once you know the message or content you want to transmit, you need to codify it in the language you're using, according to the rules of that language. Afterwards, the receiver will decodify your language to understand the message.

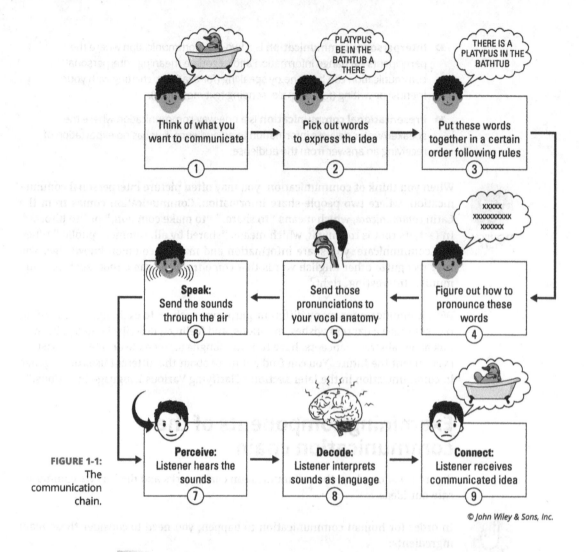

FIGURE 1-1:
The communication chain.

© John Wiley & Sons, Inc.

> Obviously, for communication to be successful, the interlocutors need to know the code: its sounds (or its written form), the meaning of the words used, and how words are conveyed in sentences (grammar).

>> The *medium* is the channel used to transmit the message from the sender to the receiver. Nowadays, cell phones are a very popular medium used to transmit messages.

>> The *context* (setting) is the physical place where the communication occurs. The context may affect the message or the way you use the code. For

instance, think of the way you would explain the reason for a sick day if you're at a bar with friends as compared to being in the office with your boss. You would express it differently, right?

>> *Feedback* is the verbal or nonverbal response you give to the other interlocutor(s) to indicate that the message was received (or not), or to ask for clarification and the like. Feedback helps the interlocutors ensure that the communication was successful.

You can see how these components work together in Figure 1-1.

Recognizing special design features

Communication has a series of characteristics called *design features* (a term coined by linguist Charles Hockett in the 1960s). Although both animals and humans communicate, our communications don't share the same design features. In fact, only humans use a sophisticated form of communication: language.

Table 1-1 provides an overview of all the design features of communication. You can see which features are shared by all communication systems and which ones are special to humans.

TABLE 1-1 **Overview of Communication Design Features**

	Design Features
All communication systems	A mode of communication
	Semanticity
	Pragmatic function
Some communication systems	Interchangeability
	Cultural transmission
	Arbitrariness
	Discreteness
Only humans (language)	Displacement
	Productivity
	Prevarication
	Reflexivity

What all communication systems have

All communication systems have these three characteristics:

>> **A medium/mode of communication:** This design feature refers to how messages are transmitted — how they are produced and perceived. Most humans and animals communicate using an *auditory-vocal* mode of communication: The vocal system transmits sounds, and the auditory system receives them.

Other modes of communication used by some animals and humans are *visual-gestural* (used in sign languages, where messages are transmitted via hand, arm, head, and facial movements and received visually) and *chemical-olfactory* (some moths communicate messages with a chemical medium called *pheromones*).

You'll use a new language mainly by communicating through sounds (auditory-vocal mode), but you'll also use the visual mode (to read print, watch video, or use sign languages).

>> **Semanticity:** This feature assumes that all signals in a communication system must mean something and that the interlocutors can understand it. For instance, if I say *book* to you, I expect that you and I have a similar idea of what *book* means.

>> **Pragmatic function:** This feature refers to the fact that we use communication systems for a purpose. We produce messages to inform or influence other community members, to keep them alive, to learn new information, and the like. For example, animals use signs to indicate alarm and to indicate the source and quality of food, and humans can convey a wide variety of intentions.

What some communication systems have

While the preceding design features are shared by all communication systems, other design features are found only in certain communication systems. Of course, human communications have all these features:

>> **Interchangeability:** The users (sender and receiver) can exchange roles: I can be the sender of the message first, and a moment later I can be the receiver of some other message. Moreover, the same person can be the sender and the receiver (when you talk to yourself, for example). Not all organisms can have both roles. For instance, male silkworm moths are only receivers; they cannot send messages.

>> **Cultural transmission:** Even if it's true that humans are preprogrammed to acquire languages (the *Language Acquisition Device*), we need social interaction and input from other users to learn a language and its conventions. These interactions also transmit the culture of the speech community. You cannot acquire a language in isolation; you need to be in contact and interact with other users to learn it. For example, male white-crowned sparrows learn their "dialect" songs from older males during their first three months after birth; male humpback whales also have their own song that evolves in contact with other humpback whales. Find out more about cultural transmission in Chapter 2.

>> **Arbitrariness:** Why do we call a certain four-legged animal *dog* in English? That same animal may be called *perro* in Spanish or *chien* in French by another person. The reason behind all these names is that words (linguistic signs) are arbitrary. No intrinsic (underlying) association exists between the form (signal, what something is called) and the meaning (what it refers to), or among the elements in the communicative system and their meaning. Some animals show some variations or "dialects," such as the songs used by humpback whales in the South Pacific.

>> **Discreteness:** Some communication systems are formed of small, discrete (separate), and repeatable units (sounds, words) that connect to form meaningful messages. For instance, languages have sounds that, on their own, don't mean anything. However, when they're combined in a linear sequence of smaller discrete units, they can form words with their own meanings. These individual units differ from one another, and together they create syllables, words, sentences, and ultimately messages. This feature allows simplicity and linguistic economy. Some apes, dolphins, and parrots show some signs of discreteness.

What only human communication systems have

And now we get to the design features unique to humans, and only possible using language:

>> **Displacement:** Humans can use language to talk about events that happened in a different place and time from the here and now, or the moment in which they're speaking. All languages have ways to express temporal and spatial displacement, because indicating time and space is important information to be shared among speakers. Some languages use *inflections* (changes in form) to indicate time displacement (for example, the *-ed* in *worked*), or they can use prepositional phrases (for example, *at home*) or adverbs (for example, *yesterday*) to indicate displacement in space and time.

Although displacement is a human communication design feature, some people think that bees can also express displacement. To a certain extent, that's true. Bees can indicate the orientation and distance to a food source, as well as its quality, through certain dance moves. However, bee dances are very strict and can use only certain postures and gestures to express very specific information.

>> **Productivity:** Obeying the rules that govern each language (to combine sounds and form morphemes, words, and sentences), humans can give new names to new items, actions, or events and create completely brand-new sentences never heard or produced before. Only humans can use a finite number of linguistic elements (although these elements may change) to produce an infinite number of sentences. Animals, on the other hand, have a closed system of communication, and they cannot combine the diverse, discrete units to create new ones.

>> **Prevarication:** Humans can use language to lie (*prevarication* is just a fancy word for lying). In general, animals cannot lie. (Interestingly, however, linguist Charles Hockett has proposed that some primates, including gibbons and guenons, can lie to achieve a goal.)

>> **Reflexivity:** This term refers to using the code to talk about the code. For instance, I use language to explain features of language itself. This is a communication design feature that only humans have.

Clarifying Various Language Functions

The members of a linguistic community use language to communicate and to accomplish certain goals. For instance, you can use language to communicate messages, ideas, or needs, to convey emotions and desires, and to bring about certain actions, as well as to just have fun with the language (telling jokes, creating poems, and so on).

To be more specific, linguist Roman Jakobson proposed six language functions: referential, emotive, conative, phatic, metalingual, and poetic. The following list goes over what each function entails. (Note that in some descriptions I use terms I introduce in the earlier section "Examining components of the communication chain.")

>> **Referential:** Language is used to share knowledge or information, to communicate observations and thoughts, to describe people/places/things, or to talk about things in general.

>> **Emotive (expressive, affective):** The focus of this function is the sender, or *I*. Language is used to express how the sender feels and their attitudes toward things.

Because cultures vary, you need to be aware of cultural and social norms when you express your feelings in a new language. You need to understand how and when you can express your feelings, and consider the context of where you are and to whom you're expressing your feelings and emotions. If you already know which language you want to learn, you may want to do a quick search online to find some of the culture's rules or expectations about expressing emotions. For instance, you can check how to say you're full and don't want to eat any more without hurting anyone's feelings.

>> **Conative:** The focus of this function is on the receiver of the message: It's a *you* function. The sender uses language to persuade or to influence others. They may use *vocatives* (direct address) and *imperatives* (commands and requests) to persuade the receiver (for example, "Girls! Come here now!").

>> **Phatic:** This function refers to the small talk that keeps social communication going. It's the language people use in everyday interactions when they say, "Hi, how are you?" and respond, "I'm okay, thank you!" or pick up the phone and say *hello* in English or *dígame* (tell me) in Spanish. In these exchanges, the intention is to say, "I am here, I acknowledge your presence, and I am ready for communication."

Your everyday communications are full of examples of this function. Sometimes you talk just for the sake of talking and having a conversation, without paying much attention to the information you're sharing. You normally use phatic words to open communication (hello), maintain communication (okay, aha, hmmm), verify information (really?), or end a conversation (bye). Search online for ways to start or end a conversation in the language you're planning to learn.

>> **Metalingual (metalinguistic, reflexive):** In this function, language is used to explain or talk about language itself. That's exactly what I'm doing here. Dictionaries also have a metalingual function.

>> **Poetic (aesthetic):** The focus of this function is on the message and how it's used. For example, language can be used creatively or artistically (in poems, literary pieces, wordplay, slogans, titles, and the like). People can also use language to entertain themselves or others (telling jokes, riddles, and so on).

The poetic function can be hard to grasp as a novice language learner. Many jokes are especially difficult for a new speaker to understand because of the cultural and historical references they normally have.

But language functions aren't just black-and-white: One sentence or phrase can have multiple functions at the same time. For instance, if I enter my classroom and say to the students sitting there, "Oh no! It's hot in this classroom," my statement may be interpreted in different ways, or I may intend different outcomes, such as

>> I may be informing the students of the fact that it's hot.

>> I may be expressing how I feel about the heat in the classroom.

>> I may want someone to open the windows or turn the air-conditioning on.

So, that single sentence entails different goals and has different functions: referential, emotive, and conative, respectively. In other words, it's doing a lot of work!

Embracing Essential Branches in Linguistics

In this chapter I explain and discuss a lot about language and communication, but I don't refer much to linguistics — until now! *Linguistics* is the science that studies language and communication. Linguists want to understand how language works. In this section I briefly explain some of the most important branches of linguistics.

Phonetics and phonology: Working with sounds

Phonetics and phonology are two branches of linguistics that study speech sounds, but in different ways:

>> *Phonetics* studies the physiology of sounds; in other words, it dissects speech sounds, and it studies how to pronounce them and how you perceive them. These individual sounds are called *phones*.

>> *Phonology* studies how sounds combine with each other to convey meaning.

TIP

Phonemes are sounds in a language that trigger a difference in meaning, and each language has its own set of phonemes. For example, in English, exchanging the sounds [k] (used to pronounce the "c") and [p] respectively in *can* and *pan* triggers a different meaning. In linguistics, we say that these two sounds are *contrastive*. When learning a new language, you need to be familiar with all the contrastive sounds. You may find some of the same contrastive sounds in your native language (*L1*), and some other sounds may be new to you. You'll have more difficulty learning sounds that aren't contrastive in your L1. Learning to distinguish and produce contrastive sounds is essential to gain proficiency in a language.

Morphology: Building words

Morphology is the branch of linguistics that deals with how words are formed. These parts of the words are called *morphemes*, and they are the smallest units in a language that carry meaning by themselves.

For instance, consider the words *cat*, *talk*, and *small*. Each word has its own meaning, but you can add extra morphemes to these words and get more meaning out of them, as in *cats*, *talked*, and *smaller*. The *-s* in *cats* is a morpheme that indicates more than one, the *-ed* in *talked* is a morpheme that carries the meaning of past tense, and the *-er* in *smaller* indicates a comparison with another entity.

Learning how to produce/comprehend meanings with the different morphemes of a language helps you enlarge your vocabulary repertoire quite a lot and enhance your language proficiency. However, these morphemes take time to acquire.

Syntax: Creating sentences

Syntax is the branch of linguistics that studies the rules and patterns we follow to combine words to create sentences. Using a finite number of vocabulary words, we can create billions of different sentences that can be understood by other speakers of the language. These sentences will vary in their complexity, but all of them will follow certain rules and patterns. If speakers don't follow these rules and patterns, people cannot understand each other.

Keep in mind that the sentence structure of some languages already tells you a lot about meaning. For example, if you read the following sentence in English, you'll probably know more than you think at first glance:

The cateps spoared the motkishes.

Can you guess who does the action (the subject) in this sentence? Which word is the verb? Who receives the action (the object) of the verb? I'm almost certain you guessed that *the cateps* is the subject of the verb *spoared*, and the receiver of the action of the verb is *the motkishes*. Not only that, by looking at the morphemes that end these unfamiliar words (*-s*, *-ed*, and *-es*), you know the subject and the object are plural, and the verb is in the past tense. And you can even test yourself a little more and form a *passive-voice* sentence (the object of the verb comes first, and the subject goes after the verb) out of the first sentence:

The motkishes were spoared by the cateps.

You can do all that thanks to the rules that govern the English language, both morphological rules (adding -*s* or -*es* to nouns to make them plural or -*ed* to verbs to indicate past tense; see the previous section) and syntactic rules (in *active-voice* sentences, such as the first sentence, the subject goes before the verb, and the receiver of the action goes afterward).

If you're thinking you still don't know the meaning of these two sentences, that's normal, because I used made-up words to give you this example. I just wanted to show you that you know a lot more about syntax and morphology than you may have thought.

Semantics: Understanding meaning

Semantics is the branch of linguistics that studies the meaning of words. Besides the definition you find in dictionaries, the meaning of words can be linked closely to your personal and cultural background. For instance, if I ask you to think of a house and describe it, your description may differ from the description someone in China, the Congo, or Alaska would give me.

Pragmatics: Getting meaning in context

Pragmatics studies meaning in conversations within the context where the conversation happens. It focuses on how language (and nonverbal communication) is used in conversation, and how a conversation works (think about principles or maxims, and turn-taking).

For example, if I ask my friend, "Do you have any chewing gum?" what I am actually asking is that my friend give me a piece of gum. So, if my friend answers *yes* and doesn't give me a piece of gum, they don't understand the pragmatics of this sentence in English.

Other branches of linguistics

Many other branches of linguistics exist, including the following:

>> *Sociolinguistics* examines how different social aspects affect the use of language, and even how language helps individuals represent their identity. Sociolinguists look at the way people of different age groups, economic status, genders, professions, and so on speak and use language. For instance, it's very possible you associate the expression *What's up?* with a certain age group, gender, and/or another identity.

>> *Historical linguistics* studies language change over time, and it can trace back some relationships between languages.

>> *Neurolinguistics* is the branch of linguistics that studies brain activity as people receive or produce language, and how the information moves in the areas of the brain that process language.

>> *Psycholinguistics* analyzes how the different linguistic processes happen in the brain, the mechanisms that help us produce and comprehend language (for example, sentence processing and speech perception), as well as how we acquire languages (first and second). Psycholinguists also look at how other cognitive capacities, such as short-term and long-term memory, help language processing.

Chapter **2**

Understanding Terms and Key Elements for Learning a Language

I n this chapter, I provide you with some foundational tools to start discussing and understanding language learning. Specifically, this chapter helps you understand some terms related to languages and language speakers, including the terms used to describe the different types of bilingual speakers. I also go over some of the key elements that affect your language learning: input, interaction, and output opportunities.

Getting Familiar with Key Terms about Languages

In this section, I invite you to get familiar with the terms used to refer to the languages you can speak.

REMEMBER

Input is the language you encounter (through listening, reading, and/or viewing) and need to process to comprehend its meaning. So, as you read the language terms in this section, I invite you to consider what language input you've received in each case. (I discuss input in more detail later in this chapter.)

First language

Your *first language*, normally labeled L1, is often called your *mother tongue*. It's the language your parents or caregivers spoke to you after you were born and exposed you to throughout your childhood.

Second language

Your *second language* (also known as L2) is any language you learn/acquire after you acquired your first language. It can be your second, third, or fourth language, and still be called your second language.

REMEMBER

You may hear two different terms that refer to another language you learn after your first one: *second language* and *foreign language*. These terms emphasize the context in which you learn/acquire and use the new language:

>> A *second language* is spoken in your immediate environment that you may need to use in your everyday communications. For instance, if you're an immigrant living in the United States, English is your second language, because you use it in natural communications in your environment.

>> A *foreign language* is usually learned in an academic setting. Normally, it isn't the language you hear outside the classroom, in your community. For instance, if you're in the United States and you learn German in a language class, German can be considered your foreign language. Because it isn't spoken in your immediate environment, you won't have many opportunities to use it in a communicative situation outside class.

TIP

In this book, I use the term *second language* to refer to both second and foreign languages, unless I need to emphasize and distinguish the learning context difference.

Heritage language

REMEMBER

Your *heritage language* (also called *home language* or *community language*) is the language you acquire at home that's different from the dominant language used in the social context where you live or go to school. For example, if your French-speaking family moved to the United States and you've been receiving input in

French in your household since you were born, but you use English outside your home (with friends, at school, or while running errands), you can say that French is your heritage language (and also your L1), whereas English is your second language (L2).

TIP

The quantity and quality of the input received in a heritage language may determine the maintenance or attrition (loss) of that heritage language. If you speak a language different from the language spoken in your social environment (outside your house), I encourage you to speak your heritage language with your children or any little ones you are taking care of. For instance, if you speak Italian as your L1 and are living in the United States, you should use Italian with your little ones at home so your heritage language isn't lost. There are many advantages to speaking more than one language, as I explain in Chapter 4.

Checking Out Key Terms about Language Speakers

In the following sections, I explain some of the labels used to name speakers of one or more languages. Specifically, I focus on the terminology employed to distinguish types of bilingual speakers. The various bilingual labels depend on diverse factors, such as when you started learning the language, the language abilities you can handle in your L2, your proficiency level, and how the two languages are represented/stored in your brain.

Monolingual speakers

Monolingual speakers refers to language users that know and use only one language (that is, they have one L1). For example, if you were born and raised in the United States and haven't taken any foreign language classes, you're almost certainly a monolingual speaker of English.

Bilingual speakers

The term *bilingual speakers* refers to language users who know and use two languages (or varieties). When someone knows more than two languages, they may be called a *multilingual speaker,* but using *bilingual speaker* in this case is also appropriate.

Bilingual speakers can be categorized in different ways, depending on factors such as the age at which you started acquiring/learning a language, the L2 skills you have, the proficiency you gain in these languages, or the way the two languages are represented in your brain.

TIP

When referring to a bilingual speaker, you specify the languages they speak. For example, suppose you're a Chinese-English speaker. The order in which you list your two languages can refer to

>> **Order of acquisition:** You acquired Chinese first, and English later.

>> **Language dominance:** Your dominant language is Chinese, and your nondominant language is English.

Onset of L2 learning/acquisition

Depending on when you start learning/acquiring your second language, you can be classified as an *early bilingual* or a *late bilingual:*

>> **Early bilingual:** You acquire the two languages from birth until around age 12. The two types of early bilinguals are

- **Simultaneous bilingual:** You acquire the two languages from birth to around age 3.

- **Sequential bilingual:** You acquire one language before the other, but you learn both languages before you're 12 years old.

>> **Late bilingual:** You acquire a language (your L1), and after age 12, you start learning a second language (your L2). Late bilinguals can only be sequential bilinguals, because you acquired one language before the second language.

REMEMBER

You can become bilingual at any age. Start learning a new language as soon as you can and take advantage of all the benefits of bilingualism. Being bilingual (despite the native/non-native proficiency you achieve) improves your life in many ways, as I explain in Chapter 4, so don't wait to start!

L2 language skills

Depending on your language skills in the second language, bilinguals can be classified as

>> **Receptive bilingual:** You can understand what you read or hear, but you cannot respond in the second language (in writing or by speaking).

> » **Productive bilingual:** You can speak (and/or write) in the second language, in addition to understanding what you read or hear.

L2 language proficiency

You may hear the terms *balanced bilingual* and *unbalanced bilingual* in reference to your language proficiency in the L2:

> » **Balanced bilingual:** Roughly speaking, you're a *balanced bilingual* when you're equally proficient in the two languages. In other words, you have the same skills in each language as a monolingual speaker at your age, meaning you have native-like command and proficiency in both languages. Some researchers suggest that balanced bilinguals are prone to be more understanding and receptive to cultural differences.

> » **Unbalanced bilingual:** As its name suggests, an *unbalanced bilingual* shows more proficiency in one language than in the other.

L2 representation in the brain

Bilingual speakers are also classified according to how languages are represented and organized in the bilingual brain.

In 1954, researchers Susan Ervin and Charles Osgood published a paper in which they considered that the context in which the two languages are learned/acquired has an impact on the representation of the languages in the bilingual brain. They divided bilinguals into *coordinate* and *compound*:

> » *Coordinate bilinguals* learned/acquired their L1 and L2 in different contexts (for example, Spanish at home and English in school). They tend to attach a slightly different meaning to similar words in each language. Thus, coordinate bilinguals link a meaning to *casa* and a different meaning to *house*. In Figure 2-1, *casa* and *house* look different to a coordinate bilingual even though they mean the same thing in both languages.

> » *Compound bilinguals* learned/acquired the two languages in the same context. So, a Spanish-English bilingual has a single representation for the meaning of *casa* and *house* (see Figure 2-2). This kind of bilingual may show more transference of pronunciation, grammar, and meaning from one language to the other than a coordinate bilingual.

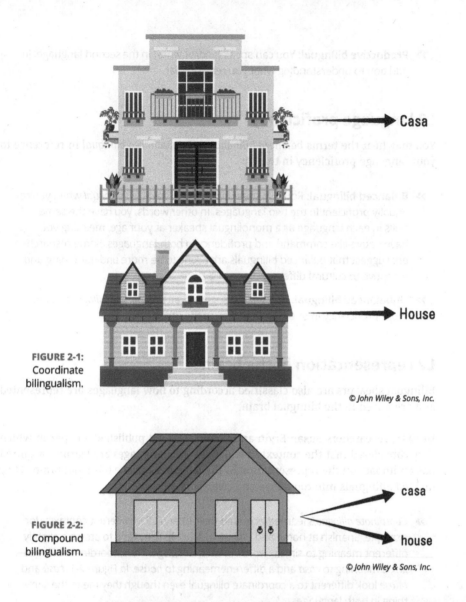

FIGURE 2-1:
Coordinate
bilingualism.

© John Wiley & Sons, Inc.

FIGURE 2-2:
Compound
bilingualism.

© John Wiley & Sons, Inc.

Linguist Uriel Weinreich identified another type of bilingual: *subordinate bilinguals*. To understand subordinate bilingualism, consider a person who acquired Spanish in their home country and moved to the United States. As a subordinate bilingual, they link the L2 word *house* to its L1 counterpart *casa*, which they later link to the meaning. Thus, they don't make a direct connection between the word *house* and its meaning before it goes through the L1 filter (*casa*). This type of processing takes longer than directly connecting words with their meaning. Translation methods of teaching are based on subordinate bilingualism, which Figure 2-3 depicts.

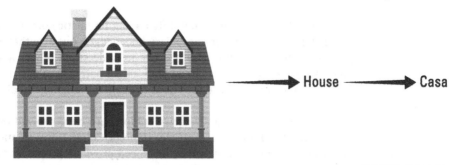

House ——————➤ Casa

FIGURE 2-3:
Subordinate
bilingualism.

© John Wiley & Sons, Inc.

More recent linguistic proposals describe the way the L1 and L2 are represented in bilinguals' brains as part of a *continuum*, or range. On one side of the continuum are coordinate bilinguals, with the two languages completely separated in their minds; on the other side of the continuum, you find compound bilinguals, who completely integrate the two languages. This continuum proposal doesn't encapsulate bilinguals under one category, but as part of a continuum that keeps changing and evolving, and it can go in either direction.

For example, if you use language A at home and language B outside your home, you may separate the two languages (like a coordinate bilingual), whereas if your living situation requires you to use both languages all the time, you'll have a more integrated approach (like a compound bilingual). Or, you may keep the two languages separate in pronunciation, but integrate the meaning of words.

Recognizing Key Terms about Communicative Competence

Most language learners would say that they want to learn a new language so they can speak and use it in different situations. What most people pursue is communicative competence, as the researcher Dell Hymes called it.

REMEMBER

What's that, you ask? *Communicative competence* refers to the actual use of a language in different communicative contexts and according to cultural norms. In other words, it's your ability to express and interpret messages adequately — for example, in a conversation, knowing how to show politeness, greet the participants, and acknowledge the turn-taking rules among the participants in the conversation. This includes not only having linguistic competence (grammatical competence and lexical or vocabulary knowledge), but also the use of intonation, gestures, and other strategies you use to understand others and make yourself understood. Under normal circumstances, all native speakers develop communicative competence because they need to use their language in different contexts.

The components of communicative competence have evolved over the years. In 1995, some scholars (Marianne Celce-Murcia, Zoltán Dörnyei, and Sarah Thurrell) published a paper in which they advanced previous proposals to describe communicative competence. In their model, communicative competence was divided into these five components:

>> *Discourse competence* — how you put words and phrases together to express meaning in an appropriate and coherent way — is the core component.

>> *Sociocultural competence* refers to the knowledge you need to have about the culture, social norms (for example, style or formality), nonverbal cues, and context where the communication happens.

>> *Linguistic competence* refers to how you use the language itself (its sounds, vocabulary, and structure for forming words or sentences) to express the desired meaning.

>> *Actional competence* refers to how you can express your intent using the appropriate linguistic forms (words and sentences).

>> *Strategic competence* is your ability to communicate your messages and intentions when you have deficiencies in any of the other competencies.

For example, imagine you have a job interview. Here's how the components of communicative competence may play out:

>> As you enter the room for the interview, you use your sociocultural and actional competence to acknowledge the people in the room appropriately (politely and with formal greetings).

>> Then, you use your linguistic and discourse competence to talk about yourself and your accomplishments, using appropriate connectors (*furthermore, to conclude*) and language forms (present and past tense). You may also use your actional competence to persuade the other participants.

>> If you forget the name of one of your former employers and you're trying to remember it, you rely on your strategic competence. For instance, you may

remember the first letter of the company's name, so you start uttering it to buy some extra time to think about it (and prompt someone to say the name for you), or you start describing it, hoping someone helps you with the name or you remember it.

>> Finally, after the interview you use your actional competence to thank your interviewers and ask them about the next steps.

By default, all native speakers of a language have communicative competence because they can effectively converse and interact with others in their everyday communications and get their message across. Of course, you acquire these competencies as you have more experience with the language. For instance, children may lack some sociocultural competency and address others using the wrong style or formality.

Uncovering Some Key Elements for Learning a Language

Several factors can affect your success in acquiring an L2, which brings up an old debate among developmental proposals: What is innate (inborn) and continues to be accessible in the L2, and what is affected by the learning environment and circumstances?

Under normal circumstances, all adults develop native fluency in at least one language, their L1. The consistency of such a successful final product (native fluency in at least one language) can only be explained by accepting that nature provides humans with some innate abilities. But you also need to consider the role of surrounding factors — your environment and your interactions with other speakers — in your language learning/acquisition. In this section, I go over some of the main ingredients, both "nature" and "nurture," that you need to develop a new language.

Nature: Understanding your innate language abilities

The following sections discuss a variety of innate language abilities proposed by different linguists.

LAD and UG

Professor and linguist Noam Chomsky's proposal from the 1960s suggested that humans are born prepared to process languages, with a language-specific mechanism (he calls it the *Language Acquisition Device,* or LAD) that takes the input you receive and processes it to form and develop your language (known as your *implicit linguistic system*).

In the 1990s, Chomsky added that a *universal grammar* (UG) shapes and dictates the grammar rules all languages follow. Briefly explained, the UG is composed of common principles, and each principle has two *parameters,* or ways to deliver that principle. Setting the parameter in one way or another triggers a series of rules that accompany that parameter setting.

For example, one of the UG principles is that all languages must have subjects in sentences (linguists call it the *Extended Projection Principle,* or EPP). Some languages, like English, require that the subject be overt (stated), whereas other languages, including Spanish, don't require an overt subject. Consider the sentence *I read* in the English parameter compared to *leo* in the Spanish parameter, which doesn't require you to say *yo,* or I, as the subject.

General learning mechanisms

To build your language (your implicit linguistic system), some researchers contend that you need only the LAD and UG that Chomsky proposed (see the previous section), but other scholars suggest that you need the *general learning mechanisms* you use to learn other skills.

Certain linguistic forms occur repeatedly and frequently in input (for example, plural endings or verb endings), and your learning mechanisms help you find patterns and generalizations that you can then apply to continue forming your internal language system. You learn words you're frequently exposed to faster, better, and sooner than you learn words you encounter less frequently, because frequent exposure creates a more powerful representation of those words in your head.

Likewise, you rely on the number of times you see the same features (the *co-occurrence* of features) to label an item; you will connect meaning to a form (a way to call it). For instance, you learn the word *cat* after observing that an animal with certain characteristics that always co-occur (pointed ears, whiskers, purring and meowing sounds) is called a cat.

Developmental stages and acquisition order

It's important to note that our innate language ability follows a specific order and pattern, which we cannot alter through nurture or instruction. Imagine these stages and orders as stairs. You cannot be at the top of the stairs without going up the first steps.

Language acquisition goes through a series of developmental stages and follows an acquisition order that isn't affected by the context (classroom or nonclassroom) in which you acquire the language. These stages and the order of acquisition are part of your natural language ability:

>> **Developmental stages** mark your acquisition of one grammatical feature over time. For example, you follow different developmental stages as you learn how to express negation (from uttering a simple *no* in front of a verb to using *don't* and *doesn't*). It takes years for language users to work through the different developmental stages.

>> **Acquisition order** refers to the predictable order in which you acquire and use different language features over time. As you learn a language, you will acquire some grammatical forms before others. For example, in English, you'll use present participles and gerunds (*-ing* verbs) before you use third person singular present tense verbs (*-s* verbs). Thus, you can use *Joe is eating* before *Joe eats*.

Nurture: Building on your innate language abilities

Definitely, to learn a language you need to nurture your innate language and general learning mechanisms. You can do so by providing yourself with input and interaction opportunities. Other factors that directly affect your language-learning ability include personality features such as your motivation and attitude, the capacity of your working memory, and personal traits like being open to others. You can find out more about these factors in the following sections as well as in Chapter 3.

The most essential element: Input

Input refers to the language you receive (through listening, reading, and/or viewing) and need to process to understand its meaning. To acquire language, you need to feed your internal mechanisms (LAD and UG, covered earlier in this chapter) with quality linguistic data.

What do I mean by *quality linguistic data*? It's input that you understand (comprehensible) and that's compelling and communicatively embedded (it has a communicative intent). For language acquisition to happen, you need continuous exposure to quality linguistic data. Your internal mechanisms will receive this linguistic data, and if appropriate (in other words, if it's relevant for your internal developmental stage and acquisition order), you'll process it and use it to construct your internal language system. (Linguists call this linguistic input that becomes part of your system *intake*.)

Little by little, with input, interaction, and output opportunities, you'll form your own internal linguistic system (your *interlanguage*) as you're learning your L2. Your *interlanguage* is a personal evolving language system that you create and adjust as you receive L2 input and use language to communicate. It's a linguistic system that's in between your L1 and your L2. Because of the in-between nature of interlanguage, you may sometimes mix the two languages and transfer elements from your L1 into your L2 production. And you may also get stuck (or *fossilize*) in some spots of your interlanguage between the two language systems. Both transfer and fossilization are a normal part of interlanguage.

REMEMBER

Language acquisition is pretty selective, and your internal language acquisition system makes the most of input that's

>> **Comprehensible:** You need to understand the input, and it needs to be at your proficiency level (although it can go a little beyond your level — what linguist Stephen Krashen calls *input + 1*).

>> **Communicatively embedded:** The input needs to be meaningful, relevant, and send messages or have an intent.

>> **Abundant:** You need to receive great quantities of quality input.

>> **Compelling:** The input needs to be so compelling, interesting, and engaging that you forget you're getting it in a different language.

>> **Appropriate for your internal system:** It needs to fit your developmental stage or acquisition order.

When you process input, you first process its meaning, and later you process its form (specifically, grammatical forms). In other words, you pay attention to *content words* (nouns, verbs, adjectives, adverbs, and so on) before you notice other language forms (prepositions, articles, and the like).

So, suppose you hear the sentence *My daughter played tennis yesterday*.

>> You first note the words *daughter*, *play*, *tennis*, and *yesterday*.

>> Once you process the meaning of those content words, you start processing their grammatical forms. Since past tense is indicated in the sentence by the *-ed* in *played* and the adverb *yesterday*, you'll pay attention to *yesterday* before you even notice the *-ed* in *played*.

REMEMBER

Processing and producing meaning should be your first goal when learning a new language. With time, you'll begin focusing on and polishing your grammatical forms. So, the more content words you can learn, the easier it will be to communicate with others. Don't worry if you sound like Tarzan during the early stages of learning a new language. The most important step is trying to communicate and employing all the strategic competencies you can (pointing, mimicking, using synonyms, and so on).

You won't acquire all the languages you hear, read, or watch. If you don't understand the input, it becomes noise, and it's useless for the language acquisition process. Furthermore, if the input isn't relevant for your developmental stage or acquisition order, you won't internalize it or use it to build your interlanguage. You can find out more about input in Chapter 8.

Back-and-forth: Interaction

Interaction happens between you and other participant(s) in a communicative exchange, such as a conversation on the street or text messages on your phone. This exchange requires that both participants pay close attention to what's being communicated so you can interpret its meaning and react to it — for instance, producing language, or *output* (see the next section for details). The effectiveness of your L2 learning is linked to how strongly the language you use is tied to meaningful experiences.

Several researchers have highlighted the importance of the *interaction hypothesis.* This hypothesis emphasizes the role that interacting and participating in L2 exchanges with other L2 users has in L2 acquisition. During these interactions, L2 experts (like native speakers, teachers, and more proficient L2 users) may adjust and modify their production to adapt to the level of L2 learners.

During a communicative exchange, you and your interlocutor(s) take turns producing output, modifying and adjusting your output to make it comprehensible for the other participant in the conversation. Sometimes you may need to negotiate meaning. Most misunderstandings and requests to negotiate meaning have a *linguistic source* (such as vocabulary or grammar not being understood), but the miscommunication may also arise from a cultural or contextual misunderstanding, or both. For example, in Spanish *Bebí champú* means *I drank shampoo,* but *champú* is also the name of a drink in Colombia, so being aware of the context and cultural knowledge will prevent miscommunication.

REMEMBER

Both input and interaction rely on common language acquisition rules: The language needs to be comprehensible and have a communicative intent.

What's produced: Output

Output isn't simply anything that comes out of someone's mouth; rather, *output* is the language you can produce that has a communicative purpose. To produce output, you need to think about the content of what you want to say, and then access your interlanguage to find the words that produce the content you want to express.

The importance of output for language acquisition has been backed by many researchers. In 1985, linguist Merrill Swain proposed the *comprehensible output hypothesis,* which emphasizes the importance of *pushed output* opportunities to advance language acquisition. In other words, you need to be pushed to produce language and verify whether it's used correctly or if you need to adjust your output. Thus, it's a way to shape your internal system (your interlanguage). Find out more about output in Chapter 8.

Chapter **3**

Recognizing Personal Factors for Learning a Language

You may wonder whether some people have a special talent for learning languages, whether they were born with that talent, whether anyone can work toward getting that ability, or whether certain factors affect it (age, motivation, and so on). In this chapter, I give you an overview of how some of these personal factors affect your language learning journey.

Balancing Individual Differences in Language Learning

Language learning is influenced by human nature, as I mention in Chapter 2, as well as by the *input* you receive (the language you're exposed to and need to process), the social opportunities you have to use your second language (L2), and some individual differences that I discuss in the following sections.

AGE-RELATED LANGUAGE RESEARCH PROPOSALS

The idea that you can learn a new language as a native speaker when you're a child and not when you're an adult is based on neurobiological processes happening in your brain as you grow. Some researchers have pointed out the importance of *lateralization* of the brain. As your brain matures (between age 2 and puberty), different functions get distributed between the right and left hemispheres. This lateralization may also explain why a native-like pronunciation is so difficult to acquire after puberty. Before puberty, the brain's *plasticity* (the ability to change and adapt) helps in the acquisition of both your first language (L1) and your L2.

However, some researchers disagree with the idea that the two hemispheres of brain have specialized functions because the brain can adapt to new functions, as shown in research with people who suffered lesions on one side of their brain.

Several researchers have addressed the idea that reaching a particular age lowers or blocks language-acquisition success: The strictest approach talks about a *critical period* for language learning, others propose a *sensitive period* for learning, and some others suggest a *linear decline hypothesis*.

- The *critical period*, first used to explain L1 acquisition and later also used to describe L2 acquisition, states that people are biologically predetermined to have a cutoff period that blocks language acquisition from happening. One of the most fervent backers of this *critical period hypothesis*, Eric Lenneberg, claims that once you pass that period (around puberty, at 12–13 years old), you cannot develop certain language skills.

- The *sensitive period* accepts that people are more receptive to learn language before puberty, but once this preferred window of opportunity has passed, you can still learn the language, although you may not be as receptive or successful.

- The *linear decline hypothesis* doesn't mention a start/finish point in the language-acquisition period, but rather talks of a performance decline, meaning a change in the quantity and quality of learning success.

Age

REMEMBER

I'm sure you've heard statements that link language and age, such as *Children are better with languages than adults* or *Only children can learn languages* or *Adults have a difficult time learning languages*. Well, I have good news for you! Although many scholars agree that age plays an important role in language-acquisition success, it's also true that everyone can learn languages. Furthermore, the role of age in language acquisition is still being debated among researchers (see the nearby sidebar "Age-related language research proposals" for details). Despite the debates, many researchers agree on these proposals:

>> Acquiring a native-like *phonology* (sound system) is difficult for adult learners.

>> Adult learners can achieve a native-like *syntax* (combining words to create sentences).

>> In the beginning stages of language learning,

- Adolescents and adults are better and faster than children at learning and using a lot of language early on.

- Adolescents outperform adults and children.

- Adults get more vocabulary and grammar control than children.

But in the long run, those who started to learn a language as children get better end results than adults, becoming more proficient and fluent than those who started learning a new language as an adult.

>> After puberty, learners may need to make a more conscious and deliberate effort to learn a language; the *automaticity* (unconscious ability) that naturally happens when children acquire languages may not be as active in older learners.

>> Children who acquire languages before ages 10–12 obtain a native-like proficiency and are more open to other cultures.

Some other differences related to age and language learning are as follows:

>> In general, children are keener than adults to use the language (even if their proficiency is low). Moreover, some adults and adolescents get stressed when they cannot use the language to express themselves as they would like to.

>> Adults and older learners rely on their cognitive maturity to solve problems and on their previous *metalinguistic awareness* (knowledge of language rules and structure) to participate in conversations about the language.

REMEMBER

So, if you've already passed the critical period mentioned in the sidebar "Age-related language research proposals" — the start of puberty, around age 12 or 13 — you should start your language-learning journey as soon as possible. In fact, some scholars have demonstrated that the onset of your language journey can affect your success: The earlier the onset, the better your language learning. Thus, starting to learn a new language at 30 is better than starting at 50, and starting at 50 is better than starting at 70. The goal is spending the maximum amount of time possible learning and using the L2. The more years you use it, the more language you'll learn and acquire.

Motivation

In 1985, psychologist Robert Gardner defined motivation in learning an L2 as "the extent to which the individual works or strives to learn the language because of the desire to do so and the satisfaction experienced in this activity." Motivation shows in the strong positive feelings you have toward the activity you're doing (in this case, learning a new language), and it normally relates to the reasons you're doing that activity (for example, to travel and visit a new country or to talk to certain people).

REMEMBER

You'll be more successful in any learning activity you embark on if you're motivated by it, and if you keep cheering yourself on for your accomplishments.

And although motivation doesn't affect the acquisition path (it doesn't alter the developmental stages or the order of acquisition you follow), it can affect how fruitful your language learning is. For example, if you're a motivated learner, you'll probably constantly seek opportunities to learn and be in contact with the L2: more input sources, diverse situations to converse with L2 native speakers and produce output, or ways to gather L2 cultural information.

Obviously, everyone doesn't have the same motivation. Also, your motivation may evolve depending on the context, the task at hand, the people you're communicating with and their motivation, group dynamics, and so on. Sometimes, social factors can affect your motivation toward learning the language. For example, your motivation may change because of how you respond to your instructor's teaching style or how you feel when you're with other L2 users (inside or outside the classroom). Likewise, your social and psychological distance from (or closeness to) the L2 language and culture (or political views) can affect your motivation and success.

Gardner's *socio-educational model* or *Motivation Theory* looks at two main types of motivation for learning a new language: integrative and instrumental. These two types of motivation can coexist:

>> *Integrative motivation* is the motivation you feel when you really want to learn the L2 and learn about its culture so you can integrate with and become part of the L2 community. For instance, if you have a significant other who speaks another language, you have a strong integrative motivation to be part of your partner's language community (for example, to get to know their family and friends who speak the L2). This motivation is one of the key elements affecting your success in your L2 learning. This type of motivation results in the most successful learning and the most fluency in pronunciation.

>> *Instrumental motivation* is your motivation to learn a language to achieve certain practical, short-term goals. For instance, you may learn an L2 to get a pay raise, enter a certain education program, complete the requirements in your undergraduate education, or access information/material in the L2.

Some researchers cite another type of motivation, what they call *resultative motivation*. You feel this motivation when you see positive results and accomplishments in your L2 learning journey.

TIP

If you haven't considered your own motivation for learning a new language, stop and think about what motivates you. For example, it may be

>> Your desire to feel part of an L2 community

>> Your willingness to speak the L2 with someone special

>> Your passion for traveling

>> Your need to satisfy certain job or education requirements

>> Your curiosity to learn/know more

>> Your wish to accomplish certain tasks

>> Your feelings of satisfaction and accomplishment after putting in the effort and successfully achieving your goal

Attitude

Researchers have found a correlation, or connection, between language-learning success and the learner's attitude. You'll be more successful in your language learning (and reach a higher proficiency level) if you show a positive attitude and a positive mindset toward the L2 language, the L2 community, the L2 culture (products, practices, and perspectives), and even the way you face the language-learning process.

TIP

Your success (or lack thereof) in the language-acquisition process is clearly linked to your attitude, and one feeds the other. When you see successful results in your learning, your attitude positively influences your desire to continue learning; if you don't see much success, your attitude toward learning the L2 sours. For that reason, here are some suggestions to help you keep a positive attitude along your language-learning journey:

>> Focus on learning language that helps you accomplish tasks that are

- Meaningful

- Engaging

- Practical for your everyday life

- Integrated within the L2 community, when possible

- A bit challenging

- » Focus on setting short-term goals.

    - Keep track of your daily/weekly goals so you feel in control of your own learning.

    - Celebrate your progress toward your goals.

    - Reflect on and celebrate your achievements.

- » Promote your self-awareness.

    - List your strengths.

    - Be aware of your weaknesses.

    - Embrace your mistakes (which are normal and expected in your learning process) and learn from them.

Anxiety

REMEMBER

Many students in regular L2 classrooms have an uncomfortable feeling of anxiety when they are asked to participate in class and don't feel ready to do so. If you studied languages in a classroom setting, you may have experienced that anxiety. According to a 2009 study, a third of U.S. students in a language class experience this uncomfortable feeling. This feeling has a label among linguists: *foreign language anxiety* (proposed by Elaine Horwitz, Michael Horwitz, and Joann Cope in 1986). It appears when your L2 proficiency isn't at the level that allows you to express your true self. Because language classes normally center upon describing or narrating personal experiences, views, and feelings, you may feel anxious and vulnerable if you cannot express what you'd like to express in the way you'd do it in your L1.

Out of the four language-learning skills, speaking and listening normally trigger the most anxiety, although reading and writing can also trigger anxiety. In general, if you're a perfectionist, you may experience more foreign language anxiety than someone who's not a perfectionist.

Linguist Stephen Krashen refers to that feeling of anxiety in the affective filter hypothesis (see Chapter 6). In broad terms, this hypothesis explains that language learning needs to happen in an environment where learners don't feel defensive or anxious; they need to feel secure and comfortable to use the language and make mistakes.

Although anxiousness and fear may be uncomfortable feelings, they're necessary for language learning if you can keep them at a certain level. When they're at the right level, the adrenaline these feelings provoke can help you in your L2 performance; however, when your adrenaline level is over the top, your performance can be completely blocked.

TIP

You may be wondering how to lessen or lower your anxiety level. Here's my advice:

>> Focus on communicating your message, transmitting the content, and being understood, even if the message sounds like something Tarzan would say.

>> Be aware of how much you can say in the L2 and try to push yourself, bearing your limit in mind. Going a little beyond your proficiency level is fine, but if you are a beginner and try to speak in the L2 the way you would in your L1, you're pushing yourself too much, and you may become frustrated and abandon the task.

>> If you try to go beyond your proficiency level, you'll make mistakes. Accept your errors and use them in your favor to enhance your learning. But don't punish or blame yourself for errors. Mistakes are an expected part of the learning process.

>> Play with the language when you're on your own: Practice saying things out loud, describe what you see, name objects you encounter, model the way you'd talk and interact in different situations, and the like. Playing with the L2 on your own gives you the opportunity to practice the new language and be more ready and less anxious when you need to use it in real situations or in class.

Aptitude

Aptitude is related to the popular idea that some people are good or bad at languages. Some scholars have challenged that idea and demonstrated that anyone, under normal circumstances, can learn languages. However, you may not be able to achieve native-like fluency, especially when it relates to pronunciation. In fact, linguistics professor Larry Selinker suggested in 1972 that only 5 percent of L2 learners achieve a native-like proficiency.

In order to study people's aptitude for language, some researchers focus on the learner's intelligences, learning style, memory, and strategies, which I cover later in this chapter. Find out more about possible L2 learning strategies in Chapter 10.

TIP

Researcher John B. Carroll in 1991 defined *aptitude* as a way to learn fast. The higher your aptitude, the faster you'll learn. In case you're wondering how to improve your aptitude, here are several strategies that affect the aptitude of learners (although you don't need to excel in or have them all):

>> Paying attention to the input you receive

>> Identifying and remembering new sounds and words (if you don't identify sounds and words, you won't be able to retain them in your short-term memory, nor will you learn them)

>> Decoding the language input you receive

- » Using your short-term memory to process input

- » Sharpening your memory and retrieval skills

- » Finding opportunities to encounter similar input at different times (spaced repetition opportunities)

- » Using *inductive* and *deductive* learning (see the later section "Processing grammar rules") by

  - Analyzing sentences and understanding the function of words

  - Identifying and noticing language patterns and rules

- » Memorizing language

TECHNICAL STUFF

Researchers have developed many tests to assess people's aptitude to learn languages, such as the Modern Language Aptitude Test (MLAT, created by John Carroll and Stanley Sapon in 1959), the Pimsleur Language Aptitude Battery (PLAB, created by Paul Pimsleur in 1966), the Defense Language Aptitude Battery (DLAB), and the Cognitive Ability for Novelty in Acquisition of Language - Foreign test (CANAL-F). All these tests have some pros and cons, and some are no longer used.

Working memory

You acquire a language when you can store it in your long-term memory. But language isn't stored in your long-term memory right away. Before that, the information you receive through input is stored in your short-term memory until you're able to process it into your working memory, and later it's moved to your long-term memory.

As you start your language-learning journey, your working memory will focus on processing mostly content words or vocabulary (like nouns, verbs, and adjectives), and not function words (like articles and prepositions). The input that your working memory processes is called *intake*.

If you have high working-memory capacity, you'll be able to easily handle meaning and forms (the way you pronounce or write a word) and figure out some patterns in the L2. However, if you have low working-memory capacity, you'll benefit from receiving explicit instruction in the L2 or looking up the rules (deductive learning, which is covered in the later section "Processing grammar rules").

Your L1's influence

Learning an L2 depends on already having an L1. As such, it's normal to resort to your L1 if you face difficulty communicating in your L2 or when you lack the tools in your L2 to express what you want to say.

For instance, when a communication problem arises, L2 learners normally transfer features from their L1 into the L2 system they're building (their *interlanguage*). Transfer occurs at all levels in language: *phonology* (sounds), *syntax* (grammar rules), *semantics* (meaning), and so on. This transfer from your L1 can benefit your L2 learning and acquisition or interfere with it:

>> **Positive transfer:** Your L1 helps your L2 production or understanding, because the vocabulary, sounds, or patterns are similar in the two languages.

>> **Negative transfer or interference:** The L1 obstructs your L2 production or understanding, because the two languages differ in the way they use certain structures, vocabulary words, sounds, and so on.

For example, the [r] and [l] sounds exist in Spanish and in English and they differentiate words. So, an English L1 speaker learning Spanish as their L2 will transfer these sounds to their L2 (positive transfer). However, Mandarin Chinese L1 speakers do not differentiate [r] and [l]. So, Chinese speakers learning Spanish or English as their L2 will have some interference from their L1 when trying to differentiate and produce these L2 sounds in Spanish or English.

TECHNICAL STUFF

With this idea in mind, the *contrastive analysis hypothesis* (CAH) gained importance in the 1960s, prompting many error analysis studies. Based on the CAH, some scholars emphasize the importance of comparing the two languages and evaluating the areas in which the L1 and L2 are similar and the areas in which they differ.

Personality traits

Your personality may also affect the success of your language learning. Here are some personality features that can affect your language-learning journey, according to scholars:

>> **Passion:** The best language learners are passionate about learning the language and its culture. This is part of your motivation. (I discuss motivation in more detail earlier in this chapter.)

>> **Diligence:** The most successful language learners are hard workers who put time and effort into learning the language and exploring its culture. So, if you want to acquire a new language, you need to be willing to work hard.

TIP

Keep track of the vocabulary you're learning and need for your daily use (you can make flashcards to review new words). Search for opportunities to practice the L2; conversation groups that meet in person or social media groups that share your language and cultural interests offer the chance to use what you've learned.

WARNING

If you start learning a language with the belief that you aren't good at languages, you may not put in enough work and effort to learn it.

>> **Independence:** You should be *autonomous* (independent) in your learning. Set realistic goals and create your personal plan to achieve them. Don't expect others to push you.

>> **Consistency:** You should find a way to get some exposure to the language every day. You can study, read, search the web for information using your L2, listen to music, watch a movie or TV program, or view any other audiovisual material you can find (including ads and videos on YouTube).

>> **Perfectionism:** If you're a high achiever or a perfectionist, you may end up overanalyzing your L2 production to avoid errors, which can affect your fluency and language development, and will almost certainly give you foreign language anxiety. You should be proud of your progress in the language journey and accept that errors are normal. Just focus on delivering the meaning!

REMEMBER

Have communication as your main goal, and leave accuracy and perfection on the back burner, especially if you're a novice learner.

>> **Fearlessness:** Along the lines of the previous characteristic, you'll benefit from being a risk-taker and using your L2 without any fear or concern about making errors. It's very important to accept that errors are a normal part of the learning process. Use your miscommunications to improve your language proficiency. Don't feel anxious about mistakes — just go ahead and take risks in your L2!

>> **Creativity:** If you're creative, you can use outside-the-box strategies to communicate messages above your L2 proficiency level. For instance, you can mime, draw, point, and so on. Creativity develops higher aptitude (covered earlier in this chapter), so find different ways to experiment with the language and culture (such as preparing a recipe from a cookbook or playing a video game in your L2).

>> **Resourcefulness:** Use various strategies and techniques to communicate in the L2, such as contextual and linguistic cues; *mnemonics* (associations that

make things easier to remember); and rephrasing or substituting all-purpose words like *thing* or *stuff* for words you don't know or can't remember. Find out more in Chapter 10.

>> **Perceptiveness:** If you have good guessing skills, you'll be able to deduce meanings and grammar rules easily.

>> **Confidence:** Being self-confident and embracing your mistakes as a normal part of the learning process encourages you to see the great progress you're making.

>> **Sociability:** The more social interactions you have, the better you'll become at your L2, so be open to finding opportunities to socialize with other L2 speakers.

>> **Open-mindedness:** Learning a new language means also learning a new culture and a new way of thinking and seeing the world. You'll have more success if you're able to accept those differences and tolerate ambiguity (uncertainty).

Multiple intelligences

Intelligence can be defined as your capacity to process information. For instance, if you have logical-mathematical intelligence, you'll learn a grammar concept better if it's presented as a formula (for example, *subject + am/is/are + -ing verb*), whereas if you're a linguistic-verbal learner, you prefer encountering a grammar concept while reading it in a book or writing it in a notebook. Everyone differs in the way they learn best.

Intelligence (and what IQ, or *intelligence quotient*, measures) has normally focused on assessing people's linguistic-verbal and logical-mathematical skills. But intelligence goes beyond that.

Educators Howard Gardner and Thomas Armstrong proposed that there are eight multiple intelligences. You have all the intelligences (and they work together), but some of your intelligences are more developed than others, and you can develop your underdeveloped intelligences. Table 3-1 explains how you can use multiple intelligences to your advantage when you're learning a new language.

TIP

If you're wondering what your strongest multiple intelligences are, I suggest that you complete a free questionnaire available online. Just search for "multiple intelligence inventory test" to find some options. Or you may use the information in Table 3-1 to consider what resonates with you.

TABLE 3-1   # Multiple Intelligences and Language Learning

Multiple Intelligence	You're Good At	Find Opportunities To
Linguistic-verbal	Using new words in sentences Repeating, imitating, and rehearsing language (out loud or silently) Using language memory strategies to recall information Communicating with others	Read, tell, and listen to stories in the L2. Write stories, poems, and ideas in the L2. Play word games in the L2. Read, listen to, and verbalize words and phrases in the L2. Make contextualized lists (for example, by topic) and create mnemonics in the L2. Interact with L2 speakers.
Logical-mathematical	Classifying and categorizing things Analyzing the language and finding patterns	Organize the information in the L2 — for example, in Venn diagrams, in graphic organizers (visual tools that help you lay out information), by topic, by function (like phrases that serve as sentence starters) and so on. Create charts or tables in the L2. Create/read/analyze surveys in the L2.
Visual-spatial	Remembering locations Creating mental images of places	On Google Maps, find places where the L2 is spoken and use Street View to pretend to walk around these locations. You can find plenty of technology tools in Chapter 14. Draw/sketch/design cities and label the buildings in the L2. Label your surroundings in the L2.
Bodily-kinesthetic	Linking motion to actions and ideas Acting/role-playing Linking the L2 to dance moves Using real objects you can touch and naming them in the L2	Role-play and act out situations using the L2. Watch music videos in the L2 and sing/dance along. Name everything you touch in the L2.
Musical-rhythmic	Perceiving patterns of tones and intonation Creating pitch and rhythmic patterns Creating melodies	Imitate words (especially if you're a child learning a tonal language, such as Chinese). Create melodies/rhymes in the L2 for everything you encounter. Access L2 audio or audiovisual sources (use L2 closed captions if available).

Multiple Intelligence	You're Good At	Find Opportunities To
Interpersonal	Interacting with people	Find L2 speakers to communicate with.
	Understanding people	Organize group meetings to use the L2.
	Cooperating with others	Find how to ask for feedback in the L2 and how to negotiate meaning (how to ask speakers to repeat themselves, paraphrase, give you examples, and the like).
	Asking for clarifications and using them as models	
	Receiving feedback	
Intrapersonal	Thinking to yourself	Journal your feelings and experiences in the L2.
	Working on your own	Read and write or scribble in the L2 and create a portfolio.
	Setting goals and planning	Assess your strengths in the L2 and use them.
	Self-evaluating	
	Focusing/concentrating	Consider your weaknesses in the L2 and plan for them.
Naturalistic	Contemplating/observing and analyzing nature	Photograph nature and label what you see in the L2.
	Photographing nature	Classify what you see in nature in the L2.
	Categorizing things	Compare and contrast nature in the L1 and L2.
	Pinpointing cultural products (such as architecture, art, or any other product you normally find in the L2 culture)	Try to visit a country/countries where the L2 is spoken.

Language-learning style

Not every person learns or works the same way. For instance, you may learn better when you discuss the topic with others (*extroverted learning*), or you may prefer working on your own (*introverted learning*). Everyone gathers and processes information differently and prefers one style over another, depending on the task or the situation.

REMEMBER

Learning style is the way in which people perceive and process information (voluntarily or not). Learning styles account for both emotion and cognition (reasoning ability), which is a great approach for dealing with L2 learning. No learning style is better than another; they're just personal preferences, and they may change as you age. Learning styles don't alter the way you acquire language (your language development), but they can affect the way you manage input or the type of input you benefit most from.

Learning styles can be divided into several categories, depending on the way learners process new input/material. I present some common language-learning styles in the following sections.

Using your senses

Some learning styles are based on the senses (visual, auditory, and kinesthetic/tactile) you prefer using in order to learn the input you receive (*sensory preferences*). Although you may learn better when you receive input in more than one way, you normally prefer using one sense over another.

TECHNICAL STUFF

Some research has found sensory learning differs according to learners' cultural background. For example, Korean students are more visual than English-speaking American students, and Chinese students are more auditory than Japanese students.

Here are the different learning styles related to your senses:

>> **Visual learners:** You remember content better when you see/watch something, receive written input, or write it down (even better if it's color-coded). You benefit from getting information from graphics, charts, maps, graphic organizers (tools that help you arrange written information visually), drawings or other images, TV, video, or books. You prefer receiving written directions over oral directions. You like linking images to new concepts and creating semantic maps. You prefer reading (silently).

>> **Auditory learners:** You're good at keeping sounds in your memory, so you remember better when you hear the input. You learn by having verbal interactions with others (speaking, interviewing, debating, discussing, role-playing) and listening (to lectures, audiobooks, and the like). Background sound/music can help you learn. You need to listen to a word several times to learn it, and pronouncing it out loud may also help you.

>> **Tactile/kinesthetic learners:** You remember better when you touch and manipulate objects, draw or doodle, or make things with your hands. You like doing projects or experiments and working with *realia* (real objects). You need physical activity and body movement (walking, standing up, and so on) to remember new words or language concepts.

Processing grammar rules

When it comes to grammar rules, you may be a deductive learner or an inductive learner. Here's how these learners process language rules better:

>> As a *deductive learner,* you prefer knowing the grammar rules from the beginning, and then applying them to specific examples. This is a more teacher-centered approach.

>> As an *inductive learner,* you prefer starting from examples and trying to notice or discover commonalities or patterns, and then coming up with the grammar rules. Thus, you're good at using inferencing strategies to guess meanings, guess rules, and form hypotheses to create your internal language. This is a more student-centered approach.

Organizing the material

Another learning style is based on how you prefer the input to be presented and organized to help you learn it. Some linguists call this *intuitive/random learning* and *sequential learning:*

>> If you're an *intuitive/random (nonlinear) learner,* you learn better when you look at the global picture in a nonsequential way. You're good at abstract thinking, and have a vivid imagination and original ideas. You prefer having a general idea before getting into the details. For example, you prefer reading a chapter summary or skimming the section headings before reading the text in detail. You're also good at connecting random L2 information that you've been getting from different sources.

>> On the other hand, if you're a *sequential (linear) learner,* you learn better when the information is presented to you step-by-step in an orderly way. You cannot easily see the big picture. You prefer to focus and analyze things as they are (not imagining how they can be), and work with what you can see and with concrete facts and items. You aren't the type of person who tries to put together a piece of furniture without reading the instructions. You don't like to change plans, and you prefer to follow the patterns you're given. You learn better when you organize the L2 information by themes or following an order (like chronology, steps, and so on). For example, you benefit from learning and practicing one grammar rule before moving to another.

Having an end goal

Some learners need to have a clear conclusion/goal to guide their learning:

>> If you're a *closure-oriented learner,* you learn better when you have an ending point, closure, or goal in sight. You try to meet deadlines, and you aren't good at letting uncertainty take over. You like knowing the meaning of vocabulary from the beginning (not guessing it) and being exposed to grammar rules so you understand how to use them and why. You like planning your learning,

and assessing your progress. You benefit from using advance organizers (tools that help you brainstorm information you already know to connect it more easily with the new info that is about to come) so you have a general preview of what you're about to learn. You carefully organize your learning and your lessons. Sometimes, this kind of learning can interfere with your ability to use communication openly.

>> If you're an *open-ended oriented learner,* you don't necessarily expect to have a goal in sight, reach a conclusion quickly, or meet a deadline; you learn by exposure to the language through communication, without consciously analyzing everything. You aren't stressed out about understanding everything from the very beginning; you prefer relaxing and picking up the language naturally.

Working with others

Working with others or group participation can help some learners. Other people prefer to learn on their own.

>> If you're an *extroverted learner,* you open up to others easily, and you like activities that make you interact with others or use social communication (role-playing, conversations, debates, and the like). Discussing new material with others helps you learn. You're outgoing and sociable.

>> On the other hand, if you're an *introverted learner,* you're quite reserved, not very open to interacting with many people, and prefer working on your own (for example, reading and writing alone) or with just one person you feel very comfortable with. You may be seen as a shy person.

Getting your bearings

Getting your bearings in the linguistics context refers to whether you need to have access to all the details of the language when you receive input. Some linguists call this *analytical–global learning.*

>> If you're an *analytical learner,* you pay close attention to grammar details and examples, so you're good at picking up new phrases you may get from input. You excel at grouping and classifying input based on common features. You don't like guessing based on context but prefer knowing meaning beforehand.

>> If you're a *global learner,* you see the overall picture easily. You prefer short and simple answers (not long and detailed ones) or main ideas over specifics. If you retell a story, you often forget many details because you focus on the main points, or the gist. You're intuitive and spontaneous, and you like interacting with others, even if you don't understand everything. You're okay with trying to guess meaning on the fly.

Advancing Your Language Proficiency Level

Your *language proficiency level* determines what you can do with the language, not how much you know about the language. For instance, knowing all the grammar rules and concepts, or when to use one tense or another, isn't equivalent to higher language proficiency. However, using different rules and forms to perform diverse language tasks (such as asking questions, narrating events, describing things, and giving an opinion) shows your proficiency.

REMEMBER

The foundation of language proficiency is using the language in context and accomplishing real-life tasks.

When the linguistic task you're trying to perform surpasses your actual proficiency level, processing and producing language becomes difficult, and proficiency suffers. In that situation, your working memory is maxed out because you're trying to process lots of information that isn't part of your internal language system, or *interlanguage*. In the beginning, your language repertoire is mainly formed by *lexical items* (content words such as nouns, verbs, and adjectives). As more of the L2 becomes part of your interlanguage, your proficiency level grows.

TIP

If you're wondering how to advance in your language proficiency, check out these suggestions:

>> Spend more time learning and practicing your L2.

>> Concentrate on accomplishing tasks (such as asking and answering questions, narrating, and describing) and the language tools (vocabulary and grammar) needed to complete them.

>> Focus on finding lots of quality input.

>> Search for opportunities to interact in the L2 that are meaningful and goal-oriented.

TIP

If you can travel to the country where the L2 is spoken and you immerse yourself in the language and culture, you'll be able to target these suggestions. However, if you cannot travel, make a plan to constantly use the L2 (at your proficiency level) to discuss topics that interest you, and find opportunities to socialize with other speakers.

Different organizations have their own guidelines to differentiate proficiency or competency levels, and different ways to name these proficiency levels. The following sections give you the scoop.

CEFR proficiency

In Europe, the Common European Framework of Reference for Languages (CEFR) dictates how to measure the competence or proficiency level of L2 learners. This framework emphasizes the importance of building plurilingualism and pluriculturalism (interconnecting and using multiple languages and cultures), and its focus is assessing the linguistic competence of L2 users and how they can use the language in social interactions. So, the CEFR's focus is not only language, but also its use in certain cultural contexts and circumstances.

CEFR divides proficiency into three broad levels (A, B, C) and six sublevels (1 and 2):

>> Basic user (A-level: A1 and A2)

>> Independent user (B-level: B1 and B2)

>> Proficient user (C-level: C1 and C2)

The most advanced proficiency level is C2, whereas the lowest is A1.

TIP

Find out more about CEFR at www.coe.int/en/web/common-european-framework-reference-languages/.

ACTFL guidelines

In the United States, the organization that dictates curricular decisions and proficiency guidelines is ACTFL (the American Council on the Teaching of Foreign Languages). ACTFL assesses all language skills, including oral and written proficiency, as well as listening and reading ability. As its *ACTFL Proficiency Guidelines* (2024) spell out, proficiency is assessed by looking at four major criteria (known by the acronym FACT):

>> **Functions and tasks:** This criterion measures the linguistic tasks you can accomplish. For example, can you list words, ask and answer questions, narrate and describe situations in all major time frames (past, present, and future), hypothesize, and support your opinions?

>> **Accuracy:** This standard looks at how appropriately you use the language to accomplish the task at hand. It assesses your vocabulary, grammar, pronunciation, pragmatics, fluency, and so on. One way to check accuracy is by considering how well someone who isn't used to dealing with L2 speakers can understand you. For example, is the language you produce understood by someone not accustomed to dealing with non-native speakers? Do you repeat patterns of errors?

>> **Context and content:** This measures proficiency in situations where you need to accomplish tasks (for example, ordering food in a restaurant, filing a report at a police station, or buying groceries at a supermarket) and how you use the L2 to talk about topics that are predictable and familiar, personal, general, specialized or specific, and so on.

>> **Text type:** This criterion examines the type of language you produce to accomplish a task. For example, do you use words and phrases, sentences, paragraphs, or discourse (stories or conversation)?

The ACTFL levels of proficiency are

>> Novice

>> Intermediate

>> Advanced

>> Superior

>> Distinguished

TIP

Find out more about the ACTFL's proficiency guidelines at https://www.actfl.org/educator-resources/actfl-proficiency-guidelines.

Chapter **4**

Enjoying the Advantages of Learning Languages

L earning more than one language (being *bilingual* or *multilingual*) benefits individuals as well as societies as a whole. When the push to learn second languages reaches a social level (as happens in many European countries, where the target for people is learning two other languages besides their first language), societies are more open to differences, appreciate other cultures, and can become more economically competitive. In fact, research has shown that when you learn a second language and its culture, you can improve in many areas: academically, cognitively, personally, emotionally, and economically.

However, you may have also heard of parents, teachers, or even some pediatricians who encourage parents to keep their kids *monolingual* speakers (fluent in only one language) because they're afraid of many unfounded myths. For instance, they may believe that learning two languages will confuse children, or that their brain has a limited capacity to store information, and once it's full, they cannot add anything else or whatever they add will be at the expense of removing something else. The effect of learning another language is actually quite the opposite, as I explain in this chapter.

REMEMBER

Early exposure to two or more languages and sustained learning of the two languages are key elements to obtaining and benefiting from the *bilingual advantage*, but later language learners also benefit from being exposed to and using the two languages. The quantity and quality of your exposure and your motivation to learn languages and their cultures are necessary factors in obtaining the benefits of bilingualism.

Strengthening Your Academic Success

Research shows that in general, language learners have greater academic success than their monolingual counterparts. In fact, some studies found that high school students who studied languages did better academically in college than those who didn't study languages.

One obvious advantage for language learners is that their language skills provide them with opportunities to access information in that language that they otherwise wouldn't be able to access. But that's not all! Knowing another language normally gives you advantages in different subject areas: metalinguistic awareness and first language (L1) skills, language arts (reading comprehension, writing, and literacy in general), mathematics (and math problems) and statistics, and science. Bilinguals also usually get higher test scores (such as in standardized tests) than monolingual speakers.

Additionally, when compared with monolinguals, bilingual speakers normally have higher levels of abstract thinking, are better at using logic and formulating (scientific) hypotheses, are better at decision-making, and have more creativity. Considering all these academic advantages, I understand why you want to learn a new language! The following sections go into more detail on all these academic benefits.

Access to more information

REMEMBER

Knowing languages gives you access to more people, resources, and sources of information. Being able to communicate with people from other cultures in their languages, and reading information sources in other languages, allows you an opportunity to understand the world from other cultural perspectives, find out more about your own culture, and consequently get a better understanding of the human experience.

Here's an example to demonstrate the importance of being able to access more sources of information: When an influential event is happening in a country (such as a terrorist attack, a political campaign and election, or a war, to name a few), the news you receive from newspapers or TV while living in your own country reflects a particular view of the events (your country's view). Sometimes it's just a way to maintain calmness in society. But if you think about it, don't you want to know everything that's really happening? Well, being able to access information about these events as reported by different countries (in their language and through their news media) gives you that wider overview.

Knowing different languages not only gives you access to more information but also opens up the possibility of enjoying art (films, books, music, and so on) in its original form, in the language that art was created. When you access art in its original form, you can really go deep into its meaning.

Test scores

In general, bilinguals have more intellectual flexibility than monolinguals, which may explain why, in general, bilinguals show better results in both verbal and nonverbal tests of intelligence.

So, if you're thinking of going to college and you need to take an entrance exam, studying a second language (L2) can help you. In fact, research has shown that students learning a second language obtain higher scores in standardized college entrance tests than students who don't learn a second language. Studying a language for more than 4 years helped students get higher scores on the verbal section of the SAT (the Scholastic Aptitude Test). And although it may be unexpected, learning a second language also helps students get better in their first language, as demonstrated by bilinguals' high scores in English language arts achievement tests.

But that isn't all! Diverse research studies have demonstrated that bilingual speakers obtain higher scores in standardized tests of different subject areas, such as math, reading, writing, vocabulary, science, and social studies.

Metalinguistic awareness and better L1 skills

Metalinguistic awareness is being able to think, reflect, and know about the nature and functions of a language. It shouldn't be confused with being able to use the language. And the great piece of news is that when you learn a second language, you also get metalinguistic advantages in your first language (as proposed in the threshold hypothesis), even when the two languages don't share the same alphabet. For instance, it helps you in your writing competence and spelling development.

In 2001, Jim Cummins, a well-known researcher and professor in Canada, proposed the *threshold hypothesis,* which states that bilingualism is most beneficial when a balanced bilingualism (equal knowledge) in the two languages exists. Thus, bilingual speakers gain the most from their bilingualism when they show language proficiency, develop similar literacy skills, and have academic access in both languages.

Young bilingual children develop metalinguistic awareness earlier than monolingual speakers. Thus, they can get some insights of the nature of language and understand that language is a system. For instance, bilingual children are really good at the following:

>> **Analyzing different aspects of language (sounds, the concept of words, *syntax* [the way words are put together], and so on) and even explaining them to a certain extent, if required:** For example, they are good at judging whether a sentence is grammatically correct even if the meaning isn't the one expected. Iin other words, they recognize that *Oranges grow in racquets* is grammatically correct even though it doesn't make sense.

>> **Understanding that language has a structure underneath:** They're aware that words have sounds, and that sounds can be written with certain letters.

>> **Understanding that the form and the meaning of language is arbitrary:** They easily get the random nature of words as they look at and compare their L1 to another language. An English-French bilingual child understands that a dog can be called *dog* or *chien,* for example.

>> **Attaining semantic development 2 to 3 years before monolinguals:** Bilingual children link similar words based on their meaning (semantics) sooner than monolingual children do. For example, in a set of words such as *cat, cap,* and *hat,* bilinguals link *hat* and *cap* as similar words, whereas monolingual children would consider *cat* and *cap* as similar words (because they sound similar). As expected, bilingual children outperform their monolingual counterparts in word tasks such as word awareness.

One very important skill needed to advance academically is learning how to read, which requires having certain metalinguistic awareness. For example, kids need to know that language has an underlying structure, that words have sounds, and that sounds can be written with certain letters. In fact, one of the first things children must learn before reading is the concept of a word — that a combination of letters (or sounds) represents an idea or object (a meaning). Fortunately, reading skills are transferable from one language to another, enhancing kids' L1 skills. And as mentioned in the earlier section "Test scores," language learners show high scores in their English language arts achievement tests.

Increased creativity

Have you ever found yourself in a situation in which you had a problem to solve and you weren't sure what to do? Did discussing it with others help you solve the problem? Possibly yes, right? Finding solutions to problems is usually easier if you discuss the issues with other people. And it's even more beneficial if the group of people discussing these issues have different cultural perspectives.

Being multilingual and having a multilingual/multicultural background contributes to developing a creative personality and undertaking creative activities. Forming teams or groups of people with diverse linguistic and cultural backgrounds enriches these groups and their discussions because the various members bring their unique creativity and problem-solving skills to the table. Creativity blossoms within groups of people with different languages and cultural perspectives and experiences.

Furthermore, multilingual speakers' creativity enhances their problem-solving skills because they excel at

>> Generating ideas and thinking outside the box

>> Showing openness to other languages and cultures (and to the world as a whole)

>> Having divergent ways of thinking and coming up with new and innovative solutions, not just the expected ones

For example, if the assignment for a history class is to make a presentation about World War II, a bilingual speaker may give this assignment a more creative touch by recording a video in which they interview different fictional historical people in that war who give their personal perspectives about how they lived through the war.

Other academic benefits

Knowing more than one language offers you several academic benefits in addition to those in the previous sections:

>> **Decision-making:** Bilingual speakers' decisions are more reason-driven, especially if you make the decision in the second language. For example, in a situation where you have to choose what to do next, as a bilingual speaker, you'll select the most logical and common-sense option. In a multiple-choice exam, you can have less difficulty choosing answers drawn from logical and reasonable choices, especially if the exam is in your L2.

>> **Objectivity:** When you're in a challenging situation, dealing with it in your second language allows you to assess it more objectively (and distance yourself emotionally). You undergo some systematic thinking and pick objective and unbiased choices. For example, in a classroom debate assignment, when you're tasked to defend an idea and support your position with objective and fact-based ideas, you'll be able to do so more easily than monolingual speakers.

>> **Interpretation:** Bilinguals outperform their monolingual counterparts in analyzing and guessing word meaning based on the verbal context. For example, when bilingual speakers are reading a text with unfamiliar words, they can use some strategies (such as checking surrounding words and analyzing word parts) to interpret the meaning of those words.

>> **Resiliency:** You become a more resilient learner because you'll make mistakes (many of them!) in front of others (native speakers, your teacher, your classmates) when you're learning a new language. Some errors may happen because you take risks to produce (orally or in written form) something you're still learning. This trial-and-error process may seem uncomfortable, but I promise it makes you grow as a person and as a more proficient speaker, and it helps you mature. You'll have a great feeling of accomplishment when you clear some of these hurdles and find yourself conversing with other speakers of the language.

Making mistakes is part of the learning process, and it's normal to hit some bumps on the road to becoming a more proficient learner. So, don't despair!

REMEMBER

>> **Problem-solving:** As I mention in the previous section, when you're bilingual, you have an advantage in problem-solving, especially when it depends on selective attention or inhibitory control (which are part of the executive control system), and when creativity comes into play. For example, when reading a math or physics word problem, where there are several factors and steps to consider, bilingual speakers may be better than monolinguals at organizing the order in which the different parts of the problems need to be solved and focusing on them. They can focus their attention on each individual part and not be distracted by extra details until it is time to look at them.

>> **Task-initiation:** Bilinguals can start an activity and generate ideas independently better than monolingual speakers. Normally, bilinguals also have a quicker reaction time. For example, they tend to be among the first ones to give ideas and solutions (mostly very creative ones) either in a class or in a job.

Improving Your Brain Power: Cognitive and Health Benefits

The way language works in the brain is still being studied. Although a lot of research has been done in the last few decades, many questions remain unanswered.

Because learning a language and gaining proficiency is a constantly evolving process, some researchers suggest that people don't have either a monolingual or a bilingual brain, but the process is seen as a continuum that goes from being monolingual to becoming bilingual.

Brain changes are correlated with the proficiency level you attain in the new language. Therefore, the frequency, intensity, and duration of your bilingual experience has an effect on your brain's structure and function. The following sections describe some of the ways in which your brain changes when you learn a new language.

REMEMBER

What all studies seem to suggest is that learning another language and becoming bilingual enhances your *neuroplasticity* (the brain's ability to change and reorganize its connections). But if you stop learning and using the new language, your brain may revert to its structure and function before you were bilingual.

Executive function

One of the most influential researchers of how bilingualism affects the brain is Ellen Bialystok, a Canadian psychologist and professor. Among her many findings, she emphasizes the advantage bilinguals have in their *executive function,* or ability to inhibit distractions and focus on tasks. (In other words, bilingual speakers are *really* good at multitasking.)

The truth is, your executive function (also known as cognitive control) does a lot! Executive function oversees several brain processes that you use to control your behavior to reach a goal. You develop executive function with training and practice, so you can always get better at it! Executive function helps you

>> Organize and plan

>> Direct your attention

>> Remember instructions

>> Prioritize tasks

>> Filter distractions and keep focused

>> Control impulses and manage emotions

>> Be (cognitively) flexible

>> Multitask

Bilingual speakers' advantage in executive function is illustrated by a very interesting study that assessed the executive function of both bilinguals and monolinguals.

The two groups of participants in the study had to drive in an arcade-type simulator while receiving commands to perform different tasks (for example, turn off the radio or eat some pizza). Thus, both groups — monolingual speakers and bilingual speakers — had to focus on the driving task while dealing with distractions. Bilinguals were better at multitasking, outperforming the monolingual group because they were able to inhibit the distractions and focus on the main goal (driving in the road).

REMEMBER

Actually, if you think about it, bilingual brains are in a constant state of dichotomy (division), where more than one language is ready to be used. So, a bilingual speaker's brain has to inhibit one of the languages to concentrate on the other.

The development and maintenance of executive function can be affected by several factors, besides use and training:

>> Your intelligence

>> Your level of education

>> Your lifestyle (social and leisure activities — for example, exercising, playing music, and having an active social life)

>> Your socioeconomic status

>> The languages you know

Bilingualism can train children's brains to develop their executive function. As a result, they can perform more challenging tasks than monolingual children.

You have an advantage in executive function if you're a balanced bilingual and start acquiring the L2 at an early age. The more balanced your proficiency in the two languages, the more enhanced executive function you'll have, the better you'll be at completing executive functioning tasks, regardless of your socioeconomic status, and the better you'll be at performing nonverbal tasks.

REMEMBER

Balanced bilinguals are equally proficient in two languages. You can read more about the different ways to classify bilinguals in Chapter 2.

Working memory

Working memory is a key part of executive function. Professor Nelson Cowan refers to *working memory* as a series of cognitive processes that allows the brain to store and manipulate or use information temporarily. Your working memory can hold only a certain amount of information, so it deletes information as soon as possible. Normally, working memory isn't fully developed until the age of 6.

You use your working memory when you memorize the number on a license plate, a verification code, or a phone number for a short time, and you do so by manipulating that information (linking it to known patterns — for example, you may recall 2413 by remembering that the two first even numbers are followed by the two first odd numbers). The information in your working memory doesn't get into your long-term memory right away, unless you work toward remembering that information.

So, if you have a sizable working memory capacity, you may be good at learning languages because you're able to keep a lot of information in your head, at least momentarily. Bilingualism can strengthen your working memory because you need to store and retrieve information in the two languages constantly. For instance, your working memory holds the sounds you hear for some time so that you can make comparisons between sounds or identify patterns. Being able to make these comparisons helps you notice feedback and learn from it. You can find out more about short-term memory, working memory, and long-term memory in Chapter 3.

Inhibitory control

Inhibitory control helps you ignore distractions and temptations. As mentioned in the earlier section "Executive function," inhibitory control is a key part of executive function. In 1998, professor David W. Green proposed the *inhibitory control model*, which states that when bilinguals produce or comprehend words, the two languages they know are active, and they need to control their activation to produce or comprehend the target language they aim to use in each case.

Bilingual children show more inhibitory control than monolingual children. Adult bilinguals who started learning the L2 earlier in childhood show greater inhibitory control than later bilinguals, because they have been exposed to or have spoken the L2 longer.

Mental/cognitive flexibility

Mental/cognitive flexibility refers to the ability to think about things in diverse ways. Bilinguals have enhanced cognitive flexibility mechanisms, so they can adapt more easily to new situations or current task demands than monolinguals. For example, as professor Nachshon Meiran noted in 2010, when bilinguals carry out more than one task or when they interact socially, they can adapt and switch between tasks more effectively than monolingual speakers.

REMEMBER

Learning a new language and culture, and consequently having an emotional attachment to more than one country, is associated with having more flexibility and creativity.

Attentional control

Attentional control makes you pay attention to relevant objects and locations, be alert and maintain a state of readiness, and select the best response to address any goal you may have. The ongoing bilingual experience especially helps *selective attention*, or focusing or filtering your attention to the information that is relevant and ignoring the rest. For example, in a conversation on the street, where many other sounds may be happening at the same time (cars, birds, other conversations, and so on), bilingual speakers are good at focusing their attention on their specific conversation — ignoring those cars, birds, and other conversations — and can still be attentive to other issues happening around them.

Delayed cognitive decline

Bilingual brains provide a way to hold off natural cognitive decline for a longer period because they have a bigger cognitive reserve (thinking abilities, processes, or mechanisms used to compensate, improvise, and offset brain functional problems). Bilingualism doesn't prevent dementia, but it delays the onset of symptoms. Alzheimer's disease is delayed an average of 4 years among bilingual speakers compared to monolinguals.

Psychologist Ellen Bialystok suggests that bilinguals simply don't show signs of dementia at the onset of the disease. Rather, because of their cognitive reserve, bilinguals with dementia can function well for a longer period of time than monolinguals who have the disease. Thus, they don't show signs of cognitive decline right away, as monolinguals do. A bilingual person in the first stages of Alzheimer's may not have any symptoms and may even function as if they don't have Alzheimer's. So, when the symptoms show up, the bilingual speaker may be at a more advanced stage of Alzheimer's than a monolingual speaker showing the first signs of the disease.

TIP

The delay in bilinguals' cognitive decline is linked to their ability to focus on the details of their languages. Some ways to keep up your cognitive reserve and obtain the same delay (besides learning a new language) are as follows:

>> Stimulating your brain

- Receiving formal education (The more formal education you get, the more you can postpone the onset of cognitive diseases)
- Being involved in activities related to alphabetization, such as book clubs
- Pursuing musical training

>> Managing stress

- Resting, relaxing, and sleeping well
- Not being hard on yourself and cheering on your efforts and progress

>> Maintaining an active lifestyle

- Pursuing an active social life and being involved in many social gatherings/events
- Exercising

Accentuating Personal, Social, and Cultural Benefits

Language is the essence of social interactions, and interactions in your new language help you develop your language skills and your understanding of the culture. So, you want to be able to use your new language as soon and as proficiently as possible to communicate with other community members, learn from them, and find out more about the culture.

REMEMBER

Don't forget that learning another language entails more than just learning new words; it also offers you insights into another culture and into the way others think and relate to the world. Learning another language and its culture gives you the opportunity to see the world through an extra pair of lenses. In fact, language encodes and reflects its culture, so to gain a deeper understanding of a culture, you need to have access to its language.

The more years you spend learning and practicing a language, the more cross-cultural awareness and communicative competence you develop. Thus, you're able to use the second language in a more culturally appropriate manner and understand the other culture better. Learning about another culture enhances your understanding of your own culture, because you're able to compare and contrast cultural products and practices and understand cultural perspectives better.

Due to their access to two languages and cultures, bilingual speakers adapt better to diverse social situations and interactions, have a wider worldview, show more social flexibility, and adapt more easily to expectations. As a result, bilingual speakers show great tolerance and sociability. The following sections describe other personal, social, and cultural benefits of learning a new language.

Improved communication skills

As I mention earlier in this chapter, you can transfer certain skills from one language to another. Actually, learning a new language helps you create a broad repertoire of linguistic tools and strategies that you can share between the two linguistic systems.

Having previous knowledge of a language influences and improves the way you process and reason in another language. This previous knowledge also helps you work with lexical and sociopragmatic cues (such as using language that is appropriate to the formal or informal social context, and that helps you reach an intended communicative goal). For instance, you can become better at understanding messages, even when some vocabulary is new to you, by using strategies such as relying on context, reading linguistic or social cues, recognizing similarity to other known words, and so on.

Enhanced intercultural competence

Language and culture are intermingled, and to know a culture better and empathize with its members, you should learn its language. Likewise, if you want to master a language, you need to learn about its culture.

I imagine you're wondering where to start. I suggest that you start by studying and reflecting upon your own culture. How can you learn about another culture without being aware of your own? You may be thinking that you know your culture well, and I believe it, but here's an activity to check the depth of your knowledge.

Think for a second about your car and what you can find inside it. Are there cupholders? Are there food remnants in the cupholders or on the floor? If so, what are they from? What kind of food do you eat in the car? Why do you eat in the car instead of eating at home or in a restaurant? Is it a matter of being pressed for time? You may say, *I can't spend time eating at a table. I have lots to do.* What does this tell you about what's valued in your culture? Have you ever thought about why you use the verb *spend* with time *and* money? Does *spending time* equal *spending money?* Wow! So many questions to answer to get a deeper understanding of your own culture! If you do this kind of questioning frequently, you'll discover a lot about your culture.

Understanding your culture definitely helps you understand a brand-new culture. In fact, you'll understand the other culture better when you compare it with your own culture. As you compare both cultures, you also learn more about your own culture. Surely, there are areas where both cultures align and other areas where they differ.

As I explain in Chapter 3, the American Council on the Teaching of Foreign Languages (ACTFL) recognizes three main components within cultures: products, practices, and perspectives. Being familiar with a wide variety of cultural products, practices, and perspectives helps you admire and understand human nature and behavior, being aware of what you know and willing to grow your understanding in new ways. You begin to realize that your own *cultural perspective,* or the way you see the world, is only one possible worldview, and many other perspectives exist.

REMEMBER

Bilingual speakers can easily accept different cultural perspectives thanks to their positive attitudes and enhanced knowledge. Also, children who study and learn a second language show more respect, empathy, and tolerance for that culture. In fact, the number of years someone spends learning languages normally correlates with the positive development of cross-cultural awareness and communicative competence.

Social-emotional connection

Learning languages makes you feel exceptional, accomplished, and welcomed into a new community or culture; you feel you're part of a superpower team!

Obviously, the reasons behind your decision to learn a new language affect the way you feel about it while you're learning it. You may be learning another language because of family ties, your job, an academic requirement, or a desire to travel and get to know new people and places. Whatever the reason behind your decision, when you realize that you can communicate in another language, you'll feel accomplished.

Learning the language of your family (or the language spoken in the place where you or your family came from) helps you complete your identity and connect with your family and your community of origin. It also helps you communicate with family members living in your country of origin, and eases your experience when you visit the place you or your family came from.

REMEMBER

The truth is, if you communicate with speakers of another language in their own language, you'll be able to connect more deeply with them. And it can open the door for lifelong relationships with friends, coworkers, or members of a community. Furthermore, you'll feel humbled by how strangers may behave toward you when they perceive your effort to communicate with them in their language.

Travel benefits

Traveling to a place where you can speak the language gives you a different experience overall: You find yourself in more dynamic situations, and you have more opportunities to interact with people, places, and the culture. You won't just be visiting the place as a tourist; you may feel you're a member of a language community.

Knowing the language gives you the ability to read labels, street signs, and reviews to find great experiences and locales that you may otherwise never find. You can converse and communicate with native speakers, immerse yourself in their culture and its products (food, art, and the like), and understand their cultural practices.

Participation in the global community

Due to huge advances in technology, the ease of traveling around the globe, the rise in international migration, and the tendency toward a global economy and a globalized world, contact with people from other countries has become an everyday occurrence.

In our multicultural and multilingual societies, communicating with people with other languages and cultures has become a fundamental need that requires us to develop linguistic and intercultural competencies.

Although English is seen as a *lingua franca* (common language) in this globalized society, monolingual English speakers are less competitive and at a disadvantage compared to others who speak two or more languages.

Enhancing Your Economic Possibilities

Speaking two languages opens up the possibility of diverse job opportunities, greater financial profits, and unique economic opportunities. Knowing more than one language and being familiar with its culture can help you become more economically competitive and qualify for more jobs, as you find out in the following sections.

More employment opportunities

Knowing more than one language is among the top eight skills listed by employers posting a job announcement, regardless of the economic sector, job title, or experience required. Any worker in any sector (from engineers to salespeople, restaurant servers, and business owners) benefits from being bilingual or multilingual. Little by little, knowing more than one language is becoming a job requirement. In fact, 90 percent of U.S. employers rely on their bilingual or multilingual speakers, according to a study (commissioned by ACTFL, Pearson LLC, and Language Testing International) in which 1,200 U.S. employers were surveyed. (See www.languageconnectsfoundation.org/programs-initiatives/research/making-languages-our-business for more information.)

Several studies show that most employers believe that knowing another language gives their employees more growth opportunities within the company, and helps them build better and stronger relations with customers.

Eighty-eight percent of job recruiters agree that being bilingual opens up and enhances your career and professional possibilities, and is a pivotal skill for success. Your knowledge of another language and culture will help your company participate in international trade (see the earlier section "Participation in the global community").

Higher earnings

Having the ability to speak at least two languages gives you the advantage of not only having more employment opportunities but also enjoying higher levels of income. Different economic publications cite figures for bilingual employees that range between 5 percent and 20 percent more income per hour than monolingual workers earn, or as much as $128,000 in a bilingual employee's lifetime.

Of course, the specific numbers depend on several factors, such as the languages you speak, the location of your job, and the skills of other workers in the area. But you may receive a pay raise or a bonus for having superior language skills and being able to communicate in more than one language.

2

Laying the Groundwork for Language Learning

Have a peek at how your first language (L1) and second language (L2) develop.

Review the main proposals that explain L1 acquisition and L2 learning.

Consider the most popular language teaching methods and find one that fits your needs and preferences.

Chapter **5**

Examining Language Development

My main goal in this chapter is to help you understand that your first language (L1) and your second language (L2) develop following a natural order that is common for all speakers of that language. The language-learning process will be accompanied by errors, and many of them are unavoidable and an integral part of the process. In general, these natural sequences cannot be altered by explicit language instruction or any other factor.

The main stages you'll see in language development include a silent period where you listen to the language and try to comprehend the input you hear, an early speech stage in which you start producing one- and two-word utterances, and finally the emergence and ultimate attainment of speech. The last step differs between L1 and L2 users. Under normal circumstances, all L1 users acquire native proficiency, whereas L2 learners may end up with very different proficiency levels.

Understanding the Natural Order of Language Development

Languages are structured and organized, so when you're acquiring a language (either your L1 or an L2), you follow a particular order in your development, and you follow those steps unconsciously. Both L1 and L2 acquisition requires you to go through natural developmental stages and acquisition orders that cannot be changed or altered, despite explicit or deliberate teaching. In addition, all L2 learners show similar developmental processes (regardless of their L1), and many of them are similar to what L1 speakers do. This natural order idea was first proposed by professor Stephen Krashen in the 1970s with his *Natural Order Hypothesis*.

Some interesting features of natural language development are as follows:

>> The natural order can't be changed with deliberate teaching or explicit knowledge (such as explanations of grammar rules, exercises, and repetition and drills). This natural order applies to what you learn first and what you learn later (for example, passive voice is acquired late), and the order you follow when you're learning to say a negative sentence. I mention these internal language development processes later in this chapter.

>> What may seem "simple" or "complex" in grammar isn't related to when you acquire them. For example, using an article (like "the" in English) seems simple, but it's acquired late.

In the following sections, I describe ordered language development, I give you an overview of the U-shaped language development behavior, and I explain the general role of implicit and explicit knowledge in language development, as well as what interlanguage is.

Natural stages in language development

REMEMBER

As you learn a new language, you pass through these natural stages:

>> **Comprehension:** The first requirement of learning a language is *comprehension* or understanding. You need to find great sources of comprehensible input, be exposed to it, and understand it. During this first stage of language development, you'll normally pass through a *silent period*, in which your production of the L1 or L2 is nonexistent or almost nonexistent, but language learning is still happening. In this first stage, while you comprehend the language, you're unconsciously paying attention and observing how the language works, and how certain words or structures (grammar) are linked

to objects and functions (for example, commands such as "Give me" are used to request things). During this first phase, your brain is constantly trying to make sense and find patterns in the input you receive.

>> **Early speech:** Once you've been exposed to a lot of comprehensible input, you'll notice *early speech* begins to emerge. You'll form this early speech by uttering words (*one-word stage*), phrases (*two-word stage*), and prefabricated chunks of words or formulaic phrases, such as *How are you?*

>> **Speech emergence:** Finally, speech will emerge. You'll get more communicative competence (including grammatical competence), and you'll be able to create with the language and produce brand-new messages. Some researchers add extra stages to refer to the level of fluency you gain once speech emerges (intermediate and advanced fluency), but for the sake of simplicity, I consider this as part of the same "speech emergence" stage.

Internal language development processes

When you acquired your L1 and as you learn your L2, your brain processes language in a specific natural order that cannot be altered. You can pass through some of these stages quickly, but you can't alter the order. This natural order applies to acquisition orders and developmental sequences, which I explain in the following sections.

TECHNICAL STUFF

Overt manipulation (such as explicit teaching or error correction) to change these ordered internal processes doesn't seem to work. For that reason, both L1 and L2 learners repeat errors despite being corrected.

Acquisition orders

We all follow some predetermined *acquisition orders.* These orders refer to the order in which you acquire different grammar forms. For example, in English the progressive form with *-ing*, as in *You are reading a book*, is acquired much earlier than the passive voice, as in *The book is read by you*. However, there is no consensus on these orders, and research proposals are scarce and limited to a few languages.

For instance, in 1973, studies presented the following acquisition orders for English as an L1 and as an L2. Language researchers Heidi Dulay and Marina Burt proposed this order of acquisition when L1 Spanish children were acquiring L2 English, and developmental psychologists Jill de Villiers and Peter de Villiers refer to the order in L1 acquisition. In Table 5-1, number 1 refers to the first grammatical feature to be acquired, and number 8 is the last feature that L1 and L2 speakers acquired.

TABLE 5-1 **Acquisition Orders in English (L1 and L2)**

Order	L1 Acquisition of English	L2 Acquisition of English
1.	Plural (-*s*)	Plural (-*s*)
2.	Progressive (-*ing*)	Progressive (-*ing*)
3.	Irregular past tense	Copula *be*
4.	Articles	Auxiliary *be*
5.	Copula *be*	Articles
6.	Possessive ('s)	Irregular past tense
7.	Third person singular present tense (-*s*)	Third person singular present tense (-*s*)
8.	Auxiliary *be*	Possessive ('s)

Some researchers also point out that in the event that you start forgetting the language or having cognitive issues that affect language (linguists call this loss of language abilities *attrition*), you first lose the grammatical forms that you acquired last. This is the essential idea of the Regression Hypothesis that professor Roman Jakobson proposed in 1941.

Developmental sequences

Developmental sequences are the order in which certain features of a language are acquired, such as sentence negation, forming questions, adding morphemes (such as -*s* in *speaks*), and so on. We all pass through the same developmental sequences as we acquire these language features, and these sequences can't be modified.

For instance, children who learn English as their L1 and learners of English as an L2 follow predictable stages to develop their skills in forming negative sentences, as shown in Table 5-2. By the way, negation is something children acquire very early on in both L1 and L2 acquisition.

TABLE 5-2 **Developmental Sequences in English (L1 and L2)**

Sequence	L1	L2
1.	*No play.* *No* appears at the beginning of a sentence or alone.	*I no sing.* The subject may appear, and *no* appears before the verb.
2.	*Mommy no play.* The subject may appear, and *no* appears before the verb.	*He don't sing. He don't can sing.* All these forms (*don't, no,* and *not*) are possible, but *don't* isn't marked by tense or person. It's also used with modal verbs such as *can*.

Sequence	L1	L2
3.	*Mommy don't play.* Other negative forms appear, such as *can't* or *don't,* but children cannot yet control when to use them based on present or past tense or the person doing it.	*He don't sing. He is not here.* *Not* is properly used with some auxiliary verbs, but *don't* is still used without being fully analyzed.
4.	*Mommy doesn't play. Mommy didn't play.* Correct forms of *don't, didn't, can't,* and so on are marked with tense and person.	*He doesn't sing. He didn't sing.* Correct forms of *don't, didn't, can't,* and so on are marked with tense and person.

U-shaped language development

When I was learning English in my high school in Spain, we practiced the present perfect verb tenses (as in *I have eaten that before*) for quite some time, and I felt I was good at it. I had studied the irregular verbs and knew their past tense and past participle forms quite well (for example, *be, was/were, been; break, broke, broken; eat, ate, eaten; speak, spoke, spoken* — you get the picture). I was even able to use these verb forms in controlled *form-focused instruction* situations (drills, grammar exercises, and controlled oral or written exercises).

After using the present perfect tense with its past participles without a problem for some time, one day, I started making mistakes, such as *I have eated that before.* I was really mad at myself because I thought I had forgotten everything. So, I talked to my English teacher and told him that I was very worried about my performance because it seemed to me I was forgetting what I'd learned. To my surprise, he replied, "Good, you are on the right track." I was puzzled by his response! But some weeks later, I was again able to form sentences using present perfect tense for irregular verbs in the correct way. Now I completely understand what my teacher meant. I was progressing because I was moving forward in what linguists call *U-shaped behavior* or *U-shaped learning.*

U-shaped behavior happens when you restructure your internal language system as you get more input. It's a three-step process, as shown in Figure 5-1, which goes like this:

1. **You produce the L2 form correctly.** When you do that, you're just repeating, like a parrot, a prefabricated pattern. For example, when you're learning comparatives and say *This photo is worse than that one,* you produce a perfect grammatical form without even thinking of the form *worse.*

2. **Then, you produce language forms that don't align with the correct L2 forms.** What's happening here is that you're restructuring your internal language system, trying to find regular patterns and applying these regular patterns to the language forms you're trying to acquire. So, you produce sentences such as *This photo is badder than that one*, adding the comparative form of regular adjectives like *tall* (where you add *-er* to get *taller*) to adjectives that require an irregular form, such as *bad*, which becomes *worse*.

3. **Finally, you "fix" the language forms you created in Step 2, and you apply these regular patterns when needed, but you're also aware of the existence of irregular patterns.** So, in this step, you come back to the correct comparative form *worse* when you're forming a comparison with *bad*, but you maintain the *-er* when forming comparatives of other adjectives that follow a regular pattern, such as *tall* and *short* (*taller* and *shorter*).

U-SHAPED BEHAVIOR

STAGE 1
worse
Correct use
(Copied and repeated)

STAGE 3
worse
Correct use
(After having restructured the rule for comparatives, and regular and irregular forms are applied correctly)

STAGE 2
*badder
Incorrect use
(Added the regular comparative ending *-er* to an adjective that has an irregular form)

FIGURE 5-1: U-shaped language behavior.

© *John Wiley & Sons, Inc.*

REMEMBER

When you're learning your L2, be aware that you may make some errors that are an inevitable result of U-shaped behavior. Rest assured that, as my teacher told me, you're on the right track!

Implicit knowledge, explicit knowledge, and interlanguage

Speaking spontaneously in a language is normally the product of having *implicit knowledge* of the language — an intuitive knowledge you have but are not aware of. That implicit knowledge develops only if you're exposed to great quantities of quality comprehensible input and have opportunities to communicate through *modified interactions* (repetition, slower rate of speech, clarification of meanings, and so on) with other L2 speakers. These modified interactions are great sources of contextualized input. You can find out more about modified interactions and input in Chapters 6 and 8.

On the other hand, some L2 learners and teachers focus on developing a conscious knowledge of grammar rules. Linguists call this type of knowledge *explicit knowledge*. The connection between explicit and implicit knowledge and the influence of one over the other is another area of debate among researchers:

>> **Strong connection:** Practicing grammar rules from explicit knowledge will influence your implicit knowledge, as researcher Robert DeKeyser proposes.

>> **Some connection:** Paying some attention to form (having some explicit knowledge) can affect your implicit knowledge, as researcher Michael Long suggests.

>> **No connection:** Explicit knowledge can never become implicit knowledge, because they are two different types of knowledge. This is the position of linguist Stephen Krashen.

Find out more about both implicit and explicit knowledge in the following sections, along with the concept of interlanguage (or internal language system).

Implicit knowledge

If you already speak an L2, you may have gone through this learning experience: In the very beginning, you often had to pause and think about what you wanted to say. Little by little, some of your output became *automatized* (subconscious), and you didn't have to stop and think about everything. This is what happens when you've acquired the language you can produce, and it's now part of your *implicit knowledge,* as language professor Bill VanPatten would say. However, sometimes you may still need to consider how to express more complex sentences, because these forms aren't part of your implicit knowledge just yet.

REMEMBER

Your *implicit knowledge* is the knowledge you have that's part of your internal language system; it's the knowledge native speakers have of their L1. When you say that a sentence, a language form, or an utterance doesn't sound right in your L1, you're using your implicit knowledge. It's an unconscious knowledge of the language.

Your implicit knowledge is part of your long-term memory, so you can use that knowledge in an automatized way, without even thinking. When you talk in your L1, you don't have to stop and think about whether your output is correct or not, because you're using your implicit knowledge of the language. You aren't aware of the language forms you're using; you just use them.

Your L2 goal may be exactly that: getting enough implicit knowledge that you can use the language effortlessly. For instance, I'm sure you've often seen many people (L1 and L2 users) having a communicative exchange like this in an automatized way, without even thinking:

Speaker 1: Hello, how are you?

Speaker 2: I'm okay, thank you. And you?

Speaker 1: Fine, thank you.

REMEMBER

You acquire implicit knowledge in your L2 when you receive enough comprehensible input, ideally from having communicative exchanges. In those situations, that comprehensible input may become part of your implicit knowledge. When it does, you'll be able to use it in an automatized, effortless way.

Explicit knowledge

If you learned an L2 in a classroom setting, you may have received a series of language rules that you studied carefully and later used in language drills and exercises. This learning of language rules is an example of what linguistics professor Bill VanPatten calls *explicit knowledge.*

When you get explicit knowledge, you must consciously think about it before using it. It isn't knowledge that comes out effortlessly and it may disappear. Many language learners use this *learned system,* or explicit instruction they received in a classroom, to monitor or check whether they're producing the L2 correctly or if they need to adjust their internal language system (this is what linguist Stephen Krashen calls the *monitor hypothesis,* as I explain in Chapter 6).

It's normal to monitor what you say (for example, by self-correcting your grammar or vocabulary) or what you're about to say (for instance, by making sure you won't hurt someone's feelings or reveal information that's supposed to be kept secret). This "auditor" idea is what underlines Krashen's proposal in the case of L2 learners.

L2 learners tend to think consciously and explicitly about their language production to make sure it aligns with what they've learned. This is especially true in the early stages of language development and when you learn your L2 in a classroom setting that focuses on the explicit knowledge of grammar rules and pronunciation (not on communication).

Using your monitor can work fine when you practice your L2 writing skills, but it can interfere with your communication when you use it in oral production. In fact, you'll notice that you're consciously using your monitor, because your oral language production is broken and your fluency suffers. This happens because you're monitoring your language form (grammar or pronunciation that are still part of your explicit knowledge) while you're still transmitting the idea (the content of the message). So, when you're producing an L2 utterance:

>> You'll use L2 that's already part of your implicit knowledge effortlessly.

>> You'll pull L2 that's still part of your explicit knowledge. This is the one that you'll tend to monitor. The more you are exposed to and use that learned knowledge in communication, the more chances you'll have that it becomes part of your implicit knowledge.

Interlanguage

REMEMBER

When you're learning an L2, you always produce language that isn't exactly the target L2 but is your version of the L2. This personal version of the L2 is what linguistics professor Larry Selinker called *interlanguage* (IL) in 1972. IL is an internal language system between your L1 and the L2 you're learning. Your IL may be simple and basic in the beginning, but you'll modify and vary it as you receive more input and practice opportunities, and as you learn more of the L2. Find out more about interlanguage in Chapters 2 and 3.

It isn't uncommon to hear adult L2 learners combining their L1 with the language they're learning (for example, through *code-mixing*, or inserting a word or phrase of their L1 into their L2, and *code-switching*, or saying whole sentences in their L1 and then changing to their L2 to produce other sentences). This mixing normally happens when you have a high proficiency level in two languages. This dynamic phenomenon of moving fluidly between your L1 and L2 in real-life situations is called *translanguaging*.

TECHNICAL STUFF

It's interesting to note that the IL of speakers with different L1s who are acquiring a common L2 shows very similar developmental sequences. Moreover, these IL stages resemble the developmental sequence L1 children follow when they're acquiring their native language, covered earlier in this chapter.

Comparing and Contrasting L1 and L2 Development

The language path you followed when you acquired your L1 in many ways resembles what you'll do when you learn your L2. That sounds encouraging, right? You already know the road! More great news: You won't get bored on your language journey. Your L2 learning experience will take you on some new roads you've never explored or experienced before. In the following sections, find out about the similarities and differences between the development of your L1 and L2.

L1 and L2 development states

According to professors Muriel Saville-Troike and Karen Barto (who published a paper on the topic in 2018), L1 and L2 development can be broken into three main states, as you find out in the following sections.

The initial state

The *initial state* of language development refers to the knowledge you have before you even start learning your L1 or L2:

>> **L1:** Professor Noam Chomsky proposed that the initial state in L1 is *innate*, meaning you're born already programmed to acquire languages. (I explain Chomsky's concepts of the Language Acquisition Device, or LAD, and universal grammar, or UG, in Chapter 2.)

>> **L2:** As an L2 learner, you start your learning process with your L1 already under your belt, some experience and knowledge of the world, some cognitive development, and an awareness of how to interact with other community members.

TECHNICAL STUFF

The debate over whether humans have access to innate mechanisms (LAD and UG) to learn an L2 is still an unresolved question for scholars. In fact, different proposals state that when you're learning your L2:

- You have access to the *same innate mechanisms* as you have in your L1.

- You have *partial access* to the innate mechanisms you have in your L1, but the access is lost as you age. For instance, you may lose the ability to produce sounds the way a native speaker would.

- You have *no access* to the innate mechanisms you have in your L1. So, learning another language is seen as learning some new knowledge, such as how to read music. Thus, you learn your L2 using cognitive strategies such as repetition, spaced learning, or guessing.

The intermediate state

The *intermediate state* refers to the phases or stages in which you develop language (L1 or L2). Both L1 and L2 learners need tons of good quality *input* (language samples that are understandable, or *comprehensible*, as linguists call it, and have a communicative purpose). Most L1 and L2 development follows an ordered and predictable pattern, and L1 and L2 learners actively participate in their language development, becoming creative with the language, not just mimicking it (as behaviorists would suggest).

>> **L1:** Children need input and interaction to develop their L1. Interaction is particularly important: Without it, a child can't learn their L1. During this state, the input received from the child's caregivers feeds their LAD and UG. The child develops both their language and their cognitive abilities as they grow up.

>> **L2:** As I explain in Chapters 2 and 3, some factors that help you develop your L2 are input and communicative interaction opportunities (and the feedback you receive), as well as certain personal factors, such as your motivation and goals, your aptitude, your attitude toward the language and culture, and the like. Two notes about it:

- A bad attitude toward the L2 language and culture will prevent L2 learning.

- According to some researchers (such as Stephen Krashen and Beniko Mason), input alone is sufficient for language acquisition — that is, interaction with other speakers isn't necessary. Other researchers consider that both input and interaction are needed.

Adult L2 learners have already developed their cognitive abilities, so they need to focus only on developing their L2 or their interlanguage. *Interlanguage* is an evolving internal language system between your L1 and your L2 that you create and adjust as you receive L2 input and use the L2 to communicate (as I note earlier in this chapter). Because you already know your L1, you can see some transfer between your L1 and your L2 in different areas of the language: vocabulary, pronunciation, grammar, and so on. This transfer from your L1 can help you learn your L2 (*positive transfer*), or it can hinder your L2 learning (*negative transfer* or *interference*).

For example, imagine your L1 is English, and you're learning Spanish as your L2. If you hear the Spanish word *televisión,* you may rightly guess, through positive transfer, that it means *television*. But if you read *pie* in Spanish, negative transfer may lead you to think it refers to a tasty treat you'd love to have with your coffee, when it actually means *foot*. Negative transfer is also the culprit of the so-called "foreign accent" that we all have when we start speaking a new L2.

The final state, or ultimate attainment

As its name suggests, the *final state*, or *ultimate attainment*, refers to the ending stage of your language learning/acquisition journey.

>> **L1:** Under normal circumstances, all children acquire a native competence in their L1. In fact, by age 5, children have already acquired their basic grammatical system and their *phonological system* (sounds). As you grow and receive

more input and explicit teaching, you can learn more about your L1. For example, you can enlarge your vocabulary with *jargon* (technical words), study the strict grammatical rules of your L1, or learn academic language or specific registers (such as formal or informal uses of the language).

>> **L2:** The final state of L2 development differs from person to person, and depends on many of the factors explained in Chapters 2 and 3 (input, interaction opportunities, personal factors, learning context, and so on). Whereas some L2 speakers may reach a near-native proficiency, others may get stuck at a much lower proficiency level. When the latter happens and the L2 learner's interlanguage gets stuck or frozen at a non-native proficiency level, linguists use the term *fossilization*.

Similarities between L1 and L2 development

REMEMBER

The range of similarities and differences between L1 and L2 learning has been intensely debated by scholars. Despite the difference in opinions, most research-ers would agree with these basic similarities between L1 acquisition and L2 learning:

>> L1 acquisition and L2 learning needs large quantities of quality comprehensible input that's at the proficiency level of the speaker and a little beyond (in Stephen Krashen's terms *i+1*, as I explain in Chapter 6). In other words, to acquire the language, you need lots of language samples you understand, as well as input that's one step above your current level of understanding.

>> L1 acquisition and L2 learning mostly happens when you're using the language incidentally to get a communicative goal accomplished, without paying attention to the language form.

>> Some of the learning errors in L1 acquisition and L2 learning are similar. This demonstrates that they follow comparable developmental sequences and acquisition orders, as I explain earlier in this chapter.

Differences between L1 and L2 development

REMEMBER

Some key differences between L1 acquisition and L2 learning are as follows:

>> **Quantity and quality of input:** The amount and variety of input L1 children constantly receive each day is quite different from the L2 input you receive when learning your L2.

>> **Silent period:** Children acquiring their L1 receive lots of input for many months without speaking (known as the *silent period*). During this silent period, they are just listening, comprehending, and storing part of that input. However, L2 learners (especially adults) are normally pushed to produce language right away, without getting enough comprehensible input.

>> **Errors:** Children acquiring their L1 have many opportunities to interact with other L1 speakers, and they do so without hesitation and without fear of making mistakes. They have no problem with taking risks to produce language, and errors aren't a concern. However, L2 learners normally have fewer opportunities to interact with other L2 speakers, and when they do, they usually are more afraid of or concerned about making mistakes than L1 children are.

>> **Linguistic and cognitive knowledge:** Children acquiring their L1 need to work on developing both their linguistic and cognitive knowledge. However, adult L2 learners have already developed their cognitive knowledge and must develop their linguistic knowledge.

>> **Reliance on previous knowledge:** Children rely on their innate language-specific mechanisms to develop their L1, whereas L2 learners (especially older ones) rely on their cognitive knowledge, their previous language learning (L1 and other L2s), and their knowledge of the world.

For instance, if L2 learners know about certain disciplines in their L1, they can use that knowledge of the world to help build their L2. Imagine your L1 is English and your L2 is Spanish, and you're playing tennis in Spain. In a training session, your coach says *buena dejada* when you make a great drop shot. Even though you don't know the word *dejada,* you can guess its meaning because of your knowledge of the world.

>> **Reliance on previous language:** Children acquiring their L1 don't have a previous language to rely on. If we accept Noam Chomsky's theories, children rely only on the innate mechanisms that have prepared and preprogrammed them for language learning. However, L2 learners already have an L1 and knowledge of how languages work. For instance, they're aware (most of the time unconsciously) that some words are the agents of action, whereas other words may serve as the receivers of action, and these roles can change depending on certain linguistic rules.

>> **Communicative competence:** L2 learners know how to interact with other L2 speakers to achieve some communicative functions, such as greeting, requesting something, apologizing, thanking, and the like. However, L1 children need to learn everything these interactions involve, such as turn-taking, difference in register, or formality in words and tone.

>> **Final state:** Ultimate attainment of the language differs between L1 and L2 learners. Whereas L1 acquisition ends up with a complete implicit knowledge of the language (in other words, unconscious and intuitive knowledge of the language) and native competency, the final competency of L2 learners is quite varied, and it can range from native or near-native competency to novice proficiency.

Hitting the Ground Running: You Already Have a First Language

When you embark on a journey to learn a new L2, you can count on having in your backpack some knowledge you didn't have when you were acquiring your L1. For example, you already have linguistic competence and communicative competence in at least one language (your L1). These competencies have helped you develop as a person and as a member of a linguistic community and culture. Your L1 helped you organize your ideas, thoughts, and ability to interact with others. The following sections give you details on how your L1 development occurred.

Characteristics of L1 acquisition

Acquiring a language is an impressive and complex feat, available only to humans. Despite its complexity, first language acquisition (FLA) happens without formal instruction, and without any apparent effort — that is, it happens unconsciously. Humans seem to have some kind of ability to create an internal linguistic system. The differences observed among children in the beginning stages of their FLA may come from their environment, the language input and interaction opportunities they have, their personality differences, or their social/cognitive maturity.

REMEMBER

Despite its complexity, FLA is a uniform process; the way you acquired your L1 follows developmental stages that are similar for all L1 speakers. Moreover, this developmental order isn't affected by external factors. That is, no social, cultural, economic, or geographical conditions affect the uniformity of the language development steps. However, some factors may affect the *speed* at which children accomplish those steps. For instance, the more interaction children have with their caregivers, and the more output caregivers require from children, the quicker they progress through the language development steps.

Some of the reasons children excel at FLA include:

>> **Silent period:** They have time to just observe other L1 speakers and process lots of input, and they take their time to produce the language (known as the *silent period*). They aren't pushed to produce language.

>> **Communication of needs:** They must continuously use their L1 to survive and get what they need. Although children can communicate their needs in other ways before acquiring language (such as crying or smiling), language is the most efficient way to communicate. So, language becomes an essential part of their lives and necessary to become members of their language community.

>> **Stress-free environment:** They acquire the language in a stress-free environment, where they aren't worried about making mistakes or people judging their speech. This aligns with Stephen Krashen's affective filter hypothesis, which I explain in Chapter 6.

But children are very busy during their first years of life. Besides getting their linguistic knowledge, they need to develop their cognitive knowledge and learn about the world in general. For instance, newborns and infants must learn many skills, such as the ones in the following list, which help them in their future language acquisition:

>> **Selecting the sounds that form part of their L1:** When babies are born, they can produce the sounds of any language. The language input they receive and the reaction of their caregivers to their production will help children select the sounds that belong to their L1, and reject the rest of the sounds that aren't part of their L1. That's why speaking to children and exposing them to input is so important.

>> **Adjusting to a new reality full of movement and objects:** For example, babies must pay attention to the names given to the different objects so they can learn those words, and understand what certain movements mean, such as blowing a kiss.

>> **Paying attention to pointing gestures by people around them:** Babies first pay attention to the finger or hand (or arm) of the person pointing, and sometime later they start paying attention to the object being pointed at. This helps them develop language by starting to label objects, or understanding grammatical forms such as *this* or *that*.

>> **Taking turns in communicative exchanges:** At a young age, children begin to figure out the give-and-take of conversations, such as keeping quiet when another person talks.

>> **Maintaining eye contact when talking to someone:** Children need to learn strategies to maintain a conversation with other speakers. This is part of the communicative competence they need to develop.

With these skills as a foundation, children establish part of their L1 system, from sounds to vocabulary to grammar, including the *morphosyntactic* features of the language (in other words, how to form words and sentences), conversational customs, sociolinguistic and pragmatic rules, and so on. This is quite a lot for little ones who are also physically growing and learning everything else about life! The following sections cover some of the important language-related concepts children absorb as they develop and acquire their L1.

Phonetics and phonology

Phonetics and *phonology* study how to produce and perceive sounds in a language, and how to combine them to form meaningful words. Before being born, babies are already acquiring their L1. During the last trimester of pregnancy, the part of the baby's brain that processes sounds is developed, which allows the baby to recognize intonation patterns from the sounds around their mom and to store them.

TECHNICAL STUFF

In fact, several studies show that within hours and days after they are born, babies prefer the language of their mother (even if their mom isn't the person talking) over languages they aren't familiar with. These studies are performed with computers connected to pacifiers that monitor babies' suction rates. When babies hear people talking in their mom's language, because of their familiarity with these language sounds, they suck faster than if they hear a language they aren't familiar with.

Before producing words, children spend some months just listening and absorbing verbal and nonverbal communication around them, reacting to people's commands, and processing the language in their environment. They pay attention to the sounds they hear, start babbling (producing speech sounds), get the rhythm and pitch of the language, and the like.

When babies are born, they have the potential to discern and produce any language sound in the world. Unconsciously, they focus on the sounds that are important for communicating and expressing meaning in their environment, and their vocal tract adjusts to allow them to produce these sounds. By the time they're 1 year old, children have developed their *phonological repertoire* (meaning they're able to produce all the sounds they'll need for their L1), although some sounds appear sooner than others because they're easier to produce. For instance, [t] and [m] are easier to pronounce than [r].

You may be thinking that a baby's first words are the names they call their parents. Well, I'm sorry to disappoint you, but when babies produce *mamama* and *dadada* syllables (which are easy to articulate), they are only trying to adjust their vocal tract to start forming their phonological repertoire. The *mamama*, *dadada*, and *papapa* sounds they make are very common in all languages, since the way you produce these sounds is easy and they are formed by a consonant and a vowel.

Before acquiring grammatical knowledge, one of the first ways babies express meaning (for example, with a question, statement, or command) is by using *intonation* and *stress*. For example, they raise their voice at the end of a word or phrase to indicate a question.

TIP

Using intonation and stress can be really useful strategies for L2 learners to compensate for the lack of language tools (grammar or vocabulary).

Word production and acquisition

In most languages, children acquire and produce nouns first, verbs next, and finally adjectives. (Interestingly, children whose L1 is Korean learn verbs first.) In all languages, children acquire these content words (nouns, verbs, adjectives, and adverbs) early so they can express their needs easily.

The number of words children acquire per day or week depends on the child and their environment, and it can range from one new word per week to two new words per day. In 1994, linguist Stephen Pinker stated that children are "lexical vacuum cleaners," with the ability to learn about 10 words a day.

However, children commonly *overextend* and *underuse* words. For example, they may overextend their use of *banana* to refer to several different fruits, or they may underuse a word like *shoes* to refer to their favorite shoes, but not to their other shoes. Children may even use words to indicate certain linguistic functions, such as using *bottle* to mean I want the bottle.

Morphosyntax

Morphosyntax is the study of morphology (how words are formed) and syntax (how words are organized to create sentences). First, children need to understand that by putting words together in a specific order (syntax), they can create and transmit messages.

Children follow predictable stages to develop their skills in syntax and morphology, and several studies demonstrate those developmental sequences. I talk about developmental sequences earlier in this chapter. It's important to notice that children don't produce perfect sentences from the very beginning (as shown in

Table 5-2). They follow certain developmental sequences, and those "errors" are just part of their natural language acquisition process.

The role of adults in L1 acquisition

REMEMBER

The early language experiences of newborns and toddlers lay the groundwork for successful language development and literacy. In fact, thanks to the input they receive through their interactions with others during conversations, storytelling, playtime, and other activities, children acquire *phonological* skills (sounds), as well as knowledge of *morphology* (word formation) and *syntax* (grammar rules) and an understanding of *semantics* (the meaning of words) and *pragmatics* (the appropriate use of language in social situations). You can review these language components in Chapter 1. So, the input children receive from adults is pivotal to their development in general, and to their language development in particular.

The input adults provide to children is quite different from the input they give to other adult speakers. This simplified input, called *parentese* or *motherese*, is characterized by using high pitch, exaggerated intonation, and a lot of repetition and clarification; providing examples; pointing to objects (which helps children bind meanings to words); and defining words.

For example, adults extend or elaborate on words or phrases to explain meaning or language forms, they encourage children to continue conversations by asking questions, they repeat what children say (and fix erroneous statements or mistakes), and they usually mark this input with certain intonations, emphasis, and adjustments or corrections.

In other words, when 1- to 2-year-old children start trying to identify and describe their environment using strings of two or three words to mention people, places, actions, and other things, they normally receive constant feedback and interaction from other interlocutors (speakers) who serve as important listeners and conversation partners.

The more adults interact with children and the more input they provide:

>> The larger the child's vocabulary will be, and the better they will be able to explain themselves.

>> The quicker they will move through the language development steps. The input won't change the order of the developmental stages and acquisition orders, but it will speed up the process.

>> The better they will understand their L1 pragmatics and social interactions. Adult guidance is of utmost importance in this area, from prompting a child with a simple *What do you say?* and expecting the child to answer with a

thank-you or *please,* to exploring more sophisticated scenarios, such as how to address and greet people (by showing respect toward those in certain age groups or occupations, for example) or when to use nonverbal communication or social norms (for example, if it's okay to greet someone by kissing them or shaking hands, the appropriate cultural practices regarding personal space or eye contact, and so on).

Developing a Second or Foreign Language

Your experience learning an L2 is different from the experience you had when you unconsciously acquired your L1. First and foremost, learning an L2 requires a conscious effort, unless you acquire your L2 as a *compound bilingual* (as a child being raised with two languages, as I explain in Chapter 2). The context in which you learn the language also makes the process different (learning the L2 in a classroom setting versus a naturalistic setting, or as a foreign or second language). However, despite these differences, everyone who's learning an L2 follows the same developmental sequences, regardless of their L1. Find out the details in the following sections.

REMEMBER

Here's a quick recap of the difference between the two terms in the title of this section (you can also read about them in Chapter 2):

>> *A second language* is a language that you learn after you acquired your first language and that you can use in social interactions in naturalistic settings. It's an L2 that you use in your everyday life. Sometimes, you may combine this naturalistic use of the language with studying the L2 in an academic setting — for instance, if you study Spanish in school while you're abroad in Spain, or if you're a student from Taiwan studying English in the United States.

>> *A foreign language* is a language you study in an academic setting after you've acquired your L1, and your only interaction with that language is related to the classroom setting — for example, studying Afrikaans in a university in the United States, but not using Afrikaans outside the classroom.

The timing of L2 learning

Despite the apparent differences between L1 acquisition and L2 learning, many of the proposals and ideal conditions used to explain first language acquisition (FLA, covered in the earlier section "Characteristics of L1 acquisition") are also used to explain second language acquisition (SLA).

One proposal to consider in the case of L2 learning is the critical period hypothesis, or CPH (covered in Chapter 6). In the 1960s and 1970s, many scholars used the critical period idea to explain that after a certain age, you can no longer acquire certain knowledge/skills. This idea was considered applicable to the animal kingdom as a whole, not just humans. In the case of language learning, linguist Eric Lenneberg proposed the CPH in 1967, suggesting that children can acquire languages during a certain time in their lives. After that period (puberty, or about age 11 or 12), you won't be able to fully develop your internal language system as a native speaker.

REMEMBER

Although the CPH is still debated among researchers, some current scholars now suggest the idea of *sensitive* periods, instead of critical ones. In other words, the ability to learn certain aspects of language (such as accent) starts fading as you age, but there isn't a firm cutoff period, so everyone can learn a language at any age! With the right motivation and attitude, adult learners can gain L2 competency more quickly than children do.

Starting with an L2 as an adult

If you learn your L2 as an adult, your L2 learning experience will differ from your FLA. As an adult L2 learner:

>> You may have less proficiency than L1 speakers (meaning less than native proficiency). However, if you're an adult learner with high motivation and language-learning aptitude, you may approach native-like proficiency in the L2.

>> You may not reach native-like pronunciation. By the time you're 1 year old, your vocal tract has adjusted to produce the sounds you need in your environment. So, if you're exposed to sounds in both your L1 and an L2 as a child, your vocal tract will adapt to produce the sounds necessary for both languages. However, if you're exposed to the L2 sounds as an adult, your vocal tract won't adapt easily or at all to produce some of the sounds native speakers produce. On the contrary, you'll have some interference from your L1 pronunciation when you're trying to produce your L2.

>> You'll be more efficient and faster in learning vocabulary than L1 children.

>> You may have less input than L1 speakers, and it may not be as diverse, especially if you learn the L2 in a classroom environment. Therefore, the quantity and quality of input will be different:

• As an adult, you'll normally receive input that's more complex and denser than the input children encounter. For example, whereas children receive *parentese,* which is a type of modified input with simple words, changes in intonation, and the like (think of the way you talk to a baby), you'll receive unmodified input in naturalistic settings, where sentences may be long, unfinished, at a regular or high speed, and so on.

- If you learn the L2 as a *foreign language*, you'll probably receive input only a few hours each week, and it will be very controlled content. Your interlocutors will be your teacher and other L2 learners.

- If you learn the L2 as a *second language*, you may have more input opportunities, including exposure to unmodified language outside the classroom setting. This unmodified language may not be comprehensible, and it will likely be over the *i+1* level that Stephen Krashen finds helpful (see Chapter 6 for more information). Your interlocutors in class will be your L2 teacher and colleagues, and anyone in the L2 community once you're in a naturalistic setting.

» You may not have the opportunity to remain silent while you're exposed to input and store part of it in your interlanguage. You'll normally feel the need to produce language from the very beginning. As an adult, you cannot (or aren't expected to) have some silent period to just listen to the L2 input and gather the language you need to form your internal linguistic system (or interlanguage).

» You may be more conscious and afraid of making errors. You'll normally monitor your production to avoid making errors, and you'll tend to correct your mistakes more than children do. This error avoidance may make you evade certain topics or situations, and it can affect your language fluency.

» You'll encounter more demanding and challenging conversations than children do, especially if you learn the L2 as a second language (used outside a classroom setting). For example, you may need to discuss work-related topics or politics. But at the same time, you'll also need to interact in potentially easier everyday situations such as running errands. There's a connection between conversational interaction and L2 learning (the interaction hypothesis; see Chapter 6 for details).

» You'll rely on previous knowledge and skills as you'll use your *cognitive skills* (association, memorization, and so on), your *world knowledge* (how to interact, awareness of various topics, and so on), and your *L1 knowledge* (transferring L1 information, finding patterns, and the like) to help you learn the L2.

Of course, language is composed of many parts, such as sounds, vocabulary, syntax, and so on. In most language areas, adults can outperform children. The only area that adults seem to have more difficulty in achieving a native-like proficiency, compared to children, is the L2 pronunciation. Normally, adults cannot perfectly imitate a native-speaker accent.

Some factors may interfere or aid in adult SLA, such as *affective variables* (motivation, attitude, and personality), as I explain in Chapter 3:

>> **Aptitude:** An adult's L2 aptitude may also affect their L2 learning. (This aptitude includes working memory and phonological short-term memory; see Chapter 3 for details.)

>> **Techniques:** Adults can learn faster than children if the strategies and techniques they use are appropriate.

- The L2 learning process for adults is mainly based on problem-solving strategies and other cognitive processes. For instance, consider what you do when you (in your own L1) are tasked to read a brochure where some medical jargon appears: You have some expectations about the content, and then you try to look for images that help you understand meaning, guess meaning from context, use your world knowledge and experience, and so on.

- Adults can use their previous L1 knowledge (or bilingualism) to understand how languages work (for example, how to recognize patterns, guess meaning from word roots or word endings, and the like).

Starting with an L2 as a child

In this section I focus on children acquiring an L2 when they are younger than 3. In this situation, acquiring an L2 is as effortless and unconscious for them as acquiring their L1.

When children acquire two languages from birth (*bilingual L1 acquisition*), each language follows its own developmental process and ends in the same competence level that native speakers of each language have.

Phases of early L2 learning

REMEMBER

A child who begins acquiring an L1 and an L2 before age 3 pays attention to the rhythm, intonation, and sounds of both languages. They need to be able to discover and differentiate sounds that affect meaning, try to replicate and produce these sounds, and adjust them as needed based on the responses they receive from their *interlocutors* (parents or caregivers). That is, if the interlocutor understood the sound, the child won't need to adjust anything, but if the interlocutor shows misunderstanding, the child will need to readjust their production of the sound.

Children acquiring their L2 before age 3 also discover in their input the different aspects of phonology, morphology, syntax, semantics, and pragmatics of their L1 and L2 (see the earlier section "Characteristics of L1 acquisition"), and integrate these features, making them work together. They process all this language information unconsciously. They follow these steps until they feel comfortable speaking each language:

1. **Comprehension in the silent period:** First, they spend some time listening and paying attention to the input around them, trying to connect the *aural* signs (what they hear, the form) with meaning (the object, activity, and so on). During this time, they are learning the new languages, adjusting their sound repertoire, and their brains are constantly working and trying to make sense of what they hear.

2. **Early speech:** When children feel they can start producing language, they will begin speaking using simple words or phrases. Some children like taking risks more than others, or are more extroverted and want to talk to other people right away. Others may prefer to store language a bit longer before attempting to speak it. So, the child's personality, interests, and needs play an important role during these first attempts to use language.

3. **Speech emergence:** During this phase, children feel more comfortable using both their L1 and L2 and creating brand-new sentences. It's important to provide them with as many opportunities and situations as possible to use the two languages.

TIP

When children have a variety of opportunities to speak two languages, their comfort level with both languages gives them the tools to think with a broad perspective and feel like powerful members of a globalized society. You can read more about the advantages of being bilingual in Chapter 4.

Input and output

Young children learning an L2 receive easy-to-process L2 input, so they can normally figure out meaning using contextual clues from the actions of their interlocutors, real objects, or drawings in their surroundings. Additionally, they receive that modified L2 input in the context of low-demand social situations, such as playing in the park or at day care.

Usually, the content of the L2 input children receive isn't cognitively demanding. For example, it doesn't require the same cognitive ability to process *I want the ball* as it takes to understand *I want you to explain further the developmental stages children go through*. The former sentence is an example of something a child may hear as part of their input, whereas the second sentence would be addressed to an adult (in their L1 or L2).

Moreover, children produce output without being worried or embarrassed about the errors they make. They focus on communicating the meaning, not on the correctness of the grammatical form.

TIP

You may be aware of some situations in which caregivers tried to teach an L2 to young children without the success they expected. To acquire an L2 as a near-native speaker, a child must feel the same connection with the L2 as they have with their L1. So, I encourage you (or your child's caregivers) to

>> Use the L2 in the same situations and activities as you'd use your L1.

>> Name objects, express actions, mention places, count items, and the like in the L2.

>> Encourage the child to feel a social and cultural connection to the two languages.

>> Make the child feel they are part of an L2 community.

REMEMBER

For families that want their children to speak more than one language, it's very important to encourage and maintain feelings of social and cultural connection to both languages. Providing appropriate input definitely requires consistency, determination, and time from everyone involved.

Chapter **6**

Explaining Some Language Learning Proposals

In this chapter I provide an overview of the main theories scholars use to discuss first and second language acquisition. Despite the effort to understand how language acquisition happens for your native language (L1) and your second language (L2), the complexity of language learning makes it difficult to reach a conclusion.

This chapter is divided into two parts, with the first part covering theories of L1 acquisition and the second part addressing theories used to explain L2 learning. In both cases, I touch on the main theories and proposals used to discuss language acquisition: behaviorism, innatism, and interactionism.

Acknowledging Main FLA Perspectives

First language acquisition (FLA) is a complex task that all children can accomplish successfully under normal circumstances. But language acquisition is only one of the many "jobs" children must accomplish as they grow and develop. During their developmental years, they are also trying to learn about themselves, the world around them, and the diverse tasks they need to perform each day, such as naming objects, expressing their needs, and being aware of danger. In this section, I give you an overview of some of the main theoretical proposals that explain how the FLA feat takes place.

Behaviorism: Acquiring language by forming habits

During the mid-20th century, behaviorist theories explaining learning in general gained great support, especially in the United States. The main idea of *behaviorism* is that you learn by creating habits. Specifically, you form these habits when you imitate what you perceive and receive positive reinforcement for that imitation.

An extreme behaviorist position claims that children are born with a *tabula rasa*, or blank slate, that contains no language or world knowledge, and their experiences and appropriate reinforcement from their environment fill and shape that tabula rasa with knowledge, including language. One of the main proponents of the behaviorist approach to acquiring languages was American psychologist B. F. Skinner.

REMEMBER

According to behaviorists, the reinforcement you get after you imitate the language around you helps you create language habits — or not.

>> If you get *positive reinforcement* (for example, you're praised, you receive an affirming smile, or you see that your message gets across), you repeat that imitated language until you form habits. Continued positive reinforcement is key, because it encourages you to practice these language samples to fill your tabula rasa with language (forming your linguistic system).

>> However, if you receive *negative reinforcement* (for example, you're corrected, you get ignored, or your message isn't understood), you must adjust the language you just produced, imitate and use new language forms, and expect to receive the appropriate reinforcement.

Although behaviorism can explain many aspects of language learning (such as routine language), it can't explain many others, such as the new language forms children create that aren't part of the L1 input they receive in their environment. For instance, why do some children say *badder* instead of *worse*? They don't hear their caregivers saying *badder*. What a child is doing when they say *badder* is using a pattern they know — adding *-er* to make a comparative — in a context that isn't appropriate (a process called *U-shaped behavior*, which I explain in Chapter 5).

REMEMBER

In general, children are creative in their use of language. They imitate and repeat some language, but this behavior is selective. One of the most important aspects of language they imitate early on is sounds. They repeat the sounds around them, discard the ones that receive negative reinforcement, and keep the ones that receive positive reinforcement. That way, they form the collection of sounds that are important for their L1.

Moreover, children normally imitate the language forms (like words and grammar) they are starting to use or trying to figure out (although they may be unconsciously doing this). So, most of the time, what they imitate is determined by their internal language system, not by their environment. Of course, you know that children are especially keen to imitate bad words and repeat information that was supposed to be kept secret!

Innatism: Language is preprogrammed in the human brain

Consider this: You're born preprogrammed to perform certain activities, such as eating and walking. Nobody has to teach you how to do these things; they are innate/biologically preprogrammed abilities that you know how to do unconsciously. These innate abilities follow certain developmental steps that align with how your brain and body mature.

In 1959, linguist Noam Chomsky challenged B. F. Skinner's proposal that language is acquired through imitation and formation of habits. Chomsky brought an *innatist* or *cognitivist* perspective (the belief that something is biologically predetermined) to the study of language acquisition and how language is stored in your brain.

REMEMBER

Chomsky proposes that humans are born equipped and pre-wired to acquire languages. He supports this claim by arguing that the way you acquire your L1 cannot be dependent only on the input you receive from your environment. In fact, he maintains that, using the L1 input from your environment along with the internal language mechanism/ability you're born with, you can discover the rules of your L1.

Getting some background on Chomsky's approach

Some of the proof Chomsky offers to support his theory of the innate nature of language acquisition is as follows:

>> **Native competence in the L1:** All children, under normal circumstances, acquire their L1. Moreover, some studies show that even children with limited cognitive ability can develop a complete internal linguistic system. In

Chomskian terms, a child's cognitive development and linguistic development progress separately.

>> **Poverty of stimulus:** Children's language input is often full of incomplete sentences, where some words are left out, or riddled with errors. Chomsky refers to those insufficient and imperfect sources of input as *Plato's problem* or the *poverty of stimulus*. Despite the limited L1 input a child may receive, they still acquire their L1.

>> **Input differences:** All children acquire native proficiency in their L1, even though language input isn't the same for all children. In fact, the interactions between parents and children are more frequent and accepted in some cultures than in others.

>> **Lack of feedback on form:** In general, children don't receive feedback on their *language form* (grammatical structure and rules) unless there's a miscommunication or an error; if they do receive feedback, it normally refers to the content of their communication. When parents or caregivers offer a correct form, children usually ignore these corrections and continue using the same "incorrect" form that's part of their internal linguistic system (see Chapter 5). So, the lack of feedback doesn't serve as a type of positive or negative reinforcement to create habits, as behaviorists believe (see the previous section).

Chomsky's innatist theory explains that humans are equipped (pre-wired) with a biological ability to acquire languages, called the *Language Acquisition Device (LAD)*. So, in order to acquire languages, what you unconsciously do is plug the input you receive into your LAD. And even though the input you receive isn't always the best and doesn't offer a perfect array of linguistic samples (there's that poverty of stimulus theory), you acquire your L1 because your LAD fills in the blanks the input lacks. (See Chapter 2 for more.)

Furthermore, according to Chomsky's theory, people are born equipped with an algorithm, or set of grammatical principles, common to all languages in the world, called *universal grammar*, or *UG* (see Chapter 2). You can think of UG as a huge spreadsheet with all the possible underlying grammatical rules of languages, where the input is imported and categorized accordingly. Thus, you unconsciously activate your UG with the input you receive. Your UG categorizes this input and selects the appropriate parameters (or options) for each principle, thus allowing you to choose the rules you need for the language you're learning.

Understanding the critical period hypothesis

One common and still unanswered question that arises from the innatism perspective is this: Do you have access to the LAD all your life? Some researchers have theorized that humans are biologically prepared to acquire certain knowledge and skills at critical periods in their development. According to scholars who put forth the *critical period hypothesis*, that's also the case with language acquisition.

REMEMBER

In 1967 linguist and neurologist Eric Lenneberg proposed the idea that humans go through a critical period in language acquisition. This hypothetical developmental period guides your final language proficiency. If you acquire a language within that time period (before puberty), you can attain a native-like proficiency. After puberty, native language acquisition isn't as likely or is impossible (especially *phonetically*, or with regard to sounds, and to a certain extent structurally, applying grammatical rules).

The critical period hypothesis used to be linked to biological factors. For several years, many researchers believed that as you grow, your brain loses its *plasticity*, or ability to create new neural pathways (a common feature in children). Thus, as you mature, each hemisphere and part of the brain loses its flexibility to become specialized in certain cognitive functions. For instance, most of the language functions happen in the left hemisphere of the brain. The specialization of each hemisphere of the brain (called *lateralization*) ends at around puberty, which is the age this hypothesis proposes as the end of the critical period.

The existence of a critical period has been supported by studies of children who were deprived of appropriate language input before their critical period was over. Consider the following case: Genie was isolated in her home in California, tied to a chair and a crib in her room for almost all her childhood, until she was found when she was 13 years old. During that time, she didn't communicate with anyone, so she didn't get any linguistic input. When she was found, she hadn't developed physically, linguistically, emotionally, or intellectually. After she was removed from the home, several people took care of her, among them some teachers and therapists. Despite her rehabilitation, her language didn't develop properly.

With the intervention and help of specialists, Genie developed her L1 a lot, but not as well as a native speaker of her age. She understood much more of her language than she produced, as is normal. And although she acquired a lot of vocabulary, her grammar suffered. In the end, she was able to progress only to a language level comparable to a 2- or 3-year-old child because she wasn't able to develop a proper articulatory system at an early age, when children normally do that. To create an articulatory system, a child needs to listen to sounds, try to imitate them, and keep the sounds that work for their L1, according to the positive reinforcement they get.

TECHNICAL STUFF

Genie's case helps scholars support the critical period hypothesis. Because children are able to develop certain linguistic features after this period, some researchers prefer calling it a *sensitive period*.

Interactionism: Developing language by interacting with the environment

Whereas behaviorism proposes L1 acquisition is an ability you learn through imitation and habit formation, and innatism considers L1 acquisition the result of a biological device you're born with, *interactionism* suggests L1 acquisition is a skill you build and develop as part of your experience interacting with the world and with others.

REMEMBER

According to the interactionist (or *developmentalist*) perspective, your brain has learning mechanisms ready to acquire skills and knowledge from your environment. In other words, language acquisition is one of the many skills you need to learn through experience and interaction with the people and things in your environment.

One proponent of this perspective was Jean Piaget, a Swiss psychologist who studied the different steps children follow in the language acquisition process. Interactionists/developmentalists see language acquisition as one of the milestones you reach as you mature and develop cognitively.

Developmentalists believe that language appears after a child's intelligence and knowledge exist, and it strengthens or perfects their knowledge and cognitive processes. For instance, you're able to use comparatives in your L1 (like in *nice and nicer,* or *tall* and *taller*) only after you understand the concept of comparing features of two things that are different.

Another influential proponent of the interactionist perspective, psychologist Lev Vygotsky, suggested that language develops from supportive social interactions between children and their caregivers, other adults, and other children. These interactions help you gain new knowledge and develop the knowledge you already have at the same time you're acquiring your language.

REMEMBER

As part of his sociocultural theory, Vygotsky coined the term *Zone of Proximal Development (ZPD).* In his words (published decades after his death in a study by other developmentalists in 1978), the ZPD is "the distance between the actual developmental level as determined by independent problem solving and the level of potential development as determined through problem solving under adult guidance or collaboration with more capable peers." Vygotsky's ZPD proposal explains that there are two developmental levels and the space in between these two levels (the Zone of Proximal Development):

>> Without any help, you are at your *actual developmental level*.

>> With the help and encouragement of experts (adults or more experienced/capable speakers), you can reach your highest potential (your *potential developmental level*). Afterwards, this potential development level can become your next actual developmental level.

In the interactionist view of language, interaction with others is key for language development, as shown, for example, in a study of a boy named Jim by Jacqueline Sachs and other researchers in 1981. Although Jim was hearing, his parents were deaf. His parents didn't communicate with him orally or through sign language, so Jim was only exposed to language on TV. At 3;9 (3 years and 9 months), he was assessed, and his spoken language ability was below what other children his age could produce (his word order was ungrammatical and not expected among children his age). After he started having some conversational sessions with an adult, his language development grew. At 4;2 (4 years and 2 months), he was producing language appropriate for kids his age.

So, Sachs's 1981 study shows that

>> Interaction with other speakers is necessary for language development, because the other speaker will rephrase or modify their input if needed.

>> In the early stages of language acquisition, watching TV, listening to the radio, and using other forms of media aren't sufficient for language learning, because there's no possibility to negotiate meaning. Your L1 or L2 will develop appropriately if you have interactions with other speakers.

Outlining Some L2 Learning Perspectives

Language learning in general, and an L2 in particular, is a complex phenomenon that must be studied from different perspectives and viewed through various lenses. Several of the theories on learning a second language in this section are related to the theories on L1 acquisition I describe earlier in this chapter. Obviously, L1 acquisition is different from learning an L2 (as a child or as an adult), as you find out in Chapter 5.

Behaviorism: Imitation and habit formation are key in L2 learning

REMEMBER

Behaviorism proposes that all learning follows a similar process. This theoretical view emphasizes the role of imitation, reinforcement, and habit formation, thus highlighting the role of external variables. In behaviorism, the process you follow as an L2 learner goes like this:

1. You receive linguistic input.

2. You associate that linguistic input with objects, people, or events.

3. You imitate the linguistic input you receive.

4. You practice using that imitated information.

5. You receive reinforcement from your *interlocutors* (other speakers) for your practiced imitation. In the case of an L2, your teachers or other L2 speakers are the ones who offer reinforcement. The reinforcement can be

   - **Positive:** If you receive positive reinforcement for your successful imitation, you're encouraged to continue repeating it.

   - **Negative:** If your interlocutors give you corrective feedback or negative reinforcement, you made an error in your imitation, and you need to try the steps again.

6. You form habits after imitating a specific language form several times and receiving positive reinforcement for the imitated language.

Behaviorists believe that you acquired the ability to speak your L1 by imitating linguistic input and forming habits. Because you already have L1 habits, you may end up transferring these L1 habits and some aspects of your L1 (pronunciation, vocabulary, word order, and so on) into your L2.

Based on the possible interference between L1 and L2 acquisition, some scholars came up with the *contrastive analysis hypothesis (CAH)*. This hypothesis proposes that the two languages be compared and contrasted to anticipate the ease or difficulty of learning aspects of each language that are different. The CAH anticipates that

>> The closer your L1 and L2 are structurally, the easier it will be to learn the L2.

>> If the different aspects of your L1 and L2 are pretty far apart, you'll find the L2 more difficult to learn, and you'll end up making more errors.

The CAH is accurate in foreseeing phonological difficulties for L2 learners. In other words, when your L1 and L2 have different pronunciation features, learning these features will be difficult. For example, Chinese uses tones as a way to distinguish meaning, whereas the meaning of words in English isn't linked to tones. So, if your L1 is English and you want to learn Chinese as an L2, you'll have a difficult time learning tones.

Behaviorism inspired the *audiolingual* teaching method (see Chapter 7), which focuses mainly on imitating dialogues, drills, or sentence patterns; memorizing them; and repeating them to form habits. The habits formed in a person's L1 can be transferred into their L2. Drills practiced in audiolingual classes are based on contrastive analysis, in an attempt to avoid negative transfer from the L1 as much as possible. Thus, behaviorism and the CAH go hand in hand.

Innatism: Realizing the importance of the monitor model

The main goal of Noam Chomsky's theory of innatism (covered earlier in this chapter) was to explain L1 acquisition, but his ideas have also been used to understand L2 learning. Some of Chomsky's most influential proposals on language acquisition are the innate existence of a language-specific mechanism that allows humans to learn languages (the Language Acquisition Device, or LAD) and a universal set of rules (principles and parameters) that applies to all languages (universal grammar, or UG). According to his proposal, the existence of the LAD and UG is the only way to explain your success in learning languages despite the incomplete input you receive in the language (what Chomsky called the *poverty of stimulus*).

Linguists and other scholars focused on the study of language learning continue to debate whether L2 learners have access to these innate features of language acquisition proposed by Chomsky:

>> Some scholars say that the nature of the UG is the same for L1 and L2 learners, and both have access to it.

>> Others agree that the UG is available to L2 learners, but it's a bit different from the UG you had when you acquired your L1.

>> Some scholars believe that L1 learners use the UG to acquire language, while L2 learners use other learning strategies, such as memorization.

One of the most significant models of L2 acquisition inspired by Chomsky's innatist theory of L1 learning is Stephen Krashen's *monitor model*, which focuses on comprehensible input. Krashen's monitor model proposal includes five main hypotheses, covered in the following sections.

The acquisition-learning hypothesis

The *acquisition–learning hypothesis* proposes that language learning and language acquisition are two different and independent processes:

>> **Language acquisition:** Acquisition is the subconscious process you followed with your L1. It requires no effort or work on your part, and it happens involuntarily. For acquisition to happen, you need to receive enough appropriate *comprehensible input* (input that you understand) so that you start picking up the rules of the language subconsciously. This input helps you start forming an internal linguistic system for the language.

The result of language acquisition is *acquired competence,* meaning you use the language effortlessly, without having to stop and think about the language itself. Your communicative fluency in the L2 is due to what you've acquired, which has become part of your internal linguistic system (your interlanguage), not due to what you consciously learn (because this still isn't part of your internal language system).

Both children and adults can acquire languages. You can acquire your L2 if you receive comprehensible input and process it for meaning, without paying close attention to the language form or structure.

>> **Language learning:** Learning is a conscious process; it's what you normally do in school when you memorize vocabulary and grammar. It requires your conscious effort and work, and you voluntarily decide to do it. Language learning is memorizing the grammatical rules of a language and applying them consciously (for example, when you write or speak), or being able to explain these rules.

Krashen claims that conscious learning (of grammar rules, for example) doesn't change or impact the language acquisition process. However, conscious learning can be used to measure your progress, monitor whether the language you produce is correct, and help you modify that output (see the next section). When someone corrects your errors, their feedback can help you fix your learning, but error correction doesn't help with acquisition. (Under this theory, acquisition follows a predetermined sequence that you cannot alter, even with feedback or error correction. You can read more about these predetermined sequences in Chapter 5.)

According to Krashen, learning can't become acquisition. So, the goal is engaging in lots of acquisition activities, where the focus is receiving communicative input at the right level, rather than learning grammar rules.

The monitor hypothesis

When you use your L2 spontaneously, you use the language you've already acquired. But sometimes when you write or speak (when you produce *output*), you have to produce language that you may not have acquired yet, and you want to make sure it follows the grammatical rules you've learned. In that case, you're using your *monitor* (your conscious learned knowledge) to check whether what you're producing is following the rules you've learned. The monitor actively watches your L2 output and helps you edit, alter, or correct your output.

Your monitor works like this: You need to say something in your L2, so you access your acquired competence to pick up the language you've already acquired, and you internally scan the form you need against your learned knowledge and correct any errors you may find before producing it. You can also use your monitor to correct your output after you produce it (*self-correction*).

REMEMBER

Krashen suggests that the monitor can help with accuracy, but it doesn't help with fluency. He considers acquisition to be the main route to getting both accuracy and fluency. To use your monitor, you need to

>> **Know the rule.** Before you can monitor your output, you should have learned or be familiar with the applicable rule.

>> **Be focused on the form to produce the correct language.** During a conversation, being focused on both the meaning of your words and the form or structure of your sentences is difficult. The constant use of the monitor in oral production can interfere with the conversation flow. To avoid that, focus on transmitting meaning and not on using the monitor to produce grammatical accuracy.

>> **Have sufficient time.** After you write an assignment for a class or for work, you normally use your monitor to make sure your writing is well done. If you use your monitor when speaking, your interlocutor may feel stressed as they watch you hesitating or looking for the correct form in your learned knowledge. Overusing your monitor indicates that the message you're trying to convey is above your current L2 proficiency level.

The natural order hypothesis

According to the *natural order hypothesis*, you follow a predictable order when you acquire both your first language and your second language. The order of acquisition for L1 and L2 is similar but not exactly the same, as I explain in Chapter 5. In any case, acquisition happens in a predetermined order that you cannot alter.

So, as you're studying your L2, if you receive lots of quality meaningful input that isn't in the natural order of acquisition, you'll subconsciously pick from that input what you need to form your internal linguistic system in a natural order. Error correction has little or no effect on this subconscious picking up of the rules.

The comprehensible input hypothesis

According to Krashen, comprehensible input is what really leads to L2 acquisition. You can acquire a language only when you understand/comprehend the messages you read or listen to — in other words, when you receive comprehensible input. For example, one way to make language comprehensible is by connecting the L2 meaning of a word to its form, such as linking the English word *apple* or the Spanish word *manzana* to the fruit itself. Linguist Tracy Terrell (in a study in 1986) named this linking process *binding*.

But for language acquisition to advance, you need to receive comprehensible input (labeled *i*) plus input that goes a little beyond your level (labeled *i+1*). This *i+1* allows you to continue enriching and expanding your current proficiency level, adding new words, new grammatical forms, and more L2 features to the input you already comprehend.

To understand this *i+1* level, you may use your previous linguistic knowledge and any extralinguistic knowledge you may have (for example, your knowledge of the world and your knowledge of the context). The important consideration is making sure that, with the extra help from your previous knowledge or extralinguistic knowledge, you can understand and decipher the meaning being transmitted.

Krashen also believes that output will emerge on its own once you acquire enough language (thanks to the *i+1* that you've received).

The affective filter hypothesis

The *affective filter hypothesis* refers to the best environment to acquire language. When you're stressed and/or nervous, you won't be able to acquire language. You can think of the affective filter as an imaginary wall that prevents input from entering your internal language system and being acquired. A stressful environment raises that wall and blocks input. So, you need to be in situations where the affective filter is low, and where you feel relaxed and comfortable, to acquire language.

REMEMBER

Language acquisition occurs when you're in a low-anxiety environment and you receive input that's comprehensible, compelling (so interesting that you forget it's not your L1), and communicatively embedded (it has a purpose).

Interactionism: Appreciating the impact of social interactions in L2 development

Psycholinguist Michael Long agreed with Stephen Krashen's emphasis on the necessity of comprehensible input for language acquisition to happen. In 1996, Long used the *interaction hypothesis* to explain how interactions with other L2 speakers help you comprehend their messages (that is, get comprehensible input). These interactions with other L2 speakers provide adjustments in the input that align with your needs as an L2 learner.

Long proposed in a paper published in 1983 that you need to participate in *modified interactions* with other interlocutors to receive comprehensible input and ultimately acquire language. When these modifications are embedded in communicative conversations, you're more prone to acquiring an L2. In modified interactions, you may need to change your output so your interlocutor understands it, and vice versa.

TIP

You can modify your interactions in many ways, as I mention in Chapter 8. For example, you may

>> **Use simplified language.** Instead of saying, "I want you to come now, please,'" you may say, "Come now, please."

>> **Speak more slowly.** Make sure you're not speaking so fast that your interlocutor can't understand what you're saying.

>> **Elaborate by giving an explanation or examples, or by paraphrasing.** For example, you can say, "She has many trips on her bucket list; what I mean is, she has a list of many places she wants to visit."

>> **Gesture or point.** Use your hands to indicate things like size or what or whom you're talking about.

>> **Use the context to help get your meaning across.** For example, you can use your location to clarify meaning, such as when you say, "I need to get some vegetables" when you're in that section of the supermarket.

>> **Check for comprehension.** You can say, "Do you understand what I mean?" after any utterance.

>> **Request clarification or repetition.** For example you may ask, "What do you mean?" or "Can you repeat that, please?"

As I mention earlier in this chapter, two names that are normally linked to the developmental or interactional approach are Jean Piaget and Lev Vygotsky:

>> Piaget suggested that linguistic knowledge comes after cognitive knowledge. For instance, children learning a second language may not have developed certain abstract thinking abilities their teacher may be requiring from them, so their L2 learning will take a while. However, the teacher can require more challenging activities with adult L2 learners, because they have completed their cognitive development.

>> Regarding L2 learning, Vygotsky's research has been very influential in the language teaching field. His main proposal was that you learn and advance in your language acquisition when you interact with and receive help from others who are more expert in the L2 than you.

In the process of learning your L2, you pass through different steps or developmental stages. When you're learning an L2, you encounter things you can do with the language on your own (they represent your *actual developmental level*) and tasks you can do only if someone gives you a hand. Vygotsky explained that with the help and encouragement of experts (teachers, native speakers of the L2, and so on), you can reach a higher developmental stage (what he calls your *potential developmental level*). The space between your actual level and your potential level is what he calls your *Zone of Proximal Development*. With time and additional help from experts, your potential developmental level can become your actual developmental level. Thus, in Vygotsky's proposal, social interaction and expert help can advance your linguistic and cognitive development.

Chapter **7**

Reviewing Language Teaching Methods and Approaches

You're reading this book because you want to learn a new language, and you may be considering taking classes in an academic setting or hiring a tutor. If that's your situation, you want to choose an approach that helps you learn the way that best works with your goals and preferences. In this chapter I offer a review of some of the main methods and approaches that have been used to teach languages. Although some methods are no longer common in classrooms, I think you can still gain insight from them and connect them to some of the learning proposals in Chapter 6.

Selecting the Best Language Teaching Method for Your Needs

Language teachers and language learners often wonder which language teaching method is the best. What's the secret recipe for teaching languages and getting students to learn and absorb the information? The answer is, there isn't one perfect teaching method that targets or benefits everyone or aligns with all students' or teachers' needs. In this chapter, I introduce you to some of the most widely used language teaching methods based on principles of second language acquisition (SLA). Once you read through them, you can ponder what works best for you, and what won't benefit you or your situation.

The discussion about the best language learning method has been going on for many decades. Each method or approach has different views on several issues, such as the role of

>> Vocabulary

>> Grammar

>> Accuracy and fluency

>> The instructor and student

>> The main linguistic abilities to be developed (listening, speaking, reading, and writing) and the strategies used

>> Teaching materials

>> Culture

>> Technology, especially in the modern methods

REMEMBER

Nearly all theorists and practitioners (teachers and learners) agree that following a *communicative approach* is the best way to teach and acquire languages. Several methodologies align with the communicative approach, as I explain in the later section "Examining Current Teaching Practices in the Communicative Approach."

Studying the Traits of Notable Early Language Teaching Methods

In this section I introduce some language teaching methods that were used in classrooms across the world for several decades, presenting them in chronological order and discussing their main principles. Although you can still find classrooms where these traditional methods are implemented, they aren't as popular as they used to be.

The grammar-translation method

As suggested by its name, the *grammar–translation method* focuses on translating the second language (L2) to your first language (L1) and learning the L2 grammar. It was a popular teaching method until the late 19th century. If you ever took Latin or ancient Greek classes at school, your teacher likely used this method.

The following occurs in the grammar–translation method:

>> The teacher uses the students' L1 as the language of instruction.

>> The instructor teaches the L2 grammar, and students need to memorize grammatical rules. For instance, students learn the different cases of nouns and adjectives by heart. Sometimes they work on exercises to practice the application of the grammatical rules. So, there's a huge emphasis on the language form (that is, on grammar). For proponents of this method, dissecting and analyzing the language and memorizing the rules is helpful because it trains the brain to recognize these forms.

>> The L2 learners need to memorize lists of L2 vocabulary words with their L1 translations. So, they receive long bilingual lists of words to learn.

>> The main goal is translating texts (normally authentic literary texts) from the L2 into the L1 using dictionaries. Occasionally students work with the texts to check for comprehension, or with the vocabulary (synonyms, antonyms, and so on).

>> The L2 learners work on reading and writing skills, whereas speaking and listening skills are mostly ignored. Because this method was very popular for teaching Latin and ancient Greek (two dead languages), it makes sense that the focus isn't on oral or aural skills (speaking and listening, respectively).

Nowadays, some language teachers and learners still rely on learning lists of vocabulary and grammar rules, as well as translating sentences. However, many researchers have proved that this isn't the most effective method to learn languages.

The direct method

The *direct method* appeared in the late 19th century and the beginning of the 20th century as a way to fill the need to practice the speaking and listening skills that the grammar-translation method (discussed in the preceding section) was missing. Two proponents of this methodology were linguists François Gouin and Otto Jespersen.

The direct method differs significantly from the grammar-translation method. Some of its main tenets are as follows:

>> The teacher uses the L2 as the language of instruction. (Use of the students' L1 is avoided.)

>> L2 grammar is learned inductively (indirectly), not deductively (explicitly). In other words, students are expected to extract the grammatical rules from the language samples provided in class by reading, listening, and speaking the L2; imitating the language samples; and repeating them. For that reason, it's important to provide lots of L2 input in class.

>> The teacher introduces the L2 vocabulary using prompts, such as images or *realia* (real objects used to demonstrate the meaning of words). For example, an apple is the realia used to teach the Spanish word *manzana*.

>> The goals of the lessons are

- Practicing ordinary conversations with the teacher and focusing on everyday vocabulary and expressions

- Using correct pronunciation and grammar

>> Some activities used in direct method classes include ask-and-answer questions, fill-in-the-blank vocabulary exercises, dictation, and the like.

WARNING

The direct method works best when teaching is individualized and targeted, but it's challenging to create those ideal learning conditions in the classroom. Specifically, it's difficult to find teachers with a near native proficiency in the L2, and to keep classes small enough that students get the direct, personal instruction they need.

Some of the tactics used by the direct method are still present in language classes nowadays. For example, using realia is an effective strategy to learn vocabulary in a new language; so is using the L2 as the means of instruction.

The audiolingual method

The audiolingual method (sometimes called ALM) was popular in the 1940s and 1950s because of a need to teach U.S. soldiers fighting in World War II to speak L2s so fluently that they could blend into the local community and not be perceived as foreigners. For that reason, one of its goals is producing error-free language, and it emphasizes learning about the L2 culture.

The audiolingual method is based on the behaviorist perspective of language learning, which I explain in Chapter 6. Behaviorists believe that language is acquired by repeating and mimicking the language around you, and creating habits in a stimulus-response setting (see the following bulleted list).

Some of the main principles of the audiolingual method are as follows:

>> The teacher uses the L2 as the language of instruction. (The L1 is avoided as much as possible.)

>> As with the direct method (see the previous section), L2 grammar is learned inductively, meaning the teacher doesn't teach grammar directly (explicitly/ deductively). Students focus on pattern drills, and this repetition is expected to help them learn the grammar inductively. When they form habits, they can pay attention to the grammar involved in the repetition.

>> L2 vocabulary is normally linked to the context of dialogues.

>> Lessons focus on these main goals:

- Forming habits through stimulus-response exercises and repetition — for example, the teacher asks a question, a student answers it, and the student then poses the same question to another student, who repeats the process. Other exercises include changing sentences from positive to negative utterances or to questions, and completing a dialogue with missing parts.

- Memorizing dialogues or paragraphs

- Avoiding errors; error correction is emphasized

- Developing listening and speaking skills

- Learning about the L2 culture

WARNING

The audiolingual method is based on practicing and repeating patterns and dialogues, with the goal of mimicking them perfectly without paying much attention to the content or meaning. The problem is, L2 learners feel lost and don't know how to proceed if the pattern or dialogue is modified, because they aren't creating with the language, but are just repeating the patterns and dialogues.

Nowadays, most teaching methods don't use audiolingual tactics. However, the emphasis given to learning about the L2 culture is commendable.

Examining Current Teaching Practices in the Communicative Approach

Although choosing the best language teaching method seems to be an impossible task, today's scholars, language teachers, and students seem to agree that focusing on communication is the most effective way to learn a new language. The communicative approach to language teaching appeared alongside linguist Noam Chomsky's proposals on language acquisition and his criticism of behaviorism and the audiolingual method (covered earlier in this chapter). Several teaching methods align with the communicative approach, including total physical response, the natural approach, task-based learning, and content-based instruction.

REMEMBER

All communicative teaching methods share one common denominator: Communication is the key ingredient for language acquisition to happen. So, L2 learners are expected to use the language to communicate. In the communicative approach, you focus first on comprehending messages, and then on expressing ideas (and negotiating meaning when needed).

Some of the main features of the communicative approach are as follows:

» The teacher uses the L2 as the language of instruction. (The L1 is avoided as much as possible.)

» The instructor doesn't focus on the L2 grammar. Grammar is only one of the tools students use to reach their final goal, which is communication and transmission of their message (the content).

» The instructor teaches L2 vocabulary using visuals or anything else that makes the vocabulary comprehensible, such as real objects (realia).

» Students work on all language abilities (listening, reading, speaking, and writing).

>> The goals of lessons are

- Developing communicative competence, not grammatical competence (in other words, transmitting the content or meaning of the message is more important than doing it error-free)

- Communicating in the L2 with a real purpose

- Developing fluency over grammatical perfection (in other words, speaking smoothly, easily, and effortlessly is more important than producing grammatically perfect messages that are choppy, unsteady, or broken)

Total physical response

American psychologist and professor James Asher developed the *total physical response (TPR)* teaching method in the 1970s, in an attempt to imitate what children do when acquiring their L1. Specifically, children respond physically to their caregivers' or parents' commands in the L1 ("Give me the ball," "Put the teddy bear on the table," and so on). They listen to and process a lot of L1 input before they begin producing it, as a large part of the input comes in the form of commands.

Students learning through TPR listen to and act out the L2 commands their instructor gives them. TPR tries to connect language with actions, thus linking the meaning (the action) with the language form (the command). Linking form and meaning helps students memorize and learn the L2. In fact, Asher focused on the need to activate the right hemisphere of the brain through motor activities before developing the language function, which is located in the left hemisphere.

TPR is perfect for people who learn *kinesthetically* (through physical activity), because students move as they learn the L2. TPR also respects the silent period of L2 learners because they aren't pushed to talk until they're ready, and it normally lowers their *affective filter* (an imaginary wall that can be raised or lowered depending on emotions like anxiety) because they don't have to produce the L2, just act it out.

TECHNICAL STUFF

The *silent period* is a phase during language learning in which you don't produce language, but you're still learning it. You're processing the input you get, trying to make sense of it, and storing it for later use. Because you go through this silent period, your language acquisition journey doesn't begin when you start producing language — it actually begins during the silent period.

Some modifications to the original TPR are also in use today. For instance, instead of just giving students one command to act out, the teacher gives several commands at once, and students must keep the commands in their working memory before acting them all out at once. Additionally, in more advanced language classrooms, students are the ones giving the commands.

These days TPR is mainly used as a classroom activity rather than a stand-alone language teaching method. Some of TPR's features are as follows:

>> The teacher uses the L2 as the language of instruction.

>> The instructor doesn't teach L2 grammar explicitly. Everything is focused on the use of imperatives, from simple commands (for example, "Stand up" or "Open the window") to more complex ones (for example, "Stand up and open the window with your left hand").

>> Students learn L2 vocabulary through commands, which can vary from simple to complex.

>> The main goals of the lessons are

- Providing lots of comprehensible input

- Linking the L2 to physical actions

- Not pushing oral production in the L2

The natural approach

Tracy D. Terrell developed the *natural approach* teaching method in the late 1970s and early 1980s considering Stephen Krashen's monitor model hypotheses (see Chapter 6). The natural approach is also closely associated with psychologist James Asher's emphasis on L2 learners remaining silent while listening to lots of comprehensible input until language emerges.

The natural approach relies on students receiving a large amount of comprehensible input and teachers keeping a low affective filter in the classroom (making sure the atmosphere is relaxed). In a stress-free environment focused on communicating messages, L2 learners pick up the language without having to analyze and study its grammatical form.

Some of the key features of the natural approach are as follows:

>> The teacher uses the L2 as the language of instruction (the L1 is avoided as much as possible), focuses on providing lots of comprehensible input that goes a little above their current level (what Krashen called *i+1*, as noted in Chapter 6), and doesn't force students to talk until they're ready.

>> L2 grammar is acquired inductively, so the instructor doesn't focus on teaching it. Grammar is only one of the tools students use to reach their final goal, which is communication.

>> The instructor teaches L2 vocabulary using images, realia, gestures, or anything else that makes it comprehensible. Because it's important to make the input comprehensible, the teacher adapts their *teacher talk* (how they provide input) to the students' level. Vocabulary and grammar are recycled constantly in communicative exchanges and spiral up. For example, if students learn how to discuss their close family members in week one, they may talk about family again a few weeks later, expanding their discussion from immediate family members to extended family.

>> All four language skills (listening, reading, speaking, and writing) are practiced.

>> Error correction is limited and mostly done through recasting what students say, because errors are a normal part of the learning process, and the goal is communicating messages.

>> Lessons target the following:

- Providing lots of comprehensible input, as well as input that's a little beyond students' level, as suggested by Krashen

- Adjusting teacher talk or *foreigner talk* (the simplified language used by native speakers when they talk to non-native speakers or foreigners) to students' level

- Using activities that facilitate acquisition, such as lots of comprehensible input, followed by opportunities to produce early speech and the emergence of speech (see Chapter 5)

- Practicing creative L2 communication about interesting and useful topics (talking to friends, shopping, reading, listening to the radio, and the like) and using everyday language

- Lowering the affective filter so students feel relaxed and comfortable receiving L2 input

- Respecting the silent period, and not forcing students to talk until they're ready

Task-based learning

Task-based learning focuses on learning a language to accomplish real-life tasks. It aligns with the communicative approach, because it emphasizes interactions in the L2. The main goal of this methodology is having students complete communicative tasks they may encounter in everyday life (for example, reserving a hotel room or writing a note to a teacher). Task-based lessons require students to complete some activities independently and work with classmates to complete other activities.

Some important facets of task-based learning include the following:

>> The teacher uses the L2 as the language of instruction, and they focus on providing lots of input, although it may not be as simplified as other communicative approaches (because it tries to reflect real-life L2 usage).

>> The instructor doesn't focus on teaching the L2 grammar. Students use the grammatical forms they need to complete tasks, and sometimes they must do grammar exercises to learn the forms they need to accomplish tasks.

>> L2 vocabulary is based on the language needed to accomplish the task at hand. Students may need to recycle some vocabulary or grammar they had already learned to accomplish this task. The goal isn't learning academic language; the idea is to acquire the language speakers encounter in everyday situations.

>> All four language skills (listening, reading, speaking, and writing) are emphasized.

>> Errors are seen as a normal part of the learning process, and the goal is communicating messages.

>> Lessons are designed so students can

- Complete a simulated real-life task

- Learn by doing: facing a task and trying to solve it

- Communicate in the L2 with classmates to complete tasks and problem-solve when needed

- Learn not only the language but also the process they followed to complete the task; when a task is finished, they can reflect on the task and the learning process

- Obtain guidance and support from the instructor in the beginning, and gradually remove that help as they can work on their own (a technique called *scaffolding*)

Content-based instruction

Another communicative teaching method, *content-based instruction*, focuses on teaching other subjects, such as math, history, and so on, through comprehensible input in the L2. Supporters of this methodology argue that learning new information in the L2 about different academic subjects is relevant, appropriate, and interesting for language learners. Moreover, students' motivation, confidence, and language proficiency increases as they learn new content.

In some content-based instruction classrooms, students are in an immersion setting, where all classes are taught only in the L2. Similar to what students do in a regular L1 school, they go to class and learn the new information, but in this case the means of instruction used is the L2.

The L2 input students get in a content-based class comes from many authentic L2 sources to help them understand and learn the subject (the content area). Content-based instruction promotes use of the four language skills (listening, speaking, reading, and writing) in the L2.

WARNING

One drawback is that the language used in content-based instruction materials may be beyond the proficiency level of students, so it may not be comprehensible input.

Digging into Proficiency and Standards

In the following sections, I discuss two popular curricular proposals used to design language plans and goals for schools: the focus on developing language proficiency, and the goal of meeting language standards.

A focus on proficiency

Whereas the goal of many language classrooms in the past was learning about the language (that is, learning its rules and when to apply them), the goal of most classrooms today is developing language proficiency (that is, using the L2 to accomplish certain communicative tasks).

Having proficiency in a language means being able to accomplish several diverse communicative tasks (such as asking and answering questions or narrating an event) in different contexts (formal and informal) using different forms (words and phrases, sentences, paragraphs, and so on) with an accuracy level that fosters understanding of the message (accuracy in vocabulary, grammar, pronunciation, and so on).

Certain tasks are more cognitively demanding than others, so as your proficiency level in the L2 rises, you'll be able to accomplish more cognitively complex tasks. For example, some of the easiest tasks (novice or beginner level) are listing vocabulary words, such as your favorite food/sport/animal or the members of your family, whereas some of the most challenging tasks (advanced or proficient level) are hypothesizing, or giving and supporting an opinion.

The more challenging a task is, the more cognitive demand it requires. When the tasks you accomplish align with your L2 proficiency level, you're using the grammatical forms in your long-term memory, and your short-term memory is focusing on the content of the task (that is, the meaning you want to deliver). However, when a task is above your proficiency level, the cognitive demand will be too high, and you'll have to focus on both the meaning you want to transmit as well as the grammatical form you need (which isn't yet part of your long-term memory).

For example, in Spanish, nouns and adjectives must agree on gender and number, such as the masculine singular *un coche híbrido* (a hybrid car). If the communicative task you need to accomplish is describing the car you have, you may say *Tengo un coche híbrido* (I have a hybrid car). However, if you're asked why it's better to use one type of car over another (gas, hybrid, or electric), in the middle of your communicative task to give and support your opinion, you may end up saying *Prefiero una coche híbrida* (I prefer a hybrid car), mistakenly using the feminine ending *-a* in *una* and *híbrida*. In this example, your communicative task is way beyond your proficiency level, and you can't keep up with both meaning and form.

REMEMBER

When the focus of language learning is on proficiency, you're encouraged to be creative with the L2 and express yourself in different contexts and on different topics — using the language to communicate and accomplish diverse tasks. So, to develop proficiency, you should have conversations in which you discuss different topics and present your ideas and opinions to others. But to do that, you need to be exposed to authentic language samples that show you how to accomplish such tasks. You can find out more about language proficiency in Chapters 2 and 3.

The importance of standards

Schools normally design their language curriculum according to their state and/or national standards. In most cases, language learning and cultural awareness are seen as a central part of students' preparation to learn, live, and work in the globalized world. Curricular plans for learning languages are designed by different entities, which I discuss in the following sections.

REMEMBER

Although language curricular plans around the globe share similar ideas, the areas of emphasis are sometimes different. One key difference between most European countries and the United States is the importance given to *multilingualism* (knowing more than two languages) and the role it has in understanding and analyzing how languages function (*metalinguistics*). Here are some of the common ideas that most curricular plans target:

>> Communication is the core piece of any second/foreign language curriculum. Communication can happen in different ways, so lessons often emphasize that language helps you

- Interpret and understand messages you receive by reading, listening to, or watching L2 input.

- Interact with other L2 speakers by exchanging information, negotiating meaning, and so on. This interpersonal interaction is more successful if social, cultural, and practical goals are taken into account.

- Present or produce language for others to process and understand.

- Explain/reformulate/clarify messages. To do that effectively, you need to be able to compare languages (specifically, your L1 and L2).

>> Culture and *intercultural competence* are also part of most curricular designs. You reflect on your own culture to understand the L2 culture better and consequently can communicate and work better with people from other cultures.

Language and culture are completely integrated parts of any language community. In other words, language reflects culture, and you need cultural knowledge to communicate properly.

Standards in the United States

In the United States, the ACTFL's (the American Council on the Teaching of Foreign Languages) *World-Readiness Standards for Learning Languages* are used to create curricular plans in many schools and universities. You can access the standards on the ACTFL website (www.actfl.org/). The main goals of the standards, known as the 5Cs, are

>> **Communication:** Using different modes to communicate in the L2, such as interpretation (comprehend the language you hear, read, or view), interpersonal interaction (using the language with other speakers to exchange information and negotiate meaning), and presentation (posing information for others to process in written, spoken, or video form).

>> **Cultures:** Learning and understanding cultural products (such as books, art, and food), practices (activities you do in different situations, such as during celebrations), and perspectives (values, attitudes, and beliefs).

>> **Connections:** Using the L2 to gain knowledge in other disciplines.

>> **Comparisons:** Using the L2 to compare, contrast, and investigate your own language and culture with the new language and culture. This should help you gain intercultural and metalinguistic knowledge.

>> **Communities:** Using the L2 to participate in the globalized world, transferring what you've learned in the L2 to your lifelong learning, and using the L2 and the accompanying knowledge in your community and in the world as a whole.

Standards in Europe

The curricular plan in Europe follows the Common European Framework of Reference for Languages (CEFR). The CEFR emphasizes the importance of speaking at least two languages, and encourages learning a third one. You can find out more at www.coe.int/en/web/common-european-framework-reference-languages/.

European countries know the importance of speaking different languages in today's world, where constant global, intercultural, and plurilingual connections occur. The CEFR emphasizes that for a democratic dialogue to exist, people need to gain communicative and intercultural competence in different foreign languages and cultures. Gaining these competencies allows speakers to understand, interact, and express themselves in another language, to understand their own and other cultures, and to be conscious of cultural differences when interacting with others.

REMEMBER

There's no doubt that being competent in at least one L2 and its culture will enable you to perform better in a wider array of communicative situations, and help you gain new understanding of your own culture, acquire intercultural competence, and enhance your learning as a whole. Acquiring a second language will allow you to access sources of information in both your L1 and your L2. Access to a variety of information sources can provide different viewpoints of how things work in the world and improve your higher-order thinking skills (evaluating, analyzing, and creating new ideas).

3

Understanding Language Learning Activities

Realize the importance of input, interaction, output, and errors in your learning process.

Get some strategies for building your L2 vocabulary and improving your listening, speaking, reading, and writing skills.

Uncover language learning strategies that can enhance your experience, and consider which strategies fit your learning style.

IN THIS CHAPTER

» **Highlighting the star: Language input**

» **Mapping the role of interactions**

» **Creating language output**

» **Knowing that errors are fine**

» **Considering where language is learned**

Chapter **8**

Juggling Key Elements in the Language Learning Process

You can speak at least one language (your first language, or L1) perfectly well, right? And the great thing is, you accomplished that feat without noticeable effort. If you stop for a second and think about the people and props that helped you acquire your first language, you may credit your caretakers (parents, grandparents, siblings, and so on), your friends and other family members, the cartoons you watched on TV, and the books you had access to, just to name a few.

Researchers continuously debate which elements are most important in the language learning/acquisition process. However, all of them agree on one thing: Comprehensible input is the essential element to learn and acquire a language. Without input, language learning/acquisition doesn't happen.

In this chapter, I tell you about some of the key components of language learning and acquisition — input, interaction, and output — and I emphasize that making errors is normal and expected during the learning/acquisition process. Finally, I explain how these components vary depending on the context in which you learn and acquire the language.

Uncovering the Essential Element: Language Input

Scholars and linguists are still debating and disagreeing about many aspects of second language acquisition (SLA). The main aspect that all SLA researchers can agree on is the essential and indisputable role that input has in language acquisition. Without input, your *internal language system* (see the later section "Understanding interlanguage") won't develop, either in your L1 or in your second language, or L2.

But even though everyone agrees that input is needed for language acquisition to happen, not everyone agrees with the idea that input is enough on its own to acquire a language. In the following sections, I clarify what input is and where you get it.

Understanding input basics

REMEMBER

Broadly defined, *input* is the language you encounter and comprehend during a communicative encounter. In other words, you make form-meaning connections. Input can be spoken, written, or signed (in sign languages).

WARNING

I want to make this clear from the beginning: Everything you hear isn't useful input; some sounds can also be noise. Think about birds chirping or dogs barking. You don't understand their communication system, and what you hear is simply noise that isn't useful for your language development. Receiving language input you can't comprehend is also noise.

Here's an example of how you get comprehensible input from your environment: Have you ever found yourself listening to your favorite radio program, hearing a song and not paying attention to its meaning? It happens to me all the time. While driving my children to their after-school activities, I'll tune in to my favorite radio program, which includes some popular songs in English. In this example, you can look at the input from the songs and the radio program like this:

>> **The radio program is an excellent source of input for me,** because I pay attention to and understand the meaning of the spoken content.

>> **The songs are often not really input for me,** because I don't always make form-meaning connections from the words being sung. But it may be input for my copilots in the car, who love the songs and pay attention to their meaning.

REMEMBER

Although everything you hear isn't input for you, it may be a good source of input for others. Language input is beneficial for you when you can comprehend it, even if you need to depend on *extralinguistic cues* (tone of voice, facial expressions, or gestures, for example), the context, or your background knowledge. Furthermore, the person speaking (writing or signing) also uses these extralinguistic cues as a way to get their meaning through. To be useful, the input you receive needs to help you build or strengthen form-meaning connections.

TECHNICAL STUFF

Linguist Tracy Terrell calls the form-meaning connection *binding,* which means that you process and associate a new word or language form with a mental representation of its meaning. For example, if you're learning Spanish and you come across the word *sol,* you picture the sun. The goal is to link the new word to its meaning, not to a translation from your L1. Binding happens in both L1 and L2 acquisition.

Receiving optimal input

One of the main proponents of the importance of input in language acquisition is Stephen Krashen, who, in the 1970s, proposed his input hypothesis as part of his monitor model (see Chapter 6). For Krashen, receiving appropriate comprehensible input (that is, *optimal* input) is enough for language acquisition to happen. Here's a look at the right kind of input that's useful in your language learning process:

>> **Input must be comprehensible and comprehended.** The input needs to be at your current proficiency level so you can understand the message it transmits. This level is different for every person, and it changes as you acquire more language.

>> **Input should be a little beyond your current level.** To understand input that's beyond your proficiency level, you can use the context, your knowledge of the world, or other extralinguistic information (such as gestures or tone of voice). If the input is too incomprehensible for you (it's noise for you), it can prevent you from understanding the message.

>> **Input needs to be compelling, interesting, and relevant to you.** Ideally, the input is so compelling and engaging that you'll forget you're receiving and understanding messages in a different language!

>> **Input has to be communicatively meaningful.** The focus of the input should be to communicate meaning, not to use specific grammatical forms.

>> **Input cannot be *grammatically sequenced.*** That is, the focus of the input can't be about using a grammatical structure, because real communication may suffer. On the contrary, the goal of the input has to be communicating meaning.

>> **You need lots of input in different communicative situations.** Encountering similar input in different communicative situations helps you acquire its meaning. But be careful: Repeating a word out of context, for the mere sake of repeating it, doesn't help with acquisition.

>> **Input should happen in a low-anxiety, stress-free environment.** In this environment, you feel safe and calm to process the meaning and to use the language when you are ready to do so.

REMEMBER

When you have optimal input in your L2, you can take the opportunity when appropriate to produce output and negotiate meaning with your *interlocutors* (others speaking the language you're learning). The later section "Factoring in the Role of Language Interactions" talks about the important role of interlocutors in language learning.

Developing your language system

Learning a new language involves developing a new language system. To do that, you need to feed your system with lots of quality comprehensible input — the type of input described in the preceding section.

When you make a form-meaning connection in real time to comprehend or produce language, that subset of the input is called *intake*. Intake is the language input you've processed, absorbed, and internalized. In fact, intake is what helps you build your new language system (your interlanguage, or IL).

Not all the input you receive turns into intake right away; language acquisition takes time. Some factors that can affect what becomes intake are

>> **The type of language form to be processed:** You'll process some language forms before others. For example, you process content words (nouns like *dog* or verbs like *play*) earlier than functional words (determiners like *a* or prepositions like *to*).

>> **The extent of your working memory:** Your *working memory* is the amount of information you can process at a time. This feature is very personal. For instance, some people can retain more information (such as a phone number, a license plate number, or a sentence) in their working memory than others.

>> **The frequency of input:** The forms of input you receive frequently often become intake sooner than the ones you get less frequently. But that isn't always the case. Your language develops according to a fixed process, so you'll acquire some language forms before others.

>> **The constancy of the language element:** Elements that have a constant function can become intake more easily than elements that change their function. For instance, a word that always works as a noun, such as *car*, will become intake before a word that can have more than one function, such as *pretty*, which can be an adjective or adverb.

Recognizing quality sources of input

Developing language proficiency takes time, but the quantity and quality of the input you receive has a huge impact on your success in the L2. So, the goal is finding lots of good quality sources of input. But you may be asking yourself: What is good quality input? Well, there's no one-size-fits-all answer.

The quality of the input depends on each learner's abilities, needs, and interests, so something that may be good quality input for you may not be so good for other learners. You just need to find appropriate sources for you: input that's at your proficiency level (or slightly beyond your level), contains topics that interest you, and has a communicative purpose.

TIP

Finding input at your proficiency level can be challenging, especially for novice learners. If you're a novice learner, you'll benefit the most from modified input (see the next section). After receiving comprehensible input (which may be modified input) for some time, you'll start filling your language toolbox with enough language resources to participate successfully in natural communicative exchanges.

L2 input may come from some of these sources:

>> **Reading, reading, and more reading:** Reading is an excellent source of L2 input. You should read any available texts that are interesting and relevant to you. Texts can range from text messages and emails from friends and colleagues, to street signs, books (including children's books and cookbooks), magazines, and newspapers.

TIP

Novice learners can start with *graded readers,* which are books written at specific proficiency levels. For more advanced learners, I highly recommend reading novels. Their episodic nature helps you with comprehension of the content, and the narration normally provides a wide array of verb tenses.

>> **Listening to messages:** You can listen to L2 messages aimed at you or others. In a classroom setting, those messages come from the teacher or from other students; in a natural setting, those messages may come from your neighbor, your friend, your boss, a clerk at a store, or any other person in your community. Some of these interlocutors (such as teachers) may modify their

input to adapt it to your level (*teacher talk*), whereas others will produce natural unmodified input.

TIP

If you're a novice learner, you can start with modified audio input sources, such as the ones created for children or for students learning the L2. Audiobooks, podcasts, radio programs, and the like can also be a great source of input if the content is at an appropriate level for you. You can search for audiobooks you're already familiar with, or podcasts that discuss topics you interested in.

» **Watching audiovisual media:** One of the advantages of audiovisual media is that you can make form-meaning connections through the linguistic and extralinguistic features (such as the context or the speakers' gestures). Movie and TV trailers, movies, TV programs, and cartoons are great sources of L2 input, especially if they're on topics you really enjoy and/or you're very familiar with. Stream a movie, turn the L2 captions on (if available), and enjoy the movie in the L2!

TIP

If you're a novice learner, start with material that you've already watched in your L1 or that you're very familiar with. That way, making form-meaning connections will be easier because you already know the content. But you shouldn't stick to only watching familiar media. Adding different audiovisual media that interest you will push you to learn something new. Novice learners also benefit from viewing children's programs and movies, because they're normally full of high-frequency language and repetition, which can help you strengthen and expand your current language abilities.

REMEMBER

Novice learners shouldn't be concerned about understanding every detail of the input they listen to, watch, or read. Just focus on reasonably comprehending the overall meaning of the language exchange. The best input is the one that is at your comprehension level or somewhere just above it. (Input is at your proficiency level when you can understand most of its content. But if you have trouble understanding its meaning or you need to constantly look up vocabulary in a dictionary, the level of the input may be way over your current competence level.)

Examining modified input

As I mention earlier in this chapter, comprehensible input is the essential element in both L1 and L2 acquisition. But the type of input L1 speakers and L2 speakers receive is different:

» When you were a child acquiring your L1, your caretakers used *child-directed speech* or *caregiver speech* to talk to you. That input was adapted to your level and needs so that it was comprehensible for you. This is an example of *modified input.*

>> L2 learners may receive modified input from their teachers, but in natural settings they normally face unmodified input from the L2 community (such as neighbors, friends, or colleagues).

The goal of modified input is to contribute to the comprehension and acquisition of the language — in other words, to make language comprehension easier and less of a burden for the learner. Modified input is tailored to the needs of the learner, adjusted to their level so they can connect the language and its meaning, with the goal that the input can become intake and be used in communication.

When you find yourself having trouble understanding your interlocutor's L2 input, you can ask them to modify their input to make it comprehensible for you. For example, if you have problems understanding vocabulary, you can ask your interlocutor to

>> Provide examples.

>> Simplify their speech by using high-frequency vocabulary.

>> Provide different options or choices.

>> Offer examples from popular culture, such as familiar products, famous celebrities, and recognizable brands.

>> Give some *semantic* details (information about meaning).

If you have problems understanding grammar, you can ask your interlocutor to

>> Simplify the grammar by using familiar grammatical structures.

>> Repeat or restate the utterance.

>> Use shorter sentences and simpler *syntax* (sentence structure).

If you have problems with an overall communicative exchange, you can ask your interlocutor to

>> Adjust their rate of speech by slowing down and/or pausing more.

>> Use extralinguistic features, such as pointing and gesturing, making facial expressions, and using props.

>> Negotiate meaning with you (to make sure you comprehend their input and they understand your output).

Noticing particular language elements

Imagine that while you and your friends are playing tennis, one of your friends mentions in your L2 that they need a new grip, and asks if you have an extra one. You notice that the word *grip* is missing from your linguistic repertoire (there's a gap in your understanding of that word). Possibly, you've encountered the word before, but it's still not part of your language repertoire yet. In this interaction, it's important that you understand the word to accomplish the communicative goal. Your friend may use some strategies to modify their input (such as pointing to the grip on their racquet) to help you understand what a grip is. After that, it's very likely that you will process and try to register that new element in your internal linguistic system.

This example demonstrates that when you're producing an L2 message (or understanding one) and your brain notices a gap you have in the L2 (either in meaning or form), you're more likely to learn the new element you noticed than if you hadn't noticed it. This distinction is part of the *noticing hypothesis*, introduced by linguist Richard Schmidt in 1990. Only when you pay attention — you are aware, process, and comprehend the linguistic input you receive (and notice the gaps you have) — can you potentially internalize that input. Without attention to and awareness of the input, learning doesn't happen.

TIP

Here are a couple notes about noticing:

>> **Familiar elements:** Don't despair if you can't pay attention to everything in the L2 input you receive. That's completely normal! Bear in mind that it's much easier to notice L2 forms or vocabulary when you've previously encountered them. If they're brand-new L2 forms for you, noticing is less likely.

>> **Type of words:** When you're learning vocabulary, you first pay attention and process meaning, and you later focus on form. Similarly, because meaning is mainly linked to content words (such as nouns, verbs, and adjectives), you process content words before you process other elements of the language, such as functional words (like prepositions and determiners).

Factoring in the Role of Language Interactions

Many researchers agree that, along with input (covered earlier in this chapter), interaction and output in the L2 are key factors in language learning and acquisition. In this section, I explain how your language learning process can benefit from your interactions with other L2 speakers. (Find out more about producing output later in this chapter.)

Looking at feedback's benefits

REMEMBER

In broad terms, *communication* involves interacting with members of a community while exchanging messages using a shared code. The goal in any communicative exchange is mutual comprehension of the message. When the goal is achieved, you may receive *positive feedback*. However, when you and your interlocutors face a breakdown in communication (either because of a language problem — the wrong language form or misunderstood meaning — or in the conversation structure), you may receive some *negative feedback* that illustrates a lack of understanding. In that case, you need to make adjustments and modifications in the interaction to negotiate, repair, and make sure the meaning is comprehended by your interlocutor.

TIP

Novice learners normally benefit the most when they focus on solving a problem with meaning or content. On the other hand, more advanced learners may not have problems with meaning, and focusing on grammar or form can help them improve their competency level.

So, your interlocutors' feedback can help you in two ways, depending on its content:

>> **Positive feedback: Identifying what matches.** By receiving positive feedback from your interlocutors, you can confirm, reinforce, and strengthen your internal linguistic system. Positive feedback is a way of ensuring that what you're producing as part of your intake aligns with L2 norms, or at least can be understood by L2 speakers. Your interlocutors may demonstrate that what you say is appropriate by using

  • Affirmative L2 words for *okay*, *good*, or *yes*

  • Nonverbal cues like nodding, giving a thumbs-up, smiling, or using any other cultural convention to show approval

>> **Negative feedback: Identifying what differs.** Negative feedback helps you pay attention to a language problem/gap you noticed in your linguistic system and make the appropriate changes to advance your development. The problem may involve vocabulary, *morphology* (word form) or *syntax* (sentence structure), cultural understanding, or even *pragmatics* (language use in context). After receiving negative feedback, you must reconsider your comprehension and/or production, figure out what the problem is, and determine how to modify your knowledge to fix the communicative breakdown.

Receiving various types of feedback

Communicative exchanges are normally accompanied by some type of feedback, either positive or negative (as I explain in the previous section). When a breakdown in the communicative exchange occurs or the interaction isn't completely successful, you need to employ some strategies to negotiate meaning. In those cases, you may receive negative feedback in several ways, but you can also request modified input (covered earlier in this chapter).

When you receive negative feedback, you may prefer *explicit feedback* (being corrected overtly so that you notice the error) or *implicit feedback* (being prompted about the mistake so that you realize the problem/gap yourself).

Some common forms of feedback you may receive from your interlocutors during an interaction include the following:

>> **Correction:** Your interlocutor tells you that you made an error, and they offer the correct way of saying the intended information. For example, if you say in your L2, "Yesterday he eat a sandwich," your interlocutor may say, "You have to say *ate*, as in 'Yesterday he *ate* a sandwich.'"

>> **Metalinguistic feedback:** The interlocutor asks you to use specific language forms, or you ask for a specific language form. For example, if you say, "Yesterday he eat a sandwich," your interlocutor may say, "You need to use the past tense of *to eat*. Remember, it's an irregular verb." Or you can just ask, "What's the past tense of *to eat?*"

>> **Confirmation check:** Your interlocutor checks to make sure they understood what you said (or heard your words correctly) or checks whether there's an error/gap. For example, suppose you say, "I just registered for the football team. I want to be as good as Lionel Messi." Your interlocutor may say, "Football? I think you mean soccer. Messi plays soccer. Is soccer what you mean? Football uses an oval ball."

>> **Clarification request:** Without directly saying that there's a problem (a mistake or misunderstood or unintelligible utterance), the interlocutor asks for clarification, hoping you recognize the inaccuracy and adjust the utterance correctly. For example, if you say, "Yesterday he eat a sandwich," your interlocutor may say, "Sorry?" or "Excuse me?"

>> **Comprehension check:** One interlocutor asks the other whether they understood/comprehended the message before a communication breakdown occurs. You may say or hear, "Do you understand me? Is my meaning clear?"

>> **Recast:** The interlocutor restates or rephrases your incorrect utterance (or part of it) using the correct L2 form, but without calling attention to the error,

and allowing the conversation to continue normally. Thus, the focus is on clarifying the meaning and keeping the communication going. If you say, "Yesterday he eat a sandwich," your interlocutor may respond, "Oh, yesterday he *ate* a sandwich. I also ate a sandwich yesterday. I love sandwiches!"

TIP

Recasts are one of the most successful and beneficial implicit feedback strategies, and therefore, linguists tend to focus on (and prefer) them. As a result, recasting is a common feedback strategy used in language classrooms.

» **Elicitation or prompt:** Your interlocutor repeats part of your utterance and stops where the error was produced to prompt you to self-correct and restate the message/utterance using a better L2 form. If you say, "Yesterday he eat a sandwich," your interlocutor may respond, "Yesterday he . . . Be careful!" You can self-correct by saying, "Oh! Yesterday he ate a sandwich."

WARNING

Prompts may cause you to freeze up if you aren't aware of the rule or don't know what's expected from you. In that case, you can ask your interlocutor to help you with the form because you don't know it or you can't come up with it.

» **Repetition:** Your interlocutor repeats your utterance (with the error) in a questioning tone so that you pay attention to their question about meaning and repeat the utterance with the correct L2 form. If you say, "Yesterday he eat a sandwich," your interlocutor may respond, "He *eat* or he *ate?*"

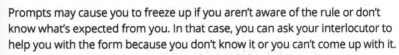

Feedback has a different effect for written and oral communications. Explicit feedback is more accepted (even expected) in written format, but during oral interactions, explicit feedback and overt correction normally interrupt the communication flow. This is why recasts are more widely accepted (as noted earlier).

Producing Language Output

In this section, I talk about another important component in the language learning process: output. Specifically, I clarify what language output is, mention some problems learners face when producing output, and highlight the benefits of producing output for your language development process.

REMEMBER

When you're learning a language and striving toward producing output, you take these steps:

1. **Before producing output, you seek out and receive lots of comprehensible input.**

   Comprehensible input, as I explain earlier in this chapter, may come from diverse L2 sources (in written, spoken, or audiovisual form), including from your interactions with other L2 speakers.

2. **You process a portion of the comprehensible input you receive.**

Out of all the comprehensible input you receive, you process only part of it, mainly the input you've encountered previously that's essential to understanding the meaning being communicated.

The portion of the input you process may become intake. When it's acquired and part of your internal linguistic system, you can use it effortlessly to understand or produce messages.

3. **You repurpose the acquired input to turn it into language output.**

You use the input that became acquired (your intake) to communicate with others. In other words, your intake becomes the source of your output. Part of your language output can also serve to assess if your L2 hypotheses are correct and identify gaps/problems in your L2, as you find out later in this chapter.

Explaining output

REMEMBER

Output is the production of language with a communicative goal, so it must have meaning and a purpose. Only meaningful and purposeful output really helps you build your internal language system. In that sense, not everything you produce in the L2 helps you in your language learning process.

>> Output occurs when you need to use the L2 tools you have available (such as vocabulary and grammar) to transmit meaning.

>> Language production that doesn't require you to pay attention to its meaning is *not* output. For example, completing fill-in-the-blank grammatical exercises by looking at sentences with the verb in parentheses, without having to understand the meaning of the sentence itself, isn't output. These exercises will make you produce language, but those forms may not become part of your internal linguistic system right away, because you're not linking them to meaning.

WARNING

So, although producing output is a common goal for many language learners, I often encounter people who studied a second/foreign language in school for several years, but claim they still cannot function in that language. Normally, this lack of output abilities can be traced back to at least one of these problems:

>> **Being forced or pushed to produce language before you're ready:** You need lots of comprehensible input in your L1 or L2 before you can produce output. (Note how much input babies receive before they can produce intelligible output in their L1.) If output is forced before you're ready, you may mistakenly believe that you aren't good at languages. But the root of the

problem may be the scarcity of appropriate input. It's like trying to grow a plant without watering it properly: You can't grow your L2 without feeding it enough comprehensible input.

>> **Trying to produce language that is above your proficiency level:** You need to accept that your L2 proficiency may differ from your L1 proficiency, and you may not have all the L2 tools you have in your L1. So, your L2 output needs to reflect the language you have available, even if that entails simplifying the language you would use in your L1.

>> **Focusing your attention on grammatical accuracy:** In instructional settings, it's common to focus attention on the grammatical accuracy of the L2 production, and transmission of meaning takes a secondary role. Although grammatical accuracy is important for some learners — and it can be especially beneficial for advanced learners — too much emphasis on it can be discouraging for novice learners who don't have enough language tools yet. For that reason, I encourage you to keep meaning at the forefront of your output.

>> **Lacking opportunities to produce meaningful output:** Focusing on meaning and purposeful communication when your produce output strengthens your form-meaning connections. As a result, your access to your internal L2 system will become stronger, and little by little, this access will become faster (which will show up in your fluency). If you're a novice learner, don't worry too much if your output is full of grammatical errors. Form (grammar) will be shaped appropriately as you receive more comprehensible and good quality input.

Here's an example of the importance of focusing on transmitting meaning (over achieving grammatical accuracy), especially for novice learners: Imagine that a tourist visiting the United States wants to buy a red dress for a party, but their knowledge of English is pretty basic. The tourist enters a clothing store and says to the clerk: "Me want dress red, please." Do you think the tourist will leave the store with a red dress? Possibly. Although their English grammar is quite off the track, the tourist has produced basic content words (the verb *want*, the noun *dress*, and the adjective *red*). So, even with very simple English grammar, they are able to get a meaningful message across and attain their communicative purpose: buying a red dress.

Checking out the benefits of output

Researchers agree that input is an essential element for language learning and acquisition, but haven't reached a consensus about the importance or role of output in the language learning process. Some researchers see output as the final result of language learning/acquisition. Many others, such as Merrill Swain, consider output a part of the process to acquire/learn a language.

I am a firm believer that input, interaction, and output are essential parts of the language learning process. Output helps you develop your internal linguistic system and your language proficiency. In fact, your L2 system develops as you produce L2 output. Through your L2 output you can

>> **Assess whether your L2 hypotheses are correct.** If it doesn't cause any communicative breakdown, then you can consider the output you're producing okay. If you have a communication problem, you need to revisit your L2 production and adjust it accordingly. For instance, if an L2 English learner produces the word *cats* and their interlocutor indicates they understand, the learner can confirm that plurals are created by adding -*s* to some nouns. However, if that same learner produces the word *childs* instead of *children*, their interlocutor may provide feedback that suggests something isn't right. In this case, the reaction of the interlocutor to the learner's output indicates that their hypothesis was correct in the first example (*cats*), but needs to be reformulated in the second example (*childs*).

>> **Acknowledge a gap/problem in your L2.** When you try to communicate an idea in your L2, you need to access your internal language system and retrieve what you need. In that process to produce output, you may realize you don't have all the tools you need to communicate your idea in the L2; in other words, there's a gap in your knowledge. If this occurs when you're communicating and interacting with other L2 speakers, you have an opportunity to negotiate meaning with them (and they may give you some modified input), which may end up helping your developing L2 system. Thus, this output opportunity allows you to recognize the areas in your internal linguistic system you need help with.

>> **Create automaticity and fluency in your L2.** The more output you produce, the stronger your form-meaning connections become. Your access and retrieval from your L2 system gets stronger, and with time, this access is easier, faster, and more automatic (which shows up in your fluency).

TIP

If you're one of those people who talk to yourself when you're alone, I have great news for you! Self-talking in your L2, playing around with your L2, or taking mental notes about how to say something (even if you got the input while eavesdropping on a conversation) can have a positive influence in your L2 learning process. Through language play, learners can experiment with different features of the language (sounds, grammar, vocabulary, and so on) that they'll later use as output in public. *Language play* is a private rehearsal and experimentation of a language being learned/acquired. Language play can be audible (heard aloud), whispered, or subvocal (only happening in your head). In language play situations, thought and language converge. Some of the activities learners do as language play include

>> Trying to produce L2 sounds

>> Rehearsing hypothetical conversational exchanges

>> Experimenting with new words encountered in input

>> Practicing grammatical rules

>> Correcting errors they produced or noticed in the input

>> Repeating or imitating what others say (which may be beyond their current competence), making those messages their own

>> Repeating and adjusting their own utterances

Understanding interlanguage

In the process of language learning, you create an internal language that seems to be in between your L1 and your L2. Linguistics professor Larry Selinker (in 1972) coined the term *interlanguage* to describe this internal personal language. Your interlanguage includes features of previously acquired/learned languages (both L1 and L2), features of the new L2, and some common features found in all interlanguage systems. But as with languages in general, interlanguages are dynamic systems that change as you receive input and test your hypotheses about the L2 system you're building.

Fossilization

Language learning doesn't advance steadily. You may notice you're progressing in your learning for a while, but at some point you may feel that you've stopped making progress and you've reached a plateau, and then something may trigger your development again or you may remain on that plateau.

During the process of learning a new language, when your interlanguage stops progressing and remains at a stable plateau, you may be stuck at a *fossilization* stage (another term coined by Larry Selinker). This fossilization stage may happen at any moment in your L2 journey.

L1 influence

As you learn your L2 and build your new language system, you normally draw on the language you already have — your L1 and any other L2s you've acquired. Your previous language(s) can interfere with the development of your new L2 system, or they may help you learn your L2 in the following ways:

>> **L1 as an obstacle:** When you're learning an L2, your L1 can be an obstacle for you in two different ways:

- If you reach an interlanguage developmental stage that shows some similarity to a structure in your L1, you may transfer this L1 feature/pattern into your interlanguage and stay in that developmental stage for longer than other learners (or you may even fossilize with that L1 pattern, especially if the errors don't affect your communication and aren't corrected).

- You may avoid using an L2 feature when it seems very different, difficult, or distant from your L1 (a concept known as *avoidance*).

>> **L1 as an aid:** Your L1 can help you notice aspects of your L2 and make sense of the feedback you receive (especially when it's implicit feedback; I discuss feedback in the earlier section "Receiving various types of feedback"). Furthermore, sometimes you can rely on your L1 knowledge to learn academic content in your L2.

REMEMBER

Although your L1 can influence your L2 learning process (serving as an obstacle or an aid), it's important to note that all L2 learners follow the same developmental sequences, regardless of their L1 background or the context where the L2 is learned (in a natural or a classroom setting). See Chapter 5 for more details on developmental sequences and acquisition orders.

Recognizing That Making Errors Is Totally Normal

Errors in language learning may irritate some parents and teachers. However, when children produce errors in their L1, nobody really worries that they'll keep repeating these errors throughout their life. Making errors is part of their natural language acquisition process.

Consider this example: A child whose L1 is English says that something is *badder* than some other thing. Despite being corrected by their parents, the child says *badder* for quite some time. As they grow and reach the appropriate developmental sequence, they stop saying *badder* and fix the error — perhaps without even realizing they've begun to use the correct word, *worse*. Guess what? L2 learners make similar errors!

REMEMBER

Language acquisition and learning follow a developmental sequence (see Chapter 5), so it's expected that you'll produce errors as you progress through the different developmental stages.

When you produce an L2 error proper of a developmental stage and someone corrects it, their error correction won't be effective in rearranging your internal L2 system (similar to the example of a child saying *badder*). Thus, it's very likely that you'll repeat the error until your internal linguistic system reaches the appropriate developmental stage to fix it in your internal L2 knowledge.

It's important to note that some of the errors L1 and L2 learners make are developmental errors, some are overgeneralization errors (like adding -s to *tooth* to form the plural *tooths*), and some are simplification errors (such as asking someone *You like to read?* instead of adding the auxiliary verb *do*). All these errors are normal and expected in the language learning process.

Even though correction of developmental errors may not be effective (because you can't alter developmental stages), some learners expect and are grateful to receive direct error correction, whereas others prefer not being corrected (or at least not under some conditions, such as in front of certain people). You may perceive direct correction of errors as

>> **An expected practice:** Some adult L2 learners expect error correction, especially in instructional settings.

>> **A helping hand:** Some L2 learners feel that error correction and feedback can help them develop their L2 and fix errors in their output by pointing out specific explicit knowledge of the L2 forms.

>> **A source of anxiety and stress:** For other learners, too much overt error correction can cause anxiety and stress, blocking input comprehension and output production.

Distinguishing Learning Contexts

The context in which you learn a language has a big impact on the language learning process. In this section I discuss two main contexts: naturalistic environments and instructional settings.

Naturalistic settings

L1 acquisition normally occurs in a naturalistic setting, in an immersion context (for example, at home with family). Some L2 learners also acquire their L2 in a natural setting, in social interaction with native or proficient L2 speakers in the community. Here are the key aspects of learning an L2 in naturalistic settings (what is called second language learning, as I explain in Chapter 2):

>> **Time:** You have ample time and opportunities to receive input and produce the L2 with other speakers. You may choose to be immersed in the language all day long.

>> **Input:** You receive input with limited or no errors, but it may be above your comprehension level (that is, some of the language you receive will be noise for you). You may need to use strategies to request modified input. The linguistic input doesn't follow a curriculum or a guided series of steps, and you may receive it in a variety of ways, including by interacting with L2 speakers or listening to language exchanges among L2 speakers; by reading flyers, newspapers, and ads in your community; and by watching audiovisual media. As a result, your vocabulary and grammar input is extensive and varied.

>> **Interlocutors:** You can receive input and communicate with interlocutors at work, at the store, on the playground, and the like. In general, your interlocutors are native or proficient L2 speakers.

>> **Output:** Your everyday use of the language may include a wide array of tasks: greetings, commercial transactions, information exchanges, interactions at work, arguments, and more. In all those communicative exchanges, the goal is getting the message across or accomplishing the task. In other words, the focus is communicating meaningfully.

>> **Errors:** Linguistic or pragmatic errors won't be corrected as long as they don't interfere with communication, or unless you ask your interlocutors to correct them. Some interlocutors may believe that making corrections is rude.

Instructional settings

Many L2 learners start their language learning in a classroom setting, which can be a great option for novice learners. A good language classroom can provide you with modified input, which may boost your confidence to continue learning the L2. In my opinion, some of the best instructional settings resemble a naturalistic environment (such as classrooms that follow the natural approach to teaching, which I explain in Chapter 7).

Some key features of instructional settings are as follows:

>> **Time:** The amount of time and opportunities you have to use the language are minimal, compared to a natural setting. This is especially true when you're learning a foreign language. (See Chapter 2 for the difference between a second and a foreign language.)

>> **Input:** You receive only a few hours of input per week. The advantage is, you normally receive high quality comprehensible input, because the teacher produces modified input without errors. But input also comes from your peers (and may contain errors) and from sources the teacher selects for the class. The input normally doesn't include a wide array of real-life scenarios, and it normally follows a grammatically-sequenced curriculum.

>> **Interlocutors:** In class, your interlocutors are your instructor (often the only proficient speaker) and your peers. The interactions with your peers may come with errors (typical of their interlanguage).

>> **Output:** Fortunately, many modern language classrooms focus more on communicating meaning, and not so much on achieving grammatical accuracy. However, some language classrooms still emphasize grammatical accuracy over everything else. I provide an overview of some instructional methodologies in Chapter 7.

>> **Errors:** In communicative language classrooms, teachers are expected to focus on meaningful interactions, and when students make errors, instructors may use recasts or other error correction techniques (covered in the earlier section "Receiving various types of feedback"). However, because they're in a classroom setting, some learners may expect explicit correction of grammatical errors.

Chapter **9**

Digging into Diverse Language Skills

earning a new language and all its components is a challenging but very rewarding experience. The task may seem overwhelming, but with the appropriate tools, goals, plan, and motivation, you can succeed.

You may have heard the terms *passive skills* to refer to reading and listening and *active skills* to refer to speaking and writing. Second language (L2) learners usually consider the active skills more difficult to master. But as you find out in this chapter, all four skills require some action on your part, because everything related to language learning is an active process. Here, I provide several strategies to get better at reading, listening, speaking, and writing.

Advancing Your L2 Reading Skills

REMEMBER

Reading is a great source of L2 input because you encounter language in real communicative contexts, and it's a skill that normally isn't limited by time, so you can read and reread the input as many times as you need. (Don't know what I mean by *input?* Check out Chapter 8.) As such, reading is an essential part of your language development journey. In this section, I help you understand how to advance your L2 reading skills.

Knowing how reading helps you acquire language

As you read, several areas of your L2 develop:

» **Vocabulary:** Reading gives you the opportunity to encounter more high-, mid-, and low-frequency vocabulary words incidentally and repeatedly. You strengthen the vocabulary you already know and enrich the vocabulary you partially know by adding new features.

» **Grammar:** You get used to and absorb the grammatical structure of the language.

» **Text and discourse features:** You learn how the different text types (such as descriptions, narratives, poetry, and argumentative essays) are structured, the purpose of each text type, the language (vocabulary, sentence structure) used, and some other features of each text (like characters).

Reading requires you to have a certain level of language knowledge as well as some understanding of how languages work. For example, you need to understand that the written symbols in the text represent words, that to decode and recognize words, you can sound them out (overtly or in your head), that words are separated by spaces, that punctuation helps you understand the meaning of the text, and that you read in a specific direction (left to right, right to left, horizontally, or vertically).

So, your reading success is determined by several factors, such as

» Your L2 knowledge (vocabulary, grammar, and so on)

» Your world knowledge, which can be activated before or while reading the text

» Your familiarity with text types and their organization (for example, descriptive or narrative texts)

» Your short-term memory capacity (ability to keep the information you're reading in your memory)

» Your use of reading strategies to understand the meaning of the text

TIP

Several studies show that an efficient way to retain L2 words is by inferring (or guessing) their meaning from context while reading (instead of learning words and meaning in isolation). So, as you encounter new words in your reading, you need to activate some learning strategies: Guess the meaning, check your guessed meaning (using a dictionary or asking an expert like a teacher or native speaker), focus on the form of the new word, and try to find its relationship to other words you already know. I talk more about strategies for successful L2 reading later in this chapter.

Comparing alphabetic and logographic languages

Because you're reading this book, I can safely say that you're familiar with *alphabetic* languages (like English and Spanish), in which words are written using a specific set of letters (an *alphabet*). Some of you may also be familiar with *logographic* languages (like Chinese), in which a symbol represents an entire word.

As an L2 learner, you may face some challenges when you need to read in a language that doesn't align exactly with your first language (L1). For example, you may need to read a language that doesn't have phonological representations (sounds) for symbols, or you may find symbols that you recognize in written form but can't pronounce, or you may even find languages where vowels aren't written or the direction of the writing (right to left, for instance) differs from your L1.

In logographic languages, such as Chinese, every symbol represents a word or a unit of meaning, but these symbols aren't directly linked to singular pronunciation units (the way letters are linked to sounds in English). In other words, these languages don't have *phonological transparency*. So, figuring out how to introduce literacy in logographic languages is always difficult.

One solution is *romanization,* which is the use of alphabetical symbols to indicate how to pronounce logographic characters. For Chinese, the Romanized system is called *pinyin,* and the Romanized version of Japanese is called *romaji.* The symbols used in pinyin to represent sounds are close to the ones used in English (although they aren't exactly the same) with some *diacritics* (accent or pronunciation marks) added to indicate tone. Pinyin is also used to type in Chinese.

TECHNICAL STUFF

Some researchers and teachers support romanization of logographic languages so that learners can start accessing the language and its pronunciation as soon as possible, without having to first learn the new script (characters). Other scholars emphasize the importance of using logographic symbols from the very beginning.

Transferring your L1 reading skills

You don't need to start from scratch as you begin your L2 reading. When you read in your L2, you've already learned how to read in your L1, so you have some *literary experience.* Of course, you need some L2 linguistic knowledge so you can recognize and comprehend the meaning of the symbols you're reading, but you don't have to relearn everything you did for your L1 reading (for example, that written symbols represent words, or the role of punctuation). You can piggyback much of that knowledge.

Some researchers support the hypothesis that your reading ability in your L1 influences your reading ability in your L2, so there's an interdependence between the two languages. This is the idea behind the proposal that a common central processing system exists for both your L1 and L2. In other words, what happens in your brain with one language affects the other. Based on this hypothesis, the more developed your L1 reading skills, the more you can develop your L2 reading abilities.

The *linguistic distance* between the L1 and the L2 normally affects your L2 reading skills. That means the closer the two languages are (the more similar they are), the easier it is for you to transfer many of the skills you use in your L1 to your L2. This distance also affects the rate at which you develop your L2 reading skills.

Some linguists believe that decoding skills are more easily transferred between languages with phonological transparency (see the previous section) than languages without phonological transparency. For example, when your L1 and L2 have an alphabetic writing system, even if they don't use the same alphabet (such as English, which uses the Roman alphabet, and Russian, which uses the Cyrillic alphabet), aligning your L1 reading skills with your L2 skills will be easy, and you'll be able to decode the L2 by very slightly modifying your L1 skills. However, if you're dealing with an alphabetic language and a logographic one, such as Chinese, you can't transfer your L1 skills so easily to your L2.

Your L2 proficiency level also affects your reading skills:

>> For novice L2 learners, your L2 knowledge influences your L2 reading comprehension more than any other factor. (It's important to remember that children start reading in their L1 only after they have a certain command of the spoken language.)

>> For advanced L2 learners, your L1 reading skills influence your ability to read at higher levels in your L2 more than your L2 language skills do.

When they're reading and listening, L1 users benefit a lot from *discourse signaling cues*, which are linguistic mechanisms that help you anticipate the information you're about to receive. Likewise, recognizing discourse signaling cues in your L2 can improve your L2 reading skills. These signaling cues are especially important when you're reading or hearing certain types of texts, including expository texts (such as news articles or textbooks). Here are some examples of discourse signaling cues:

- » *Emphasis markers,* which try to get your attention (for example, *This is the most important feature.*)

- » *Logical connectors,* which organize series or events by importance or in chronological order (for example, *first, second/later, in the end*), or add elements or opposing views (for example, *and, or, but, on the other hand*)

- » *Previews,* which prepare you to receive specific information (for example, *This recipe has five steps.*)

- » *Summaries,* which indicate that a recap of ideas or conclusion is being presented (for example, *to sum up* or *in conclusion*)

Employing strategies for L2 reading success

Your L2 reading abilities can improve when you use some of the reading strategies in the following sections.

Having a purpose or goal for your reading

Before starting, consider your goal in reading the text. It can be having a pleasurable experience, learning about something that interests you, completing a school assignment, improving your reading fluency, or enhancing your L2 input opportunities. Hopefully, by the time you finish, you've satisfied your curiosity or accomplished your goal.

Selecting a text that's appropriate in content and proficiency

Pick reading material that targets your goal and deals with meaningful topics you enjoy and/or are interested in. That way, the content will grab your attention and hook you into more L2 reading.

TIP

In addition, pick reading material that aligns with your L2 proficiency level:

- » Novice and intermediate learners benefit from graded readers and even children's books designed for L1 learning. Graded reader books are helpful because they're written with high-frequency and mid-frequency vocabulary words.

- » More advanced learners benefit from all types of reading material. Extensive reading gives advanced L2 learners the opportunity to enlarge their vocabulary and strengthen their understanding of L2 grammatical structures.

Getting ready to understand the text

The following strategies and processes can help you understand the reading material:

>> **Activate your prior knowledge and make predictions.** Use the information you already have (your prior knowledge of the topic and experience, as well as your knowledge of the world) to get ready for the new reading material.

For example, if it's a detective book, you expect a certain storyline and characters: You know there's a problem and some people who need to solve it.

>> **Process the content.** Start from the broader aspects and move on to the details.

- Look at the title (and subtitles or chapter headings).

- Pay attention to the illustrations or photographs.

- Preview the material before digging in: Skim the text to locate specific information, key words you recognize, and the like.

- Predict content based on textual features (like grammatical structure and vocabulary) and contextual clues, as well as use your background knowledge (about the historical setting and cultural details) and previous knowledge of the world.

- Identify the main idea.

- Locate the details that support the main idea.

TIP

>> **Use context clues.** Using context clues is a great strategy to improve your reading comprehension skills and enlarge your vocabulary. For example, when you encounter a word or expression you can't understand, you can use these context clues to try to guess its meaning:

- Check for examples or descriptions in the text to help you understand what's being discussed.

- Determine if it's part of a *collocation* (saying), such as the word *excruciating* in the phrase *excruciating pain.* You can guess part of the meaning just from the word *pain.*

- Pay attention to *appositions* (explanatory words or phrases) in the text. For example, you may not know the word *landlord,* but you can guess its meaning in the sentence *I paid the rent to my landlord, the owner of my apartment, on May 2* by looking at the apposition *the owner of my apartment.*

Assessing your comprehension of the text

You can check that you interpreted the text's meaning correctly by trying to

>> Summarize the content.

>> Paraphrase the content.

>> Elaborate the main concepts or continue learning about them.

>> Find the sequence of events (or reorganize it).

>> Understand the characters' motivations.

>> Reach informed conclusions.

>> Use the information you learn in subsequent situations.

>> Pinpoint the following:

- Facts and opinions

- Cause and effect (or result)

- Conflict and resolution

- Conclusion of the story

TIP

You can do this in an informal way by assessing your comprehension of the text only in your head.

Improving Your Listening Skills

Listening is a great way for L2 learners to receive input. But input is useful only if you can understand the messages being transmitted. If you don't comprehend the input and process its meaning, it's just noise. (You can read more about input in Chapter 8.)

REMEMBER

Listening is often mistakenly classified as a passive skill. However, it actually requires your brain to take an active role. That is, your brain needs to actively use a lot of your working memory to process the language you hear and comprehend its meaning.

Many L2 learners, especially beginners, claim that L2 speakers talk too fast and L2 listening is very difficult. The main issue is, you aren't used to processing the L2 quickly and immediately. Unlike L2 reading, which you can do at your own pace, you must process spoken L2 input within milliseconds of hearing it, and your brain doesn't make the required connections as fast as it does in your L1.

Every listening opportunity is different, and so is every learner. So, the way you approach different situations depends on the context, your L2 proficiency level, and your goal. Also, you normally use a combination of listening strategies rather than just one.

You can use two main types of language listening strategies: global strategies, which focus on the whole message first and then move to the particulars, and local strategies, which target the details first and then move to the big picture. I cover both types here, along with some of my personal favorites.

Global strategies for listening

Global and *macro* strategies (top-down processes) work by starting from a big-picture viewpoint. Some strategies you can use to improve your L2 listening comprehension are as follows:

>> **Be prepared for the topic.** Learn about the topic and context of what you will listen to. You can write down some of the main points you expect to hear in a specific situation and ask proficient L2 users or native speakers to help you anticipate other content/information or vocabulary you may encounter. Then, you can review/study that content and be ready for it.

>> **Predict the content.** Make predictions about the content you may hear, based on the context clues, the participants, and what you already know about the topic, the situation, and so on.

>> **Activate your prior knowledge.** Consider what you already know about the topic and get that information ready to help you comprehend the new input.

>> **Focus on main ideas.** Identify the main ideas first, to get the gist of the communication.

>> **Consider organization or order.** The way the information is organized may help you understand and anticipate content.

>> **Look for nonlinguistic cues.** Pay attention to nonlinguistic cues, such as background sounds, physical objects in the communication context or setting, body language and facial expressions, and the like.

Local strategies for listening

Local and *micro* strategies (bottom-up processes) for listening work at the word or phrase level. You can use them in the following ways:

>> **Predict words/phrases.** Anticipate the language you may encounter in the communicative situation by using your knowledge of the subject, cues from the speaker, the context of the message, and the like.

>> **Decipher unknown words.** When you face completely unfamiliar words, try the following:

- **Guess meaning.** Deduce or guess word meaning using context or familiarity with other words you know in your L1 or L2. Sometimes it can be as simple as asking yourself whether the word refers to an action, a place/thing/person/animal, or a description of something. But you need to have certain linguistic knowledge to do that. Context isn't always sufficient.

- **Confirm meaning.** Determine whether your guess about a word's meaning makes sense according to the rest of the communication. Check the meaning in a dictionary when you have the time. Ask your *interlocutors* (other L2 speakers) if the meaning you guessed is correct.

- **Avoid getting stuck.** Trying to find the meaning of all the words you don't understand can be a hurdle that stops your progress, especially for beginning learners. So, you need to know when to skip unknown words and focus on the rest of the communication.

>> **Handle known or familiar words.** When you hear words that are familiar or kind of familiar to you, do the following:

- First, focus on understanding the main meaning of the word (its root), without focusing on its form.

- Pay special attention to words you already know, because they can help you understand the message's main ideas.

- Take note of recognizable key words to anticipate what the speaker will say next. For example, if you hear words like *first* or *in the end,* you can expect a list or summary will follow.

- Listen for *cognates* (L2 words that sound similar to an L1 word) and use them to help you process meaning.

A few personal favorites

TIP

My suggestions to help you get better at L2 listening include the following:

>> **Listen to music and follow along with the lyrics.** Feel free to sing the songs too! You'll be practicing your language skills in an enjoyable way.

>> **Listen to TV shows, radio programs, and podcasts.** Look for programs on topics you find interesting or entertaining. When the topic is compelling and enjoyable, you'll actively listen and try to make sense of the meaning. As you listen, you can take note of any new words that come up and later check their meaning in a dictionary or with an expert (such as a teacher or native speaker).

>> **Set up opportunities for repeat performances.** If you listen to discussions in similar communicative situations where the topics are repeated, you can anticipate and practice specific words and phrases. For example, if you like cooking, try watching TV shows about cooking, find videos online with different recipes, or listen to podcasts about cooking on your way to work.

>> **Practice, practice, practice!** The more time you spend practicing your L2 listening skills, the better they'll get. Very soon, you'll start feeling that the speed of the L2 input has slowed down a little. I'm guessing the speed will be the same, but your listening and processing skills are getting better.

Speaking Your L2 without Fear

The feelings you had when you started speaking your L1 are probably very different from your feelings about speaking your L2. Children learning their L1 speak without fear, without really focusing on the speaking task itself, and they talk when they're ready. As an L2 learner, you normally experience some kind of stress or concern when you begin speaking the L2, and you often feel "forced" to talk before you're ready.

REMEMBER

Keeping a *low affective filter* (a low anxiety level) is key in language acquisition (see Chapter 6). So, the most important advice I can give you about speaking in your L2 is this: Go ahead and try it. Speak in your L2 without being concerned about how you do it. The more you try, the better you'll become!

As author Bill VanPatten suggests, speaking is a skill, not knowledge. So, it's an ability that develops gradually over time. With time and practice, you *automatize* the procedures you need to produce output, meaning you start speaking effortlessly. You'll show improvement in your speaking skills through speed and accuracy: As you become proficient, you'll speak faster, with fewer errors and without too much effort.

Understanding two types of spoken language

When you speak your L1 or your L2, you use these two types of language:

» The language you create on the spot to communicate new content

» A prefabricated language formed by routines and chunks or patterns of language (for example, asking *How do you say . . . ?* and *Where can I find . . . ?*)

The first type, novel utterances, require you to do the extra work of accessing your vocabulary and grammatical knowledge, but the second type, prefabricated language, doesn't require any extra analysis. You just grab lexical chunks from your stored language like you'd pull an apple off a tree. Find out more about these types of spoken language in the following sections.

Saying novel content

Some of the procedures and abilities you need to produce novel, or new, L2 speech must be in place before others can develop. Only when you have control of the first procedures/abilities do you start developing and applying later ones. For example, before adding inflections (gender, number, tense, and the like) to words, you need to be able to access the words themselves. Likewise, before you can read a book, you must recognize letters and understand how to read. Linguists call this the *processability theory.*

The processability theory, proposed by professor Manfred Pienemann in 1998, explains why children and novice L2 learners can produce one- and two-word phrases much earlier than they produce sentences. Or why L2 learners can produce subjunctive verb tense in Spanish, or understand where verbs are placed in subordinate clauses in German, only after they've learned earlier L2 procedures.

According to the processability theory, some of the procedures or steps in language development include

» **Lemma access:** The easiest procedure is accessing or retrieving words. At an early stage in learning a new language, you should start producing words without being concerned about adding the appropriate inflections.

>> **Category procedure:** Next, you begin adding inflections to words to change or complete their meaning (for example, producing the past tense verb *watched* by adding *-ed* to *watch*). These simple inflections involve single words; they aren't the more advanced inflections that link one word to another (see the next bullet point).

>> **Phrasal procedure:** After that, you start adding inflections to phrases. In this procedure, the inflections depend on other words in the phrase. For example, in Spanish you need to have gender and number agreement between adjectives and nouns (as in the masculine singular phrase *el vestido rojo*, meaning *the red dress*).

>> **Simplified S-procedure:** Here, you begin moving elements within sentences. For example, you may move the adverb in *I saw you yesterday at the library* to the beginning or end of the sentence (*Yesterday I saw you at the library* or *I saw you at the library yesterday*).

>> **S-procedure:** This step is where you start carrying information from internal constituents (phrases) to other constituents within the same sentence. For example, if you say *My brother is the tall one,* you're using information from the phrase *my brother* to make sure there's agreement with the verb phrase (in other words, you won't say *My brother is the tall ones* or *My brother are the tall one*).

>> **Subordinate clause procedure:** Finally, you begin carrying grammatical and semantic information across clauses, from the main clause to subordinate or embedded clauses. For instance, in Spanish some verbs in the main clause trigger the use of subjunctive forms (verb forms that express mood — like *quieran,* or *want* — or possibility) in the subordinate clause, as in *Dudo que (ellos) quieran comprar eso* (*I doubt they want to buy that*).

Using formulas and gambits

Not everything you produce in your L1 is new or fresh. You often use chunks or memorized phrases of language (called *gambits* and *formulas*) to maximize your processing resources and improve your fluency. For example, without even thinking about them, you produce stock phrases and sentences such as *Hello, how are you?* or *As I told you before,* or *Let me explain that again,* or *I really appreciate it!*

Prefabricated gambits and formulas are language routines — in other words, they're semifixed words, phrases, or sentences that speakers use to maintain fluency and conversational flow. These *lexical phrases* (as some researchers call them) are pretty predictable for other speakers of the language. For example, if I say, "Good morning! How are you?" you'll probably answer, "I'm OK, thank you. And you?" or something similar. You don't even need to listen to the whole question to anticipate what's coming and how you'll answer.

REMEMBER

When you produce L2 speech, relying on premade chunks of language gives you fluency, because you can use gambits and formulas without changing or analyzing them. You just learn them as a single unit, to be produced in specific situations.

As you're learning your L2, you can improve your fluency by identifying and using gambits and formulas. Here are some popular gambits and formulas to use in communicative exchanges:

» Discourse organizers to introduce what's coming up in your communication — for example, to indicate that you want to

- Change topics (*I will come back to this point in a moment.*)

- Return to something you previously said (*As I mentioned before . . .*)

- Connect content in a logical or chronological order (*These are the steps you need to follow* or *Tell me from start to finish.*)

» Strategies to keep the flow going in a communicative exchange and signal different conversational acts, such as

- Interrupting your interlocutor (*Excuse me, but . . .*)

- Explaining something further (*Let me clarify that.*)

- Taking turns (*Let me add that . . .* or *Give me a minute to add . . .*)

- Adding your point of view or counterargument (*In my opinion . . .* or *On the contrary . . .*)

- Showing interest in what your interlocutor is saying (*Wow! Tell me more about that.*)

- Approving or disagreeing with what your interlocutor is saying (*Well, I agree with you* or *No, I think . . .*)

» Pause fillers to give you time to think of what you're about to say (*Well, as I was just saying before . . .* or *As you mentioned earlier . . .*)

» Politeness formulas to satisfy certain social conventions, such as

- Expressing gratitude (*Thank you* or *I really appreciate it.*)

- Requesting something (*Can I . . . ?* or *Do you mind if I . . . ?*)

- Greeting someone (*Nice to meet you, A pleasure, Hello,* or *Hi!*)

- Leaving a situation (*Bye, See you later,* or *Take care.*)

- Assenting (*I agree with you* or *I concur.*)

Working on pronunciation

When you consider pronunciation, you may think you want to sound native-like in your L2. But what exactly does that mean? Native speakers of English, for example, pronounce the word *water* many different ways — who decides which pronunciation is "native"?

Your goals or reasons for learning a new language may affect the way you view your L2 pronunciation:

>> If your goal is intelligibility and comprehensibility, you'll probably be happy with your pronunciation as long as you can interact effectively with others, even if you have a strong accent.

>> If your goal is achieving a native-like pronunciation for personal or professional reasons, you may need to focus on your pronunciation of both *segmental* features of the L2 (specific sounds) and *suprasegmental* features (rhythm, intonation, and stress). Because there are many native-like pronunciations (which vary depending on the geographical area, among other reasons), you need to select the variety that targets your goal. You can find services (such as a vocal coach) that may help you reduce or modify your foreign accent. In fact, many people working in the media industry (such as TV news anchors and radio hosts) use these types of services.

TIP

Some studies emphasize the importance of learning L2 suprasegmentals like rhythm and stress, because mastering those speech characteristics may improve your intelligibility and comprehensibility more than just focusing on pronouncing individual sounds.

Some factors that may affect your pronunciation of the L2 include the following:

>> **Exposure to your L2:** Several studies support the idea that your L2 pronunciation will improve the longer you're exposed to the language and the more you try to imitate what you hear in communicative exchanges with other L2 users.

>> **Use of your L1:** If you fall back on your L1 when you face a communication difficulty, you may have more of an accent in your L2 than if you just try to overcome the hurdle using your L2. The more you try to speak your L2 and ask your interlocutors for help and feedback, the more success you'll have with pronunciation.

>> **Motivation and goals for learning your L2:** Both integrative and instrumental motivation are at play here.

- *Integrative motivation* is your desire to demonstrate that you belong to a group and to establish your identity as part of an ethnic community. If you want to blend in with the L2 community, your motivation to be considered part of the group will help your pronunciation. For instance, if a loved one speaks your L2, you may be motivated to be part of their community. This type of motivation is very important for success in acquiring languages.

However, if you still want to maintain your link and show your loyalty to your L1 even though you're learning an L2, you may always have a strong or foreign accent in the L2.

- *Instrumental motivation* is your desire to achieve something you value or reap the practical benefits of a task. If speaking the L2 will help you obtain a better job, get a pay raise, get a government job, earn a good grade, or satisfy some other ambition, your motivation to reach that goal will play an important role in your ability to improve your L2 pronunciation.

>> **Attention to meaning:** When mispronunciation affects meaning, you should pay attention to the pronunciation of individual sounds (for example, pronouncing "sh" versus "s" in *sheet* and *seat*). However, if your communication isn't affected by your pronunciation, I recommend that you focus on transmitting meaning over perfecting your accent.

When you learn an L2 as a child (*simultaneous bilingualism*), you're able to notice and distinguish all or many new sounds, but when you learn an L2 as an adult (*sequential bilingualism*), you normally rely on your L1 to make sense of the new L2 sounds. That's why simultaneous bilinguals usually don't have any problem adopting the two sound systems, but sequential bilinguals typically have non-native pronunciation. The different types of bilinguals are explained in Chapter 2.

As your language proficiency grows, your pronunciation of strings of words becomes smoother and more fluid. Whereas novice L2 speakers normally pronounce each word separately as they speak, more advanced L2 learners start blurring the boundaries of words and linking words together. I encourage and train my students to speak fluidly and connect strings of words from the very beginning, although I understand the difficulty of doing that for novice learners.

Enhancing your L2 speaking skills with a few strategies

When you've acquired a good amount of your L2, you can focus on improving pronunciation, speed, rhythm, and so on. Some strategies to help you improve your speaking skills are as follows:

>> **Focus on transmitting meaning.** Don't worry about grammatical accuracy, especially as a novice learner. As the processability theory suggests, you

process content words first, and the grammatical aspects of your L2 come later.

» **Know and use gambits and formulas as much as possible.** This gives you a break to breathe when you're speaking, and helps you organize your communication and sound more fluent.

» **Find input by having conversations with native L2 speakers.** Here are some additional ways to find conversational input:

- If they grant permission, record conversations in which native L2 speakers are talking about meaningful topics to you.

- Search online for examples of conversations between native L2 speakers.

» **Write down what native L2 speakers say and repeat their words.** Imitate the language you hear native speakers produce, paying attention to their pronunciation, speed, pauses, rhythm, vocabulary, as well as formulas and gambits.

» **Ask for feedback.** If you have an instructor or tutor, or know another L2 speaker who can give you feedback, ask for their opinion on how you can improve your L2 production.

» **Practice the 4/3/2 strategy.** Prepare a talk about a topic that interests you and try to explain it to someone in 4 minutes. Then, talk about your topic for 3 minutes, and finally, explain it in just 2 minutes.

» **Try reading the same passage aloud three or four times.** Set different time limits to get through the reading without sacrificing accuracy or clarity. Repeating the same information at different speeds helps you automatize language, acquire procedural knowledge, and improve your speech rate and fluency.

» **Rehearse an anticipated conversation.** Language play is an effective way to practice your L2 (see Chapter 8). You can imagine L2 interactions and act out what you'd say in those situations. If you have the opportunity, practice similar conversations with different L2 users in various contexts.

» **During interactions, make sure your L2 production is clear by**

- *Checking that your interlocutors understand you:* Make sure you learn some prefabricated sentences you can rely on in communicative exchanges (see the earlier section "Using formulas and gambits").

- *Giving explanations or examples when possible:* Your examples can be as simple as a proper name.

- *Paraphrasing your words:* Try to say what you mean in a different way if you think your interlocutor is having trouble understanding you. When you don't know a word, communicate its meaning using other words you already know, such as synonyms or antonyms for the word you mean.

Practicing Your L2 Writing Skills

Unlike speaking, writing isn't naturally acquired. In other words, you speak your L1 without making any particular effort, but writing is a skill that needs to be consciously learned. Additionally, not all languages have a written form. But writing and reading are part of your literacy skills.

TIP

For many people, few activities are more frightening than staring at a blank piece of paper or computer screen and waiting for writing inspiration to strike. As you start to write in your L2, I suggest you do the following:

>> Have a clear understanding of your goal or purpose and your audience. Your goal and audience will dictate your language choice: your tone, vocabulary and grammatical structures, text type (for example, persuasive or narrative), and so on.

>> Determine whether you have all the content you want to write about or whether you need to do some research before starting to write.

>> Brainstorm some of the ideas you want to get across.

>> Use some graphic organizers to get your ideas in order. Some examples include chronological, spatial, and logical order; main ideas and details/clarifications; abstract and concrete examples; and comparisons and contrasts.

>> Write a draft, and if you have time, let it sit for one or two days. Then, read through your draft and fix anything that isn't clear.

>> Share your writing with others, if possible, and ask for their feedback (especially on the content).

>> Revise and edit your draft using the feedback you get. Pay close attention to spelling, punctuation, and capitalization.

>> If time allows, let your revised version sit for another day or two before you reread it and fix what isn't clear.

Chapter **10**

Employing Language Learning Strategies

I n this chapter, I showcase several basic learning strategies so you can select the ones that work best for you in your second language (L2) journey. Use this chapter as a self-help resource whenever you feel stuck or eager to progress a bit faster. You'll have the opportunity to choose strategies based on your needs, preferences, communicative context, and L2 goals.

REMEMBER

There isn't one perfect strategy that works for everyone in all contexts and for all languages. The effectiveness of different strategies is linked to the individual characteristics of each learner (visual learner, aural learner, kinesthetic learner, and so on; see Chapter 3), the specific L2 skills you're trying to learn (listening, reading, speaking, and writing; see Chapter 9), and the context where you're using the strategy (on your own at home, in a traditional classroom, out in the world, and so on). A strategy that may help you learn an L2 feature may not work for another learner, or it may not work when you want to learn another L2.

Using Multiple Language Learning Strategies by Yourself

Learning strategies are dynamic, and they tend to be used in clusters (several strategies employed at once) or in chains (one strategy leads to another). In this section I cover some self-regulatory language learning strategies you may use to acquire your L2.

Memorizing and retrieving information

Research shows that when you study or learn things as part of a bigger whole — that is, within a context — you're able to remember them better than when you study them on their own. When it comes to learning a new language, for example, avoid learning lists of words that are completely decontextualized (for example, lists of random vocabulary words or phrases). Learn them as part of a whole, within a topic, and you'll be more successful at remembering them.

The following are some strategies you may use to store and retrieve information about your L2 from your memory:

>> **Linking meaning (images, objects, or actions) to form (the actual words):** For example, if you want to learn the word *book* in German, make a flashcard with an image of a book and print the German word (*Buch*) under the image or on the back of the card. Or as I used to do when I was little, add L2 labels to everything in your bedroom and living room. Likewise, you can link form and meaning by mimicking the action of a verb as you pronounce it. For example, as you jump, you can say the Spanish word *saltar* (to jump).

TIP

When the meanings are obvious, avoid using translations. It's better for your L2 learning to link meaning and form as a single unit (creating a *linguistic sign*) without having to resort to stealing the form from your first language (L1).

>> **Using acronyms or mnemonics:** You may use these memory aids to remember grammatical rules or distinguish between similar sounding words. For example, two acronyms that help Spanish L2 learners remember when to use *ser* and *estar* (two forms of the verb *to be*) are DOCTOR (Description, Occupation, Characteristics, Time, Origin, and Relationship) for *ser* and PLACE (Position, Location, Action, Condition, and Emotion) for *estar*.

>> **Using the keyword technique:** In this strategy, you connect a new L2 word to a similar sounding L1 or L2 word you already know. You need to make the acoustic link between the L2 word and the word you already know first, and then you can create a mental image of the L1 word representing the L2

meaning. For example, imagine your L1 is English, and you want to learn the word *celeridad* (speed, quickness) in Spanish.

- First, you connect the L2 word *celeridad* to the L1 word *celery.*

- Then, you imagine a celery stalk running quickly. Fun, right?

>> **Memorizing phrases:** Use this trick to remember certain words, expressions, or grammatical structures. For example, English L2 learners can keep the words *principle* and *principal* straight with these phrases: *The principal is your pal* and *A principle is a rule.* The way I learned the difference between *borrow* and *lend* was memorizing these two phrases: *Can I borrow . . . ?* and *Can you lend me . . . ?*

>> **Learning through repetition and rehearsal:** Rehearsal entails having encountered the form beforehand, so that you can rehearse it. Some researchers consider that part of the learned material (explicitly taught by a teacher or self-taught) can become acquired or implicit knowledge through repetition, especially delayed repetition, and exposure. For example, if you use flashcards, review them every day for at least for ten minutes, and later try to use some of these words in communicative situations. If you don't have the opportunity to use your L2 with others in real life, rehearse how you'll use it on your own. This is called *language play*, as I mention in Chapter 8.

Organizing vocabulary in your memory

You'll find words in your memory more easily when they are linked to other words you already know. They can relate to each other in meaning, sound, or context of use. For that reason, organizing your vocabulary learning is really important. Here are some strategies you can use:

>> **Grouping words according to meaning:** In this strategy, you classify or sort sets of related L2 words or information.

- If you use flashcards to learn words, group your cards in a way that makes sense to you (for example, put words that label items in your house in one stack).

- You can also create *semantic maps,* or images in which related words are visually linked to each other. Suppose that you're learning English as your L2; the map in Figure 10-1 can help you learn the names of different pets along with some associated words.

>> **Grouping words according to use:** Note down words that normally appear together. For example, when you come across the word *collect,* you can link it to stamps and coins, and group that information with hobbies some people enjoy.

>> **Creating comparative charts:** Highlight or compare/contrast certain features of words to distinguish meaning or use. This is mostly useful for more advanced learners. For example, create a chart that differentiates words in your L2 for *tumbler, cup, mug,* and so on.

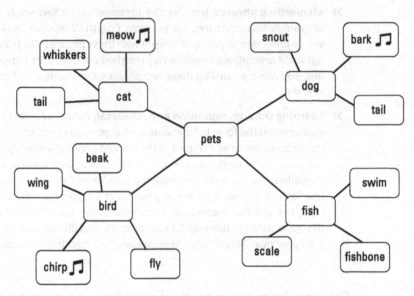

FIGURE 10-1:
Example of a
semantic map.

Activating and linking your knowledge

Your knowledge is organized in your long-term memory into *schemata*, or frameworks. One strategy you can use to comprehend what you read or hear in your L2 is activating your background knowledge — in other words, your schemata. When you're learning a new L2, refreshing what you already know about the topic, or remembering your previous experiences in similar situations, helps you process the new L2.

For instance, if you're reading your daily horoscope in the L2, you can activate your background knowledge about some of the information you may find, including words that reference different areas in your life (work, love, money) and future tenses of verbs (mostly those using the auxiliary *will*). Predicting the type of information you'll encounter and preparing yourself to comprehend it enhances your understanding of the content.

Likewise, if you know that you're going to read about, listen to, or watch someone preparing a recipe, what background knowledge can help you activate your schemata? What do you expect to find? How do you expect the text/information to be presented?

Some strategies you can use are as follows:

>> **Skim through text to activate your schemata and anticipate some of the information you may find.** Skimming helps you prepare to process information.

>> **Summarize the main ideas of L2 *input* (language samples) you read, listen to, and watch.** These summaries can help you organize your new knowledge into schemata, so you can link it to information you already have (or new knowledge you may encounter).

>> **Highlight specific information in the text you're reading.** Doing so will help you remember the information or group it with your previous knowledge.

>> **Take notes on L2 information you want to remember.** You can do this while you read or listen to input, or even when you're trying to produce language orally or in writing.

>> **Analyze the parts of new L2 words or grammatical structures to understand their components and remember them better.** For example, suppose an English L2 learner encounters the word *shopper* for the first time; they know the meaning of *shop* and have heard the *-er* ending before with words such as *teacher, singer, dancer,* and so on. By dividing the components of *shopper,* they will understand its meaning and remember it.

>> **Use deductive reasoning when you read or listen to L2 input to dig deeper into the information and deduce (guess) its meaning**. This strategy is more effective when you rely on your existing knowledge to guess meaning.

Paying attention to context

Many scholars agree on the effectiveness of learning languages in a *contextualized setting*, where you use your L2 in communicative interactions to accomplish tasks (see Chapter 7). So, a good strategy is to pretend that you're engaging in real-life L2 interactions (such as buying something at the grocery store or asking for directions) and practice those imaginary interactions repeatedly. Using L2 vocabulary and grammar in different contexts helps you learn not only the meaning of words but also their grammatical and real-life function. This is called *incidental vocabulary learning.* The following learning strategies can help you:

>> **Using words in context:** The more you use new L2 words or phrases in context, the easier it will be to recall them. If you use flashcards, you can add a note that explains the context. For example, an English L2 learner may learn the word *aisle* at the supermarket when they ask someone at the store where to find salt, and they answer, "Salt is in aisle 10."

>> **Creating hands-on experiences to use your L2:** These real-life experiences will be linked to a real context. For instance, you can write your shopping list in your L2, narrate to yourself what you're doing or watching throughout the day, change the settings of your phone to your L2, listen to podcasts or radio stations in your L2, and even create imaginary situations and role-play them in your L2. This latter example is called language play (see Chapter 8).

>> **Reading and conversing:** You also retain L2 words better when you encounter them in reading material (books, magazines, newspapers) or in conversations. This is especially true when these words are relevant to understanding a message or fulfilling a need. You retain new L2 words better when you pay close attention to them in context or make a mental effort to link them to your previous knowledge.

Planning and monitoring your learning

In Chapter 12, I explain the importance of having goals and a plan to learn your L2. One way to plan your learning and monitor your progress toward your goals is by using *metacognitive strategies* (techniques that help you monitor your thinking process and your learning). Some effective metacognitive strategies for language learners include keeping *learning logs* (oral or written reflections on what you've learned), taking notes on the L2 input you receive, and quizzing yourself with flashcards. These strategies are especially important for independent L2 learners, who plan and evaluate their own learning process and don't have a teacher to fill in any gaps in their knowledge.

I suggest that you have your own dictionary, pack of flashcards, and notebook to keep track of your learning. This will help you use metacognitive strategies to

>> **Plan your learning.** You should create a curriculum that aligns with your goals and interests, and set manageable objectives, such as learning 20 vocabulary words each week.

>> **Organize your learning.** It's important to identify what you need to learn, and separate it from what you already know or any material that isn't relevant for you. Then, group the content you need to learn by topic, situations, and so on. Repeated exposure to this content is key to learning it.

For example, you can divide your vocabulary words according to different situations or contexts. If you have a list of situations where you can use the L2, you can check off vocabulary words as you learn the language in that situation or context. Or you can organize your learning by sorting your flashcards into a particular order as you review them.

>> **Set routines.** Besides planning and organizing your learning, you need to set routines and stick to them. For example, set aside specific times during the day to learn your L2, such as early in the morning before heading to work or while you wait for your train or bus to come. You can also associate certain locations with your learning. For example, if you like sitting on your couch every night, set your books, notebooks, and flashcards next to it, and dedicate some time every day to learn your L2 there.

>> **Monitor your learning.** For example, you can check your writing (or reading) every 15 minutes, or check the words you learned after one week to make sure you're hitting the targets you planned to reach. Monitoring your steady progress is a great way to take note of your accomplishments on the path to your final goal.

>> **Evaluate your learning progress.** If you evaluate how you're progressing in your L2 journey, you can use your improvement as a source of motivation and encouragement. For example, you can compare the way you speak your L2 now to the way you spoke it two months ago, or you can keep a log of the new words you're learning so you have a visual record of your progress.

TIP

If you use flashcards, you can track and evaluate your progress easily. For example, beginning learners can start with packages of 25 vocabulary flashcards, and review them often. Soon, you'll find that you're becoming pretty familiar with some flashcards, which will give you a sense of achievement. When you progress a little more, you can start using packages of 50 flashcards. If you're using a *frequency graded list* (a vocabulary list that indexes words based on how frequently they appear in a language), you can check how many of those words you know.

Finding Opportunities for L2 Interactions

In Chapter 8, I discuss the key role of input, output, and interaction in your L2 learning journey. When you interact with other L2 users, you can use your *inter-language* (the internal linguistic system you develop as you learn the L2), test your language hypotheses, and pinpoint any L2 gaps you still have. Furthermore, as you practice your L2 with proficient L2 users in oral or written communicative exchanges (like in conversations, or via emails, text messages, and blogs or online discussions), you should start developing *social-interactive strategies.*

These social-interactive strategies provide you with the tools to use the L2 appropriately in interactions with others in different social, cultural, and pragmatic (real-life) contexts. As you participate in communicative exchanges or observe L2 speakers interacting, I encourage you to

>> Pay attention to sociocultural differences and try to notice L2 speakers' linguistic and nonlinguistic behaviors and attitudes. For example, observe the way L2 users show respect to each other.

>> Ask questions not only about the L2 content and meaning, but also about any parts of the culture that spark your curiosity.

>> Request clarifications from your L2 *interlocutors* (other L2 speakers) when you're unsure about your output.

TIP

Try to attend different community events where your L2 is spoken and pay attention to the ways native or proficient L2 speakers use the language in specific situations and contexts, as well as the way they express their cultural practices and perspectives or views.

Having repetitive encounters

It's no secret that your life can become monotonous and repetitive as you find yourself interacting with others in similar social situations or running the same errands every day (or every week). For instance, you buy your favorite foods at the grocery store each week, order your usual latte at the coffee shop every morning, go to the bank to deposit your paycheck every 2 weeks, take your kids or pets to the neighborhood park in the evening and talk to other parents, and so on. I'm sure you can anticipate some of the conversations you'll encounter in each of these communicative interactions.

But you may benefit from having these repeated interactions or social exchanges, especially as an L2 learner. Language learning in general, and vocabulary acquisition in particular, progresses when you have repetitive encounters that use the same vocabulary and grammatical structures in different contexts and social situations and with diverse interlocutors. Each time you encounter a word, an expression, or a grammatical structure, you feed your interlanguage and gather a bit more information that helps you complete the puzzle of that word, expression, or grammatical structure.

In addition, through these linguistic exchanges, you can pinpoint any language gaps you may have. In those cases, you may need to use some compensatory or conversation strategies (see the next section), and you may find yourself negotiating meaning with your interlocutors to make yourself understood or to be sure you're interpreting their message correctly.

So, finding real-life social interactions in the L2 is an ideal way to acquire the language. Although it may not be easy when you're learning your L2 as a foreign language (in other words, primarily in an academic setting; see Chapter 2), don't give up too quickly. You can search online and in social media groups for information about community events where L2 speakers meet in churches, coffee shops, parks, and the like.

But if you can't find any local events, meetings, or groups, don't be shy about starting your own social group or posting some ads seeking L2 speakers on message boards around your area (at the library, coffee shops, parks, community centers, and so on). For instance, if you like hiking, try to put together a group of people who can speak and use the L2 on long hikes through nearby woods. You'll be positively amazed with the results!

Additionally, if possible, find a conversation partner or tutor who can practice the L2 with you and ask them to correct your language and cultural accuracy as you communicate with them. Take note of their feedback and review your notes often. If you're learning an L2 in a classroom, you can ask your teacher for recommendations on conversation partners.

Finally, if you can't find an L2 speaker to talk to in many of your everyday situations, don't worry! That's when language play comes in handy. For example, recreate (aloud or just in your head) the L2 conversation you would be having with another person in that context. You can find out more about language play in Chapter 8.

Compensating and covering

As you communicate with other L2 users, you may discover gaps in your L2 knowledge that you want to hide. In such cases, coping strategies come to the rescue! You can use two types of coping strategies: *Compensatory strategies* to make up for your lack of knowledge, and *covering strategies* to hide that you lack knowledge.

L2 learners living in immersion situations (where everyone around them speaks the L2) tend to use many coping strategies, especially in the beginning, to fill in their language gaps. Some compensatory and covering strategies you may use are as follows:

» Guessing meaning by relying on

- *The context or your background knowledge of the setting:* For example, if someone says "Bon appétit" when you're about to eat, you can guess they're hoping you'll enjoy your food.

- *Linguistic and nonlinguistic cues:* You can try to understand meaning by paying attention to visual hints (gestures, facial expressions, props, images) and aural hints (tone of voice, pauses, emphasis).

» **Adjusting the message:** You or your interlocutors can convey the meaning of unfamiliar words or expressions by

   - Giving examples of the words you don't know (for instance, if you can't remember the word *newspaper,* you may say *New York Times* or mention the name of a local newspaper)

   - Using *synonyms* (similar words) or *antonyms* (opposite words)

   - Simplifying the message (for example, using two short, simple sentences instead of a long, complex one, or using common words instead of obscure or non-frequent ones)

   - Approximating the pronunciation of words by sounding them out or imitating the way you say similar words, or approximating meaning by using a broad term (*animal*) instead of a specific one (*dog* or *poodle*)

   - *Paraphrasing* (rewording) the message or using *circumlocution* (more words than you'd normally need) to explain what you mean and avoid unfamiliar L2 vocabulary or grammatical structures

   - Avoiding certain topics you don't know much about or don't feel comfortable discussing in the L2

» **Inventing words or coining new terms:** For example, you can say *air maker* for *bicycle pump.*

» **Code-switching:** When you *code-switch,* you mix languages, translating or transferring words or phrases from your L1 into the L2. For instance, a native Spanish speaker learning English as an L2 may say, "They were sitting on a *cojín* [cushion]."

» **Overgeneralizing grammatical rules or vocabulary words:** You may use the same word in all contexts, even if it doesn't apply or fit perfectly. For example, an English L1 speaker learning Spanish may say *bola* (ball) for all sports balls (tennis ball, soccer ball, and so on) instead of using the specific Spanish term for each ball (*pelota, balón, bola*).

» **Getting help from other sources:** You can check L2 vocabulary or meaning with your interlocutors, use apps or dictionaries to look words up, and so on.

» **Using memorized phrases or formulas to buy time:** This strategy can help you fill in pauses when you stop to think about what you want to say. Some useful prefabricated expressions (also called *gambits*) include phrases like "As I was saying," "That's interesting — tell me more," and "On the contrary." You can read more about formulas and gambits in Chapter 9.

REMEMBER

In any situation where you're attempting to speak your L2, your first objective should be getting the communication going. Grammatical accuracy and details come with time and practice. So, focus on understanding the overall meaning of the L2 input you receive and transmitting enough information to complete your task or achieve your goal.

Cheering Yourself On

TIP

Affective strategies address how you manage your emotions, your motivation, your willingness to do something, and your attitude toward L2 learning. Even though these strategies are important for success in language learning, most studies show that L2 learners in general don't use them much. You can benefit by using affective strategies to

>> **Develop your motivation.** When you use your L2 to accomplish compelling and meaningful tasks, you're willing to work harder and longer to get things done. So, consider your motivation when you're learning your L2 (see Chapter 11 for more details about that) and find activities that interest you.

  For instance, try using your L2 when you pursue your hobbies. Because hobbies are already a great motivating factor, using your L2 while you're enjoying them is a bonus. For example, if you like playing video games, change the language settings to your L2, if it's available.

>> **Evaluate your progress and reward yourself for your accomplishments.** Check regularly (for example, once or twice a week) to make sure you're meeting your learning goals. When you hit a target or produce output you're proud of, celebrate by treating yourself to something special (for example, a movie night with friends). Bonus points if your treat involves using your L2!

>> **Stay positive and encourage yourself to keep learning.** Patting yourself on the back from time to time helps you maintain your willingness to continue learning. For instance, after you reach a learning goal, tell yourself, "That was easy!" or "I am improving so much in so little time," or "Soon I will be able to do even X."

>> **Reduce your anxiety.** You can lower your stress level by choosing your interlocutors wisely. Work with L2 speakers who are patient and will be okay with your mistakes (which is often the case, really) and push yourself to produce difficult output when you feel comfortable. Calm yourself when something doesn't come out as expected by taking a break, using some relaxation techniques (like deep breathing), listening to music, or laughing out loud. Keep in mind that your stress is a temporary situation, and you'll feel better soon.

>> **Monitor your emotions and know how to deal with your feelings.** Pay attention to how you feel when your learning is going well or when your progress isn't happening as quickly as you'd like. It's especially important to recognize and deal with negative emotions. You can keep a diary of how you're feeling and discuss it with others. You can also practice some of the calming techniques covered in the previous bullet point.

4
Putting Your Language Learning into Action

Select a new language that aligns with your motivation and goals.

Create a language learning plan and consider activities that fit your learning style and preferences.

Think about the essential L2 vocabulary to learn first and the resources you'll need.

Browse some language learning platforms and apps, and choose the ones that match your preferences and needs.

Chapter **11**

Choosing a New Language to Learn

There are about 7,000 languages in the world, so choosing the second language (L2) you want to learn can be one of the most difficult and important decisions you make on this journey. You may have a very clear idea of the new language you want to learn. If that's the case, great! However, if you're still undecided about which new language to learn, this chapter lists some factors to consider when you're choosing the best L2 for you. You also get information on resources that help with language learning, which can affect your L2 choice, depending on how easy it is to access those resources in your community.

TIP

Once you choose a new language, you should set specific goals and plan how you'll do the work that will help you achieve them. As you work to reach your goals, you'll need to assess your learning experience and your outcomes, so you can adjust your objectives as necessary. Be sure to reward and cheer yourself on for every little milestone you attain. Flip to Chapter 10 for guidance on how to use learning strategies and turn to Chapter 12 for information about personalized learning plans.

Considering Your Motivation for Learning a New Language

Your motivation for learning a new language dictates your willingness to work toward achieving your vision of becoming proficient in an L2. Your motivation is what starts you on the path of learning an L2 and what keeps you working on it.

REMEMBER

Motivation is very personal, and it can change over time. To maintain or increase your motivation, look for experiences that are meaningful to you. For example, you may be motivated to learn an L2 because your significant other speaks it, but as soon as you break up, your motivation may end. Likewise, many students aren't motivated to learn languages in school, but after they leave school, they realize the importance of speaking another language to be successful in the workforce and life in general.

Noticing that you're advancing quickly and progressing easily in your L2 learning may also be a motivating factor. Your progress may depend on which L2 you choose to learn. You may benefit from selecting a language that's similar in some aspects to your L1 or any other language you already know.

Many researchers and studies support the idea that motivation is one of the most important predictors of L2 success. In 1972 psychologists Robert C. Gardner and Wallace E. Lambert identified two main types of motivation: *integrative motivation* and *instrumental motivation*, which I explain in more detail in this section. Integrative motivation has been linked to language learning success more than many other factors (such as cognitive abilities). And integrative and instrumental motivation may be interrelated: One can lead to the other, or they can work together.

Integrating into a community

A very strong motivational factor for learning a new language is your desire to communicate with people who speak the L2, discover their culture, and even become part of their language community. This is what psychologists Robert C. Gardner and Wallace E. Lambert call *integrative motivation*.

Several studies demonstrate that integrative motivation is the most important motivation behind your success in learning your L2. Integrative motivation can be linked to *intrinsic motivation*, which is the desire to do something because it gives you satisfaction and fulfills your internal need to accomplish a meaningful goal.

REMEMBER

Some integrative motivating reasons that may lead you to study an L2 are your desire to

- >> Communicate better with important people in your life who speak the L2, such as members of your family, your friends, your significant other, or your significant other's family.

- >> Get back to your roots as a heritage speaker of the L2, so you can improve your L2 skills and cultural understanding. (A *heritage language* is the language you acquired at home that's different from the dominant language used in your community or school; see Chapter 2 for details.)

- >> Feel integrated within the language community and culture while you live in a country where the L2 is spoken or in an area of a country where your L1 is the dominant language that's surrounded by a community of L2 speakers.

- >> Express your love of how the L2 sounds or your appreciation of a specific country's music, history, art, culture, people, and so on.

- >> Enhance your personal growth, which will also help you integrate into the L2 culture. For instance, you may want to learn the L2 in order to understand music, soap operas, movies, and other pop culture entertainment in the language or read books by your favorite L2 authors in the original language.

Your attitude and feelings toward the L2 affect your motivation to learn that language. As research has proven, integrative motivation boosts your desire to continue studying the L2 and helps your oral proficiency. The affinity you feel for the people who speak the L2 and their culture also influences your integrative motivation. When your feelings of kinship with other L2 speakers are strong, your desire to learn their language and know more about their culture motivates you to put the required time and effort into achieving your goals.

Earning practical benefits from your L2

In the context of language learning, *instrumental motivation* is the motivation to learn an L2 in order to get a practical benefit. You may want to learn an L2 because you see it as a way to achieve certain rewards, such as promotions, higher compensation, or even status.

Instrumental motivation can be linked to *extrinsic motivation*, because your motivation comes from an outside source, and it's dictated by the type of reward or compensation you get or a desire to avoid certain punishments.

REMEMBER

Some instrumental motivating reasons for learning an L2 can be classified as

- >> **Economic,** because learning the L2 will help you get a job or find a better job, keep your current job, get a pay raise, or earn a bonus in pay

>> **Academic,** because learning the L2 will help you get into a specific university or college program, fulfill academic credits, or achieve a certain score on an exam

>> **Life enhancing,** because learning the L2 will allow you to travel the world, make global connections through a widely spoken language, or enjoy the many opportunities you have to use it in your daily life

>> **Personally satisfying,** because

- You will feel unique among your friends or colleagues if you learn another L2, or you will choose a unique language (with a different writing system, a small pool of learners, or the like).

- You want to get better at an L2 you studied at school.

- You'll feel a sense of accomplishment.

- You love to test yourself, and learning an L2 will be a challenging and rewarding experience.

TIP

If your motivation is economic, you may decide to study a critical language that will open up rewarding job opportunities for you. For instance, the U.S. government is always looking for speakers of what it deems *critical languages* (such as Arabic, Chinese, Korean, Russian, and Japanese) to help with national security, global economic interests, and international diplomacy. In fact, if you're a student at an accredited U.S. college or university, you may be eligible for government-funded programs that can help you learn a critical language. These programs include the Critical Language Scholarship Program (https://clscholarship.org/) and the National Security Education Program (https://nsepnet.org/AboutUs.aspx). If you're curious about the most widely spoken languages in the world, check out Table 11-1.

TABLE 11-1   **Popular Languages Spoken Around the World**

Language	Number of Native Speakers	Language	Number of Native and L2 Speakers
Mandarin Chinese	840 million	English	1.5 billion
Spanish	405 million	Mandarin Chinese	1.1 billion
English	335 million	Hindi	609.5 million
Hindi	260 million	Spanish	559.1 million
Arabic	206 million	French	309.8 million

Language	Number of Native Speakers	Language	Number of Native and L2 Speakers
Portuguese	202 million	Arabic	Over 300 million
Bengali	193 million	Bengali	272.8 million
Russian	162 million	Portuguese	263.6 million
Japanese	121 million	Russian	255 million

TECHNICAL STUFF

Although there is no official data to corroborate the number of bilingual speakers in the world, experts estimate that between 50 percent and 75 percent of the people in the world use more than one language in everyday interactions.

CLARIFYING LANGUAGES' LEVEL OF DIFFICULTY

The Foreign Service Institute (FSI) of the U.S. Department of State has classified some of the most popular L2s into four groups, indicating the level of difficulty for English L1 speakers based on the time it takes them to reach a certain proficiency level.

- **Group 1:** Danish, Dutch, French, Italian, Norwegian, Portuguese, Romanian, Spanish, and Swedish (*around 24 weeks or 600–750 class hours*)

- **Group 2:** German, Haitian Creole, Indonesian, Malay, and Swahili (*around 26 weeks or 900 class hours*)

- **Group 3:** Albanian, Amharic, Armenian, Azerbaijani, Bengali, Bulgarian, Burmese, Czech, Dari, Estonian, Farsi, Finnish, Georgian, Greek, Hebrew, Hindi, Hungarian, Icelandic, Kazakh, Khmer, Kurdish, Kyrgyz, Lao, Latvian, Lithuanian, Macedonian, Mongolian, Nepali, Polish, Russian, Serbo-Croatian, Sinhala, Slovak, Slovenian, Somali, Tagalog, Tajiki, Tamil, Telugu, Thai, Tibetan, Turkish, Turkmen, Ukrainian, Urdu, Uzbek, and Vietnamese (*around 44 weeks or 1,100 class hours*)

- **Group 4:** Arabic, Chinese-Cantonese and Chinese-Mandarin, Japanese, and Korean (*around 88 weeks or 2,200 class hours*)

According to the FSI, mastery of languages in Group 4 may take four times longer than it takes to acquire a language from Group 1.

(continued)

(continued)

But some L2 researchers argue that the FSI's categories don't represent an exact division of languages, and there's no data to back up its levels of difficulty. For example, considerations to bear in mind are as follows:

- **The use of *cognates* (L2 words that resemble L1 words):** For instance, for a native speaker of English, Spanish has more cognates than Chinese.

- **The L2's literacy and writing system compared to English:** It's important to note that literacy is different from language acquisition. You can acquire a language and not develop literacy in it. And some languages don't have a writing system, so it would be impossible to develop literacy.

- **The L2 instructor's attitude and emphasis when teaching the language:** For example, if a teacher thinks certain word forms or grammatical rules are very difficult, they will dedicate most of the class to teaching those rules instead of providing appropriate comprehensible input and interaction opportunities — students will lack those important components for acquiring a language.

Every language has its own characteristics and peculiarities, as well as unique areas of difficulty. Some languages are harder to learn than others depending on the student's L1. For example, if your L1 shares some features with the L2, you'll find it easier to learn those features compared to other features the languages don't have in common. So, if you're an English speaker, some languages will be easier for you than others.

Surveying Available Resources before Choosing Your L2

Having access to resources in the L2 you want to study is essential to accomplish your ultimate goal of learning a new L2. So, when you're choosing a language to study, browse around and consider the resources you have at hand, which ones you'll need to get, and how you plan to get to them.

TIP

Here are some resources to consider when you're choosing an L2 to learn:

>> **Reference books:** When you're choosing an L2, consider the availability and accessibility of textbooks, dictionaries (online or printed copies), grammar books, vocabulary frequency lists, and the like. If you don't have these references at home, can you get them from your local library or borrow them from a friend? Are they easy to find online? Or, if you have the economic resources, can you find copies to buy?

>> **Access to experts:** Having access to tutors, teachers, and native speakers will help you get valuable feedback so you progress steadily in your language development. When you're choosing an L2, make sure some of these experts are available.

>> **Sources of written input:** Be sure you can find plenty of online or printed newspapers, magazines, books (novels, comic books, children's books, and so on), pamphlets, menus, advertisements, and infographics in the L2 you're considering. The public library in your area may have L2 resources on hand, or they may be able to help you access other L2 resources.

>> **Sources of aural input:** Search for radio stations, music, podcasts, and presentations/workshops that provide opportunities to listen to live or recorded input in the L2 you want to learn.

>> **Speaking opportunities:** It's important to interact with other speakers when you're learning an L2. As you decide on a language, research whether your area has many speakers of the L2 you're considering. You can search for L2 speakers online (one good resource is www.talkabroad.com) and post notices for conversation partners in public locations (such as grocery stores, libraries, parks, museums, bus stops, and the like).

>> **Cultural and social events:** A factor in your L2 choice may be whether your area has any organizations that sponsor events celebrating the L2 language and culture. L2 speakers who belong to these groups may meet up to socialize from time to time (for example, they may go to museums, meet at book clubs, watch sports, hike, take weekend trips, play board games, or play music). Also check whether your potential L2 has any dedicated Facebook groups, which can provide opportunities to practice writing your L2 or to meet up with local members.

In Chapter 14 I give you some guidance on technology to help you gain access to and navigate some of the resources mentioned here.

Chapter **12**

Tailoring a Learning Plan Just for You

The goal of this chapter is to help you start planning your second language (L2) learning experience. Throughout this chapter, you can think of the L2 you want to study (see Chapter 11) as you find out how to set learning goals, make a plan, reflect on the materials you'll need, and figure out the location(s) where you'll study, practice, and review. You can even plan the time of day you'll normally be able to work on your language learning and consider how much time you can devote to it every day. You also get guidance on where to find meaningful L2 *input* (language samples) and opportunities to interact with L2 users and produce output.

REMEMBER

As you start learning your L2, keep in mind that it's totally normal to make mistakes. So, don't expect to be perfect and don't get discouraged. Just keep going!

Ready, Set, Go! Setting Goals and Building a Plan

This section is your starting point for building your L2 learning plan. Here, I discuss pinpointing your learning goals, give you some guidance on proficiency levels, and walk you through a sample learning plan. Keep in mind that consistency is key!

Motivation is an important factor in learning your L2. The most successful language learners are motivated and passionate about their L2 and its culture. So, if you haven't yet decided which L2 to study and what your motivation is, head to Chapter 11 for help.

Stating your learning goals

If you're considering learning an L2, you probably have a specific goal you want to accomplish in that L2. Achieving your goal depends on how much effort you put into learning the language. So, you have to set learning goals and design your learning path and work plan.

REMEMBER

Consider the following questions:

>> What do you want to be able to achieve in the L2? In other words, what is your long-term goal?

- Is your long-term goal meaningful and engaging? If not, can any part of your goal become interesting to you? Can you use any part of it in real life and within an L2 speech community?

- Can you divide your long-term goal into smaller short-term goals?

- How can you measure that you accomplished your goal? When can you say that you achieved your goal? What will you need to observe?

>> Will you get a reward if you achieve your goal? What is your reward?

Once you have your long-term learning goal, you need to divide it into manageable smaller goals that help you achieve your final goal. You may decide to follow the SMART goals method if you need an explicit guide.

TIP

SMART is an acronym for *specific, measurable, achievable, realistic,* and *time-bound:*

>> **Specific:** Consider what you want to get better at. Be as precise as possible. If you're vague, you may not get your desired results.

>> **Measurable:** Set distinct targets to measure along the way so you can assess whether you're progressing as expected. The goal is to quantify your progress.

>> **Achievable:** Make sure your goals are achievable. You can't set goals that are unattainable.

>> **Realistic:** Be realistic about the results you can accomplish with the resources (materials, people, money, and the like) and time you have available.

>> **Time-bound:** Define a path for achieving your results. If you set a clear time frame for your objectives, you can take note of the progress you're making over time.

For example, if your long-term goal is being able to read recipes in Spanish, you can make this short-term SMART goal:

> Read two dessert recipes from my new Spanish cookbook during the week and take notes in Spanish on the ingredients I need to buy. Pick eight important/new words from these recipes and add them to my vocabulary flashcards. Prepare one of the recipes over the weekend for my birthday and see how it comes out!

Understanding proficiency levels

If you're not sure what your proficiency level is in your L2, you can use Table 12-1 as a guide to measure your level and evaluate your progress. Read through some of the descriptions associated with each proficiency level and note how well you can accomplish the tasks in your L2. You can get an idea of your current proficiency as well as an understanding of what it takes to become fluent.

REMEMBER

Moving from one proficiency level to the next may take several months or years. Take it easy on yourself!

TABLE 12-1   **Measuring L2 Proficiency Levels**

Functions	Novice	Intermediate	Advanced
Ask and answer questions	Ask and respond to memorized question-and-answer exchanges (such as asking for a name).	Ask and answer a variety of questions (informational and follow-up) that require you to create language (not just repeat memorized material).	Ask and answer a variety of questions (informational and follow-up), providing detailed explanations and elaborating on your answers.
Express feelings and emotions	Name basic feelings and emotions (happy, sad, nervous, tired, and so on).	Express a variety of feelings and emotions and start to explain why you're feeling that way.	Express a variety of feelings and emotions using precise vocabulary and providing detailed explanations to justify your emotions and feelings.
Express likes and dislikes	Name what you like and don't like.	Express your likes and dislikes, and start explaining your preferences.	Talk about what you like and don't like, providing detailed rationales for your choices.
Describe people and places	Use one or two adjectives or adverbs.	Use common adjectives or adverbs. Compare and contrast by using comparatives and superlatives (for example, *good, better, best*).	Use a wide variety of precise adjectives or adverbs. Include vivid and detailed descriptions, using comparatives and superlatives.

(continued)

TABLE 12-1 *(continued)*

Functions	Novice	Intermediate	Advanced
Narrate present and past events	Use memorized sentences to explain your actions, normally in the present tense. Past tense is not used or seldom used (memorized phrases).	Narrate your daily activities and some occasional tasks, using simple sequenced sentences.	Talk about present and past activities/events, using paragraph-length narration in a logical sequence.
Narrate future events	Use memorized sentences to explain what you plan to do in the immediate future.	Express your plans with some details ("I will do ____ so that I can get ____").	Talk about your future activities/events, using paragraph-length narration in a logical sequence and providing detailed explanations.
Give pieces of advice, opinions	Agree and disagree with simple statements.	Express opinions/advice using simple sentences or simple reasons.	Give pieces of advice and express opinions with reasoned arguments and justifications to support your opinion/advice.
Express dreams and hopes	State simple desires using memorized phrases ("I want," "I need," and so on).	Express your dreams and hopes in some detail.	Express your dreams and hopes with some detailed explanations, and start to express some hypothetical possibilities ("If I had ____, I would ____").

Mapping out a learning plan

In the following sections, you find out how to put together a sample language learning plan using (and building on) the guidelines in the preceding sections. In the example I provide, your L2 is Spanish.

Reminding yourself of your motivation

Ask yourself what's motivating you to learn an L2. Consider what's triggering the positive feelings you notice when you think of learning your L2. Determine whether your motivation comes from within you, as a burning desire to achieve a goal or become part of an L2 community, or whether it is an external motivation that will give you a practical gain.

For example: *I'm motivated to learn this L2 because my best friends and their families speak Spanish, and I want to feel integrated as another member of their community.* Or *I'm willing to learn this new L2 because I will receive a big pay raise.* You can read more about motivation in general Chapter 3, and I help you narrow down your motivating drive in Chapter 11.

Laying out long-term learning goals

Jot down what you would like to see yourself doing in the L2 as a long-term goal. Be sure to think about these questions:

>> Is this goal meaningful and engaging?

>> Will I be able to use my L2 in real life within an L2 speech community?

For example: *In the future, I would love to see myself participating in everyday conversations with my friends who speak the L2 and understanding some common cultural references.*

>> **Is this goal meaningful and engaging?** Yes, very much!

>> **Will I be able to use my L2 in real life within an L2 speech community?** Yes, every time I get together with my friends and their families.

Surveying your short-term learning goals

After you settle on a long-term learning goal, ask yourself what you have to do to achieve your goal. List the steps you need to take to meet that goal, and the language functions and cultural aspects to consider in each step.

For example: *In order to achieve my long-term goal, I need to converse about different topics such as the following:*

>> My first short-term goal is talking about food, because it's a very popular conversation topic in my friends' families.

- Explain the food I like and dislike, my food allergies, and the like.

  Vocabulary needed: food vocabulary

  Grammatical structures needed: *I like, I do not like, and, but, I can eat, I cannot eat,* and so on

- Accept and reject food offerings in a culturally appropriate way.

  Vocabulary needed: *delicious, tasty, full,* and the like

  Grammatical structures needed: *It looks, but, and, I would love to, thank you for the offer, I am sorry but, I just ate,* and so on

>> My next short-term goal is . . .

TIP

I suggest using a *backward design* approach, in which you start from your long-term goal and work backward to plan what you need to do in manageable chunks of work. If possible, perform a small assessment daily (*Did I learn new vocabulary that will help me with my weekly goal? Did I review the grammatical structure that will help me achieve my weekly goal?*) or weekly (*Did I complete all my goals for this week: vocabulary, grammatical structures, culture?*).

For instance, you may decide to devote each week to a different topic: food, social plans, school, trips, and so on. The amount of time you dedicate to each topic will depend on the time you have available and the difficulty of the topic. You may be focused on a topic for one week, two weeks, a month, or more. It doesn't matter! Find out more about establishing a routine in the next section.

REMEMBER

Focusing your attention on attaining specific short-term goals doesn't mean that you don't pay attention to other topics. You can focus most of your work on those short-term goals, but you should continue reading and immersing yourself in as many situations as possible and advancing in your language in general. You should keep on going with taking notes of the language you encounter in other engaging and useful communicative situations.

Setting your routine

TIP

After you've revisited your motivation, pinpointed your long-term goal, and set some short-term goals, you can put together your language learning routine. Check out these tips to get going:

>> Set a day to start. If you're ready to start today or tomorrow, go for it!

>> Pick a location and time to do most of the work, like every night in your home office or bedroom. Consider other possible locations/situations where you can work on your L2 (for example, you can listen to your L2 on your smartphone with earbuds while you're waiting at the bus stop).

>> Ask yourself what you plan to accomplish in the first week and how you plan to do it. Jot down some ideas. (I give you some pointers on picking activities in the later section "Selecting Learning Activities That Suit You," and you can jump to Chapter 14 to read about some online tools to use).

>> Decide whether you need other people's help/participation in your learning and how you'll get that help. Reach out to others if you need to.

>> Determine how to assess whether you're achieving your goal. For example, practice the language and tasks you established as your goal with others and check their response to your communicative act. Did you get the message across? Did you accomplish the task? If you did, awesome! Give yourself a pat on the back and keep up your great work! If you did not, don't get

discouraged. Continue learning and practicing a little longer. Perhaps that goal required more time than what you planned for.

TIP

Feel free to record yourself once a week or once a month to keep track of your progress. And don't forget to compare your current language performance to the one you showed one week, one month, or one year before. Be proud of your journey!

>> Have a plan B for any obstacles you encounter. For example, what will you do if you're struggling to learn something this week or you don't have much time to practice? Making a backup plan keeps your stress level down.

>> Evaluate your commitment to achieve your goal for the week on a scale of 1 to 10. If your commitment isn't at its maximum (10), consider what you can do to be more focused.

Here's what setting a weekly routine may look like for this example:

>> **When will I start?** I'll start next Monday.

>> **Where and when will I study?** I'll study in my office, both at the desk and on the sofa.

- I'll also review my flashcards while I wait for the bus and during my coffee break every day.

- I'll study every day from 7:30 p.m. to 8:00 p.m.

- On Wednesday, I'll practice speaking with my conversation partner.

- On Sunday, when I visit my friend's family, I'll converse in the L2 with them.

>> **What do I plan to accomplish in the first week?** I'll practice how to say my favorite meals/food, name the foods I don't like, and say the main phrases used to accept and reject a food offering. I'll ask my friends for suggestions and search online and in dictionaries. I'll create my flashcards from 7:30 p.m. to 8:00 p.m. on day one.

>> **Will I need the help/participation of other people this week?** I'll need my friends' help to check my word and phrase selection. I'll practice with my conversation partner for 15 minutes on Wednesday.

>> **How will I assess that I'm achieving my goal?** When I meet my friend and her family for lunch on Sunday, I'll check whether I can accept/reject meals in my L2 by their reaction.

>> **What do I plan to do if there's an obstacle in my learning?** If my friend and her family can't understand me, I'll ask them for help. I'll use my conversational formulas (see the next section) to ask for help.

>> **What's my commitment level to achieving my goal for this week?** I'm very committed (10/10), because I'll be meeting my friend's family (who only speak the L2) for lunch over the weekend.

TIP

It's a good idea to use the first day of each week to organize your learning by making note of the following:

>> The vocabulary you anticipate you will need

>> The grammatical structures you'll use repeatedly

>> Any cultural information you may need

>> Some of the tasks you want to accomplish with the language (ask and answer questions, narrate, describe, and the like)

You can also use the first day to gather or search L2 resources you can use to get input in different forms (reading, listening, and viewing), as well as find opportunities to write and speak about your topic. If you have a tutor or conversation partner, this is the time to plan a meeting with them. I talk more about finding learning resources later in this chapter (see "Accessing Input, Interaction, and Output Opportunities") and in Chapter 14.

Coming up with conversational formulas

Routines and conversational formulas are forms of communication that you should memorize so you can use them without having to stop and think. For instance, *Hello, how are you?* and *I'm OK, thank you, and you?* are conversational formulas you use when greeting people.

Using formulas helps your fluency in the L2 and gives you time to think about the content of the language you want to express next, because you aren't dedicating too much mental effort to producing these routines.

So, as you start learning a new language, find how to say some common phrases and start learning them by heart. You can search online for conversational formulas in the L2 you're learning or ask your tutor or conversation partner to help you create a list of them. For instance, find ways to

>> Greet people.

>> Say farewell.

>> Thank someone.

>> Interrupt.

>> Refer to what was previously said.

>> Agree or disagree.

>> Accept or refuse something.

>> Express your emotions. (*That's great! What a shame! I'm sorry to hear that!*)

Here are some helpful Spanish conversational formulas for the learning plan example in the previous sections:

>> **Food you like and don't like:** Me gusta la verdura, el pescado; no me gusta la carne, la leche.

>> **Greet:** ¡Hola! ¿Cómo está?

>> **Say farewell:** ¡Adiós! ¡Nos vemos!

>> **Thank:** Gracias. Muchas gracias por la comida.

>> **Accept:** Muchas gracias, uno está bien. ¡Me encanta su plato!

>> **Refuse:** Lo siento, no me gusta la carne.

>> **Express emotion:** ¡Qué rico! ¡Buen provecho!

Starting your personal vocabulary bank

Your goals, interests, and everyday encounters with the L2 are different from the ones other people may have. As I always say to my students, I want you to learn and use the vocabulary that's useful to you. In my opinion, having a passive knowledge of the vocabulary that isn't part of your interests or needs is enough.

TIP

So, create a vocabulary bank that addresses your needs and review your personal bank of vocabulary words often. Make it easy to review your vocabulary words by putting them on flashcards, which you can carry with you and review any time you have a few minutes to spare (such as standing in line at the supermarket, or sitting in the waiting room at your doctor's office).

Following with the example in the previous sections, you can create a personal vocabulary bank (in flashcards or in a notebook) with food-related words and formulas you may need to use while you converse with your friend's family during lunch.

Knowing that consistency is essential

You may have heard the expression *use it or lose it*. This expression applies to many areas in life — for example, to a tennis player who stops playing for a while, or to learning a language. You'll notice that your fluency suffers when you don't use your L2 often.

REMEMBER

So, to be successful in your language learning, you need to be consistent and work on your L2 every day. That doesn't mean you have to consciously study something new every day, but it does mean you should have some type of contact with L2 input every day, even if it's only for a few minutes.

A good way to achieve that is to dedicate a moment every day to your work in the L2. It can be early in the morning before you head to work or school, at the bus or train station, on your lunch break, before dinner, after dinner, in bed — whatever works for you! And it's even better if you have some contact with the language several times during the day. For example, review your flashcards throughout the day, talk to your conversation partner in the afternoon, and read in your L2 before going to sleep at night.

Selecting Learning Activities That Suit You

When it comes to language learning, you have endless choices of activities you can use to practice and review your L2. The following sections give you some guidance.

TIP

Keep the following questions in mind as you choose the best language learning activities for you:

>> Are you passionate about the L2 and its culture? If so, any engaging activity and topic you choose will work for you, because you have the most important elements: your passion and motivation to learn! If you aren't really passionate about the L2 or its culture, start by learning about one of your hobbies in the L2: read about it, watch videos, and participate in L2 social groups with people who share that hobby.

>> Are you a hard-working person? Do you put time and effort into what you want to do? If so, your language proficiency will improve quickly, especially if you choose activities that focus on establishing communication in the L2. But if you need some push to work on that, start by evaluating the moments during the day that you're doing nothing. Select two or three of those moments and use them to read about an engaging topic for you in the L2.

>> Are you an autonomous (self-driven) learner? Can you push yourself to study? Are you good at being consistent and following routines? If not, set some routines and reachable goals, and keep track of your accomplishments. (I talk about establishing a routine earlier in this chapter.)

>> Are you a perfectionist? Please know that you don't need to produce perfect language from day one. Leave perfectionism for other areas in your life; don't shut down your L2 communication because you're trying to speak perfectly. On the contrary, be a creative risk-taker with the language! Keep in mind that making errors is normal as you learn and acquire languages.

>> Are you willing to participate in social interactions with other L2 users? Are you open to accepting differences? Do you tolerate uncertainty well? You should be prepared to accept and tolerate uncertainty and doubts when learning a new L2.

>> Are you resourceful? Do you use anything you have at hand to get or learn about what you want to learn? For L2 learning, that involves knowing and using many language strategies. You can read about strategies in Chapters 9 and 10.

>> Are you ready to embrace errors in your L2 learning process and use the L2 to communicate with others, even if that means you're producing errors? You should feel confident that many of the errors you produce are signs of progress toward language acquisition (see Chapter 5 for details on this U-shaped behavior).

Choosing activities that align with your multiple intelligences

As you start learning your L2, you can select activities and experiences that best align with your *multiple intelligences* (*MIs*), or preferred ways of learning. If you aren't sure which MIs are most developed for you, look at Chapter 3 for some key features of each MI, or take a free MI test online to assess yourself. Just search for this test in your preferred online search engine. As a reminder, the MIs are

>> Linguistic-verbal

>> Logical-mathematical

>> Visual-spatial

>> Bodily-kinesthetic

>> Musical-rhythmic

>> Interpersonal

>> Intrapersonal

>> Naturalistic

After you determine which of your MIs are more developed (you may have more than one), check Chapter 3 for the learning activities that fit your MIs. You can use a table format with three columns to help you keep track of everything:

>> In the first column, list your most developed MIs.

>> In the second column, write what type of learning activities you're good at or what benefits you the most, using the information listed in Chapter 3 and adding your own notes.

>> Finally, in the third column, add your plan to find L2 opportunities and resources that help you put into practice what you're good at or benefit from.

For example, suppose your most developed MI is interpersonal intelligence. You're good at the following:

>> Interacting with and understanding people .

>> Cooperating with others

>> Asking for clarification

>> Receiving feedback

Therefore, in your learning plan you can focus on the following activities:

>> Find L2 speakers and communicate with them.

- Attend events and go to venues where you'll meet L2 speakers (community meetings, churches, fairs, carnivals, cultural events, and so on).

- Search for volunteering opportunities in your community where your L2 is spoken.

- Be on the lookout for people speaking your L2 (at the park, at the bus stop, in line at the supermarket, at your doctor's office, and so on) and talk to them.

- Search for social media groups that use your L2 (such as Facebook groups).

- Pay attention to bulletin boards (at coffee shops, the library, nearby universities or schools, and the like) for flyers and announcements about L2 speakers and groups.

- Find L2 conversation partners in online platforms. (You can find out more about these in Chapter 14.)

>> If you can't find established groups, try to organize new L2 group meetings.

- Create your own social media groups, and advertise them on your social media, inviting others to share the groups on their social media.

- Post flyers with ads for L2 speakers.

>> Learn how to ask for feedback in your L2. Be sure you can say key phrases such as "Can you repeat that, please?" "Can you speak slower?" "Do you understand me?" "Please, let me know if you don't understand me," and "Can you please correct me, if needed?"

Your turn! Figure out your most developed MIs and devise a plan from there.

Picking activities that fit your learning style

Your *learning style* refers to the way you perceive, process, and manage information and input, as well as the type of input that helps you learn better. Your learning style may change over time. Review Chapter 3 to understand the different learning styles and then use the following sections to select the main ways you process information. After you determine which learning style best describes you, address your learning preferences: Choose the activities you can do, and plan your strategies for receiving the input that will benefit you.

Using your senses

Which senses — visual, auditory, or kinesthetic/tactile — do you prefer using to receive input?

>> **Visual learner:** You like written input (books, newspapers, and so on), video input (TV, movies, and so on), color-coded material, graphics, charts, maps, graphic organizers, drawings, images, and the like.

>> **Auditory learner:** You prefer listening (aural) input (audiobooks, podcasts, recorded vocabulary, and so on), verbal interactions, music, repetitive pronunciation exercises, and the like.

>> **Tactile learner:** You enjoy doing projects and experiments, using real objects, moving, dancing, and so on.

Learning the rules

Do you prefer having grammatical rules from the beginning or figuring them out on your own?

>> **Deductive learner:** You need a guided (or teacher-centered) approach in which you receive the rules and apply them to L2 examples.

>> **Inductive learner:** You prefer a self-guided (learner-centered) approach in which you use L2 samples to discover common features or patterns, guess meaning and rules, and then form rules.

Organizing the material

Do you prefer processing input holistically (from a big-picture perspective) or in an orderly way?

>> **Random/intuitive/nonlinear learner:** You're good at abstract thinking, coming up with original ideas, understanding the overall (global) picture, being imaginative, finding different options, and opening your mind to others' suggestions.

>> **Ordered/sequential/linear learner:** You like analyzing concrete things, taking planned paths, and having information presented in a sequential and ordered (linear) way.

Having end goals

Do you need to have an end goal to guide your learning?

>> **Closure-oriented learner:** You prefer to plan your learning, set and meet deadlines, self-assess your learning process and progress, preview content, use advanced organizers, know the meaning of vocabulary (not guess it), and know the rules from the beginning.

>> **Open-ended learner:** You don't need to plan your learning, set deadlines or goals, analyze the language, or understand everything from the beginning. You're fine with ambiguity (lack of clarity), relaxed learning, and natural exposure to the L2.

Working with others

Do you benefit the most by working with others or on your own?

>> **Extroverted:** You're open to meeting and interacting with others. You enjoy role-playing and participating in conversation and debates. You're outgoing and talkative.

>> **Introverted:** You're reserved and shy. You prefer reading, writing, and working on your own or with only one other person.

Paying attention to details

Do you benefit from understanding all the details in the input?

>> **Analytical:** You pay attention to grammar details and examples, easily pick up words and phrases in the input, and group and classify input.

>> **Global:** You understand the overall picture and main ideas rather than the details. You enjoy being intuitive and spontaneous, guessing meaning, and interacting with others even if you don't process everything you hear.

Accessing Input, Interaction, and Output Opportunities

In this section, I present various ways you can find input, interaction, and output opportunities in your L2. Check out Chapter 8 for full details on language input, output, and interaction, which are key elements in the language learning process.

Considering available sources of input

It isn't a secret that where you live can determine the variety and availability of your sources of L2 input. Living in a community that includes many L2 speakers can give you countless opportunities to talk to L2 speakers, plenty of access to written L2 input (newspapers, signs, flyers, and so on), audiovisual L2 input (TV, radio, movies, and the like), and a variety of community events and venues where the L2 is the main form of communication (in public libraries, churches, book clubs, conversation groups, and so on). An L2 community with access to all these L2 sources has linguistic vitality that isn't likely to disappear.

REMEMBER

But don't give up on the idea of studying an L2 that isn't spoken in your community. Nowadays, technology and online tools can bridge some of the gap a lack of in-person access to your L2 creates. You can find almost all the resources you need to help you interact with the L2 online: audiovisual material, books, virtual events, conversation groups, tutors — the list goes on! I mention several of these resources in Chapter 14.

Discovering a wide range of options

TIP

Before browsing through your sources of L2 input, note the ways in which you receive input in your L1. Think about what you read, whom you listen and speak to, and when you write. Then consider which of these L1 input sources and output opportunities you can change to L2 input and output opportunities to boost your learning plan. For instance, you may have the language option on your phone (and other electronic devices) set to your L1. You can change your phone or computer settings and start getting loads of input in your L2 every day.

So, as you take note of the L1 input you receive, here are some sources to consider:

>> **Reading and viewing:** You don't read just books or watch only TV programs. For example, you read and view

- Content on your phone and computer
- Social media posts
- Text messages
- Restaurant menus
- Business service menus
- Ads on the street, in magazines, on flyers, and so on
- Posters and announcements on the street, in coffee shops, at the library, and so on
- Product containers
- Computer games
- Credits and subtitles on TV programs and movies
- Closed captions on TV programs and movies
- Instructions (for example, how to build a bookcase)
- Articles in print and online magazines and newspapers
- Hard copy books or e-books, including cookbooks, children's books, novels, and poetry collections

>> **Listening:** Consider all the sources of listening input you receive every day and on special occasions. You may find aural input coming from

- Conversations around you (at the store, school, park, bus stop, and so on)

- Radio

- Music

- TV and movies

- Online video-sharing sites such as YouTube

- Audiobooks and podcasts

- Storytelling (in libraries, classrooms, and so on)

- Voice messages (on your phone, apps, and the like)

- Events and gatherings such as talks, class lectures, debates, and religious ceremonies

REMEMBER

The more diverse the L2 input is (in terms of topics, format, and skills used, such as listening, speaking, reading and writing), the broader your vocabulary can become and the more opportunities you will have to get valuable input. So, try to participate in an array of experiences, read about diverse topics, and watch or listen to a variety of audiovisual material. For example, if you like crafts, try to read and watch videos about them in your L2; if you like traveling, find L2 sources of information about the countries you want to visit either videos to watch, books, flyers, and so on. Don't forget that online tools can give you access to a wide variety of sources. Be broad in your search for L2 input!

Understanding the special power of reading

If I had to choose the most helpful input source in language learning, I would pick reading. Reading for pleasure is the best way to learn and enlarge your vocabulary. And many well-known researchers support that idea.

So, read everything you can find in your L2: newspapers, magazines, comics, graphic novels, ads, packages, flyers, and instructions. Read anything that's at your proficiency level or even a little above it. You should be able to understand about 90 to 95 percent of the words you read (that is, 18 or 19 words out of every 20). Some researchers believe you've reached an independent reading level when you understand 98 percent of the words you read.

Reading extensively for pleasure while understanding about 95 percent of the words you come across strengthens your understanding of particular words (this is called *slow-mapping*, as I explain in Chapter 13), adds grammatical features to those words, and gives you confidence in how much you know about them.

WARNING

Don't choose reading material that's too advanced for you. If you find yourself constantly picking up the dictionary to understand the main idea of the text, you aren't reading at your proficiency level.

TIP

Beginning learners could start with *graded readers* (simplified books with increasing levels of difficulty). When you're choosing a graded reader, look over a random page, and if you see five or more words you don't understand, the reading level may be too difficult for you. If you see two or three new words, the reading level is perfect. A book with four new words is fine, although it may be a bit challenging. Try reading at least one graded reader a week, increasing the number of books you read and their difficulty level as your proficiency improves. This ensures that you continue to advance in your language learning.

You should occasionally read books that seem very easy for your L2 proficiency level. Reading these books will boost your confidence, improve your fluency, and make the reading process enjoyable. You may find yourself so immersed in the content that you forget you're reading in a new language. At the same time, you're unconsciously reviewing and confirming your understanding of certain words and grammar patterns, and adding input to your internal language system.

Seeking opportunities for language interaction and output

Although input is one of the most important elements in language acquisition (as you find out in the previous section and throughout this book), in my opinion, it isn't enough on its own. You also need opportunities to interact with other L2 users and produce language output. These opportunities for interaction and output help you assess whether the L2 you're producing makes sense to other L2 users, or if your output has some errors that interfere with your attempts at communication. If you're producing errors, you need to negotiate meaning with your *interlocutors* (other L2 users) to solve the issue.

TIP

Communicative interactions provide a perfect opportunity to encounter new words or expressions that you may find useful and don't want to forget. So, take a moment to add these words and expressions to your flashcards, your notebook, or the notepad in your phone. If you don't want to forget how to pronounce it, you could use the recording feature in your phone.

Think about the everyday interactions you have in your L1 and try to find similar situations that require L2 interactions and output, such as

>> Conversing face-to-face with people

>> Talking with people on Zoom or on the phone

>> Meeting people in online platforms and conversing orally or exchanging written messages

>> Emailing or texting others

>> Interacting with people on social media

If you can travel to or live in a country where your L2 is spoken, you'll be immersed in the language and culture, and you'll have many opportunities to interact with native L2 speakers in different real-life communicative situations. These interactions will likely encourage you to use or pay attention to meaningful vocabulary, which will help you retain this vocabulary better. No doubt, this is an ideal situation in which to practice and learn your L2.

TIP

If you don't have the desire, time, or resources to travel to a country where your L2 is spoken, you can still find ways to engage in L2 interactions with others from home thanks to the limitless reach of the internet. For instance, you can find tutors, conversation partners, or other people to practice your L2 with using online language exchange apps such as TalkAbroad (www.talkabroad.com) or HelloTalk (www.hellotalk.com). In Chapter 14, I list some online resources you can use to interact with others in your L2.

Chapter **13**

Building Vocabulary and Grammar

The goal of this chapter is to get you on the path to learning vocabulary and grammar in your second language (L2). Because I give more emphasis to the pivotal role of vocabulary in language learning, I highlight the most important words and phrases to focus on, as well as tools and strategies for learning new vocabulary.

Getting an Overview of L2 Vocabulary Learning

REMEMBER

Learning vocabulary is essential to start communicating in a new language. So, you may be wondering where to start, which words to learn first, and how many words you need to learn. The number of words and the specific words you should start with vary depending on your L2 and where and how you plan to use it. The quick answer is, start with the most frequent words, the ones you need to use in regular communicative situations.

These are my recommended steps for learning L2 vocabulary:

1. **Start with *core vocabulary*, the 500–700 most frequent words in your L2.**

TIP

To find core vocabulary, you can either consult a word frequency dictionary or, even easier, track down some premade word frequency lists. Word frequency lists are available online in different languages. You can search for some lists by typing "word frequency lists in [language]" in your search browser.

TIP

Core vocabulary words form 75 percent of everyday conversations. When you have enough core vocabulary, you'll be able to start communicating with others, even if your grammar isn't perfect. You can make yourself understood with basic grammar and imperfect pronunciation. For example, if you're talking about a past event and you don't know how to form the past tense of a verb, don't worry. Use an adverb or a phrase that indicates you're referring to the past, such as *yesterday* or *last week*, and your *interlocutors* (other L2 users) will understand, even if you say something like *Yesterday I give my friend a book.*

2. **Consider the L2 vocabulary that will be more meaningful and useful to you.**

Besides core vocabulary, you should also include the words you need based on

- Your motivations and/or needs for work, for school, to live in a country where the L2 is spoken, to communicate with a special someone, and so on (see Chapter 11)

- Your L2 learning goals (see Chapter 12)

- Your interests and hobbies (cooking, painting, sports, cars, scuba diving — whatever you like!)

3. **Try to use key vocabulary as often as possible, even if your grammar is incorrect.**

To find key vocabulary, pay attention to word frequency.

- Begin with high-frequency vocabulary (the most frequent 2,000–3,000 word families). According to several linguists, 90 percent of the words you use in everyday communication, and 80 percent of what you read, is part of the 2,000 most frequent word families. You can search for these frequency lists in your favorite search browser (use "high-frequency words in [L2]" or the like).

- A *word family* is formed by several words that have a common member, such as in the case of *nation, nations, national, nationally, nationalize, international,* and so on. Knowing one member can help you learn and guess the meaning of other members of the family.

TIP

High-frequency vocabulary includes many *survival vocabulary* words that are useful for getting by when you travel to a country where your L2 is spoken. With survival vocabulary you can produce spoken and written language that allows you to participate in everyday activities. Some of the activities you can accomplish with this type of vocabulary are greeting others and thanking them, buying items for your daily needs and ordering food, reading street signs, traveling from one place to another, and securing accommodations.

- Later, you can move on to mid-frequency and low-frequency vocabulary.

4. **Set realistic expectations to work on your vocabulary development, with a learning plan that enforces continuous work.**

I discuss this in more detail in Chapter 12.

Participating in a wide variety of L2 activities and being exposed to L2 learning situations in different contexts fosters and enlarges your vocabulary and background knowledge. The more varied your communicative contexts are, the more opportunities you have to enrich your vocabulary, because you'll encounter brand-new vocabulary and have the opportunity to reinforce familiar vocabulary you kind of knew (this happens in a process called *slow-mapping*).

TECHNICAL
STUFF

During your first few exposures to a new word, and before you have a clear understanding of what the word represents, you establish a broad idea of what you think the word means, in a process called *fast-mapping*. After being repeatedly exposed to a word, you have a better idea of what the word really means and how it's used; this is called *slow-mapping*. It's as if you were putting the pieces of a puzzle together and, with each exposure to the word, you get another piece so you can finally see the image in the puzzle.

ON THE TIP OF YOUR TONGUE

Have you ever said, "That word is on the tip of my tongue"? You may remember the first letter of the word, its meaning, or something you relate it with, but the word itself doesn't come to mind. As you learn a word, you learn its different components and features, some of them unconsciously.

For example, when you learn the word *book* in your L2, you learn the word explicitly, and you acquire some features implicitly, such as the fact that it's a noun, you can count it, it's singular but it can become plural, the sounds that form it, and other words you relate to it (like *pages, cover, index,* and *author*), even other grammatical values, such as *to book*. But suppose you can't remember the word for *book* in your L2. When you have that word on the tip of your tongue, what's really happening is that you can recognize many of these features, but not the word itself.

Surveying Key Vocabulary Words, Phrases, and Formulas

Giving you a detailed list of words to learn in every language isn't possible in this book, of course. So, in the following sections I provide a broad look at some key topics and phrases you need to learn to be functional in your L2.

Core words and phrases

Learning the 500–700 most frequently used words in your L2 should be your first goal. I encourage you to do a quick online search of "the most frequent words in [your L2]" or "core vocabulary in [your L2]," and use this list as your base for building your learning plan.

In many cases, your core vocabulary may be composed of the following main topics. But in all cases, I suggest that you start building the vocabulary that's meaningful and useful to you for each category here:

>> **Food:** Focus on the foods that you eat the most, because they're the most meaningful to you.

>> **People:** Learn the word for *person, friend, mom, dad, brother, sister, son, daughter,* and so on.

>> **Colors:** Start with your favorite color and move on to family members' and friends' favorites.

>> **Clothing:** Learn the word for basic items of clothing so you can describe people by what they're wearing, for example.

>> **Numbers:** Know the word for at least 0–10, but also for 100 and 1,000.

TIP

It's important to know that learning numbers isn't an easy task for L2 learners in general, so don't despair if you can't get them correct from the beginning, or if expressing them takes you some time. Practice makes perfect! Just try using numbers as often as possible, until you feel confident that you can do it. For example, try to count everything you encounter, and say the numbers you face in everyday situations (prices, speed limit signs, plate numbers, phone numbers, and so on).

>> **Letters:** Memorize how to say the L2's alphabet so you can spell any words you may not be able to pronounce or ask someone to spell a word you don't understand, for example.

>> **Adverbs or adverbial phrases:** Concentrate especially on the ones that help you put statements in a time frame or location, such as *today, yesterday, tomorrow, next week, later, here, there,* and the like.

>> **Places:** Know words such as *restroom, restaurant, hotel, market, bus station, airport,* and *school.*

>> **Transportation:** Think of the types of transportation you may need to use, such as *bus, metro, train, taxi, car, airplane, bicycle,* and so on.

>> **Shopping:** Learn words that will help name stores and buy things in a store, such as *pharmacy, supermarket, price, cost, cashier,* and so on.

>> **Body parts and basic medical words:** Find out the L2 words that you can use to explain if you're feeling sick or something hurts.

>> **Other everyday words:** Add any words that you use every day for work, school, leisure activities, and so on.

Some high-frequency L2 words and phrases you need to learn are highlighted in the following sections.

Basic words

Basic words to learn in your L2 include

>> Yes

>> No

>> Thank you

>> You're welcome

>> Please

>> Sorry

>> Excuse me

Greetings and farewells

Saying hello and goodbye is always useful in an L2. Check out the following greetings and farewells:

>> Hello

>> Good morning, good afternoon, good night

>> How are you?

>> I'm okay, thank you. And you?

>> I'm so-so. And you?

>> Goodbye

>> See you soon

Introductions

As you learn your L2, you may meet many native and proficient L2 speakers. Here are some words and phrases you can use to introduce yourself:

>> My name is . . .

>> What is your name?

>> Nice to meet you.

>> Where are you from?

>> I am from . . .

>> I am learning [language].

>> Do you speak English?

>> I do not speak [language].

Communication problems

Generally, native L2 speakers are understanding and patient as you try to communicate with them. If you need help, keep these phrases handy:

>> How do you say . . . ?

>> Repeat, please.

>> More slowly, please.

>> Do you understand?

>> I do not understand.

Everyday questions

Some questions are especially useful as you go about your day. Consider learning the following in your L2:

>> Where is the restroom?

>> How much is it?

- >> What time is it?
- >> Do you have . . . ?
- >> Where is . . . ?
- >> How can I get to . . . ?

Emergencies

Hopefully you'll never need the following terms used in emergencies, but knowing them is a good idea:

- >> Be careful!
- >> Help!
- >> Emergency!
- >> Fire!
- >> Get out!
- >> Come here!
- >> Call the police/an ambulance/a doctor!

Restaurant terms

Who doesn't love going out to eat? Brush up on the following phrases in case you're lucky enough to go to a restaurant where your L2 is spoken:

- >> A table for two, please.
- >> Menu, please.
- >> I would like . . .
- >> I do not like . . .
- >> I am allergic to . . .
- >> Check, please.

Formulas

If you hear *salt and* . . ., you probably think of the word *pepper*. Or if I say, "Things are not always black and . . .," you'll complete the sentence with *white*. Likewise, when you greet someone, as they hear you saying, "Hey, how are . . .," they may answer, "Good, thank you," before you even finish the question. These *functional chunks* of language are premade phrases or strings of words that normally appear together in English, and anyone who speaks English can finish them without any problem.

Words that normally occur together, such as *salt and pepper,* are a type of functional chunk known as a *collocation.* Some collocations are language-specific, so your L2 may have collocations not found in your L1 or the words may be used in a different order in your L2 (for example, *black and white* is *blanco y negro* in Spanish, which translates to *white and black*).

Additionally, languages use certain linguistic *formulas* to achieve certain goals. You don't create these formulas every time you use them; you retrieve them from your memory as chunks of language. Some formulas you can find in languages are

>> *Situational formulas,* such as what you say when you begin a meal (*Bon appétit!*)

>> *Stylistic formulas,* such as the expressions you use to start and end letters (*To whom it may concern* or *Yours truly*)

>> *Ceremonial formulas,* such as what the officiant says when a couple is getting married or what you say when someone has passed away

>> *Discourse clues,* or phrases you use to maintain a conversation or add information in a written text, such as what you say when you want to

- Greet people

- Express approval

- Take your leave

- Request something

- Thank a person for something

- Take your turn in a conversation

- Offer your opinion

- Offer a counterargument

- Show that you're interested in a topic or what your interlocutor just said

- Keep the conversation going while thinking about what you need to say (*pause fillers* like *As I was saying*)

Formulas and collocations function as building blocks that you can use in your oral and written language production. It's easier and less of a processing burden to access one of these functional chunks of language from your long-term memory than to continuously create brand-new strings of sentences. For that reason, many researchers point out the important role these preformed phrases have in your everyday speech. In fact, some linguists suggest that 45 percent to 60 percent of what you produce in your L1 is functional chunks of language.

These chunks of language also give you some sense of fluency. When you use functional chunks, you can be perceived as having an extraordinary vocabulary repertoire and control of the grammar. Additionally, these chunks give you the comforting sense that you can function in the language. Some linguists even argue that learning functional chunks of language can help you start learning your L2 with a native-like foundation to analyze and deduce grammatical regularities and improve your grammar knowledge.

You can look at learning functional chunks of your L2 as learning vocabulary. Try selecting and learning functional phrases that are

>> **Frequently found in your L2:** In other words, these are phrases you've encountered in several situations. Write them down as you encounter them, including where you encountered them (add the context), so you don't learn them in isolation.

>> **Meaningful and useful for you:** You should learn phrases that help you perform everyday conversational functions, such as asking questions, making requests, summarizing your thoughts, expressing your attitude, and providing new information. Also learn some formulaic expressions, such as *Hello, how are you?* and *I'm fine, thanks.* Consider the situations in which you can use formulas and functional phrases, and rehearse conversations or practice them with other L2 users.

>> **Easily learned:** Look for phrases you can pick up quickly and remember, such as forms that play with repetition of sounds (*make-or-break, take a break*) or *mnemonics* (strategies and tricks that help you remember; see the later section "Using mnemonics and the keyword technique"), forms you can associate with previous knowledge, and forms you encounter in songs/chants, because repetition helps you memorize them.

TIP

As with learning vocabulary in general, try using *spaced repetition* (long intervals of time between each review) when you practice formulas and functional chunks of language. The more you work with it, the more likely you are to remember the language chunk.

Gathering Your Vocabulary Learning Supplies

In this section I go over some materials that can make your vocabulary learning experience more successful. First and foremost, you need to be exposed to lots of comprehensible input, such as compelling reading material as well as many listening and conversation opportunities. See Chapters 2, 6, and 8, for more details about input.

Additionally, I suggest that you have some consultation material (like a good L2 textbook and a dictionary), and some tools to personalize your vocabulary learning (like a notebook, some flashcards, and a pen/pencil). You may prefer using a computer or some other type of technology instead of hard-copy texts and paper. (Flip to Chapter 14 for details.)

Accessing an appropriate L2 textbook

The most effective L2 textbooks to help you build your L2 should

>> Link vocabulary meaning and its form by using images and labels.

>> Be divided into topics that include communicative situations.

>> Focus on communicating ideas among students or with the instructor.

>> Spiral up the topics presented. For example, if the textbook talks about family in one chapter, you should expect to see an expanded presentation of family vocabulary in a later chapter.

>> Use the L2 exclusively or at least most of the time. If grammar explanations are offered, they should appear in your L1, so you can understand how the structural aspects work.

>> Include readings with language at your proficiency level.

TIP

Before buying a textbook, research what's available in your L2 and make sure the textbook targets the listed suggestions. I encourage you to go online to different publishers' sites and have a look at the scope and sequence of the textbooks they offer. If they have a sample chapter available, check if the items I listed earlier are covered. If not, look for a different textbook. A great advantage nowadays is that most textbooks have online materials that you can access right away and use from anywhere.

Finding a good L2 dictionary and thesaurus

You can find many types of L2 dictionaries, including electronic and print versions, specialized dictionaries (like those including slang as well as those containing terminology related to medicine, accounting, law, or the military), and monolingual and bilingual (or multilingual) dictionaries. Make sure you get one that addresses your needs and preferences.

Before buying a dictionary, look at the definitions of some words and assess whether they make sense to you. As your L2 proficiency progresses, you may want to start using more detailed dictionaries, with more entries and more information. But when you start learning a new L2, a *learner dictionary* (which targets a basic 2,000-word vocabulary) is fine.

TIP

An *unabridged dictionary* contains all the words of a language. Normally they have more than one volume. An *abridged dictionary* is a shorter dictionary, and it includes the most common words used/needed among L1 speakers.

Dictionaries may provide different word information: pronunciation, part of speech, sample sentences, synonyms and antonyms, and even notes that refer to the word's *register* (formal or slang) or the geographical location where a word is used.

TIP

Use your L2 dictionary, but don't overuse it. When you're reading a new text, you're expected to understand around 95 percent of it. You won't understand some words, but consider whether you can understand the overall meaning of what you're reading. If you can, try not to stop and look up individual words in a dictionary. In Chapter 9 I give you some hints about how to read L2 texts, and I include suggestions for some online dictionaries in Chapter 14.

I recommend that you also use a thesaurus as a reference to enlarge your vocabulary. A *thesaurus* offers synonyms and antonyms, which you can add to your flashcards.

Using a notebook

TIP

A notebook helps you organize word clusters — in *semantic webs*, for example, or *word clouds* — or you may prefer listing your vocabulary in a notebook instead of using flashcards. My recommendation is that you use the notebook for grammar notes and word clusters, and flashcards for individual words or phrases. But ultimately, you need to arrange it in a way that makes sense to you. For example, my notebook would have a section that classifies vocabulary words by topics/themes and a section that lists words that can be used more generally (like articles, pronouns, and so on).

So, to get started, select a topic and dedicate a few pages of your notebook to anything connected to that topic. For example, if you select food, you can jot down names of foods, adjectives you can use to describe food and its taste, verbs connected to eating or cooking, formulas that you would use when you're at a restaurant, and the like. Create your own semantic webs or word clouds by writing a word in the center of a page and adding words that you relate to that word, and then others that are aligned with the new words.

In another section of your notebook, you may include general and everyday language, such as articles, adverbs or adverbial phrases, and so on.

TIP

Dedicate some time every day to reviewing the vocabulary in your notebook. Always have it with you and review it while you wait for the bus or in line at the supermarket, during the commercials while you watch TV, and while you wait for the air fryer or oven timer to go off. Use your notebook any time you need to review your vocabulary lists.

Making flashcards

You may want to use flashcards to study your L2 vocabulary. Make them simple and attractive. You can color-code them by topics or word frequency or whatever makes sense to you. For example, the most frequent words can be on cards that are one color, the mid-frequency words on cards that are a different color, and the low-frequency vocabulary on cards of another color. Or you can have specialized language or academic language on different colored cards.

Here are some suggestions about using flashcards:

>> Start with a small pack of cards and increase the number as you learn the words on them.

>> Change the order of the words as you review your cards. Place the most difficult ones in the front of the pack.

>> Review your flashcards often — if possible, one or two hours a week. Review already learned words at least once every couple weeks.

TECHNICAL STUFF

Some studies have shown that learners who reviewed flashcards one or two hours a week for 8 months increased their vocabulary by more than 1,000 words, compared to 100 words for a control group who didn't review vocabulary flashcards.

>> Organize your flashcards by theme, word frequency, how well you know the words (well-known, partially known, starting to get the meaning), your personal needs, interests, and goals, or the context where you encountered them — whatever makes sense to you.

The amount of information on your flashcards may vary, depending on factors such as your proficiency level or the time it takes to create them. Flashcards are very personal and should be useful to you and your needs. If you prefer using a flashcard app, you can choose between several different ones, as I explain in Chapter 14.

On one side,

>> Write the word in the center of the card, along with its part of speech (noun, adjective, verb, and so on).

>> Underneath, include its plural form/past tense form as needed. You may add some related words (for example, *prescribe, prescription, prescriptive*).

>> If the word is difficult for you to say, add its pronunciation next to or below it. When you review your cards, say each word aloud or at least in your head.

>> Add a note about where you encountered the word (for example, during a conversation with a coworker, in a restaurant, and so on).

On the flip side,

>> Write the word's meaning. Avoid the literal translation, if possible; it's better to add an image, a definition, cognates and other synonyms, or antonyms, and provide examples. Note whether the word has some positive or negative associations.

>> Jot down a mnemonic that helps you remember the word or any associations you have with other L1 or L2 words.

>> Provide context or restrictions on its use — for example, who uses it, its level of formality, settings where it's appropriate, and so on.

Mastering Vocabulary with Some Handy Strategies

Some researchers believe that you need at least ten encounters with a new vocabulary word to fully grasp it; others think you need 16 encounters. More than focusing on the number of encounters, it's important to understand that learning a word requires multiple exposures to it (listening to it, reading it, using it in a conversation). Each time you retrieve and use the word, you figure out a little bit more about it. First, you may learn the word's general meaning, and later you may pay attention to when to use it, whom to use it with, in which context you can use it, and so on. These observations help you get better at using L2 words.

The following sections provide useful strategies for learning vocabulary in your L2.

Building semantic maps

When you link a new word to a category of words or to words you already know, it's easier to retrieve it. So, whether you use flashcards, a notebook, or both, I suggest that you organize or arrange your L2 vocabulary in some way. I encourage you to draw semantic maps (see Chapter 10) in your notebook (at least one per page) and keep adding more words as you come across them. For instance, you may write *hair* in the center of the page, and then divide it into categories such as length, style, color, and so on. As you encounter related words, add them to your categories (or add new categories).

Creating mental images

As you encounter a new word in your L2 and learn its meaning, try to come up with a mental image of the word instead of relying on a translation. Why? A *linguistic sign* (or word) is composed of two parts: its meaning (what it represents) and its form (its pronunciation or spelling). Typically, when you translate a word, your brain is linking form and meaning in your L1 first, and then trying to link that to the form in your L2. But the most efficient way for your brain to process linguistic signs is by linking L2 form and meaning together, without having to go through your L1 first.

Images can be drawings (even stick figures), or you can search for images of words online (note the Image option you have in several search engines). Once you learn an L2 word with its images, you'll be able to retrieve the mental image when you encounter/use the word. The goal is linking meaning to form (sounds/letters).

TIP

Try to create mental images when you're reading, and you'll remember the information and words much more easily.

Using mnemonics and the keyword technique

Mnemonics are common strategies that help you remember things in any aspect of life. For instance, if you want to remember a password, you may connect it to a code that reminds you of something, like your birthday or anniversary or your pet's name. For instance, you may have memorized the names of the planets in

English (Mercury, Venus, Earth, Mars, Jupiter, Saturn, Uranus, and Neptune) with a mnemonic such as "My Very Educated Mother Just Served Us Noodles."

When you're learning a language, try to link new L2 words to something familiar that sounds similar. For example, the Spanish word for *money* is *dinero*, so you can say to yourself, *Oh, Robert DINERO is rich and has a lot of money.* Linking the word *dinero* to the name of a famous actor will help you remember it. This is the way one of my friends learned that word!

TIP

Everyone has their own mnemonics, although if you and a friend share a common L1 and L2, you can share your mnemonics. You can also add a little note or drawing of your mnemonics to your flashcards or notebook.

You also may want to use the *keyword technique* I mention in Chapter 10. This technique suggests that you link a new L2 word (for example, *celeridad* in Spanish, which means *speed* or *quickness*) to a familiar sound in your L1 or L2 (in this case, *celery*). Then, visualize the word *celery* as a celery stick running in sneakers. So, now the word *celery* reminds you of a celery speeding up, which you'll connect with *celeridad*.

Inferring the meaning

When you encounter new L2 words in real-life communicative exchanges or while reading, you may need to use contextual clues and other available resources to guess and infer their meaning so the communicative act can continue and the message gets across.

Reading is a great way to expand your vocabulary (you can find out more about reading in Chapter 9). The contextual clues can help you guess the meaning of new words (and start *fast-mapping* these new words) and reinforce your understanding of words you've already encountered and are in the process of learning (*slow-mapping*). In fact, some researchers propose that language learners use a three-step process to infer meaning:

1. **Guess the word's meaning from the context.**

2. **If possible, verify its meaning (with an L2 speaker or a dictionary).**

3. **Pay attention to the word and try to connect it to other words you may know (using mnemonics or other strategies).**

WARNING

This three-step process requires a lot of attention to new words. My suggestion is that you do the three steps only occasionally or you may get bored and distracted from the main goal of language learning: communicating or receiving messages in the L2. Think about the process of learning your L1. What did you do when you encountered words you didn't know? Did you look them all up in the dictionary, or did you try to guess their meaning and only occasionally use a dictionary or another speaker to help you with the new word?

TIP

Once you know the meaning of a word, try to see whether the root of that word helps you understand other words in its family. For example, if you learn *admire*, try to guess the meaning of *admirer*, *admirable*, and *admirably* when you encounter them. Knowing the root gives you partial knowledge of other forms of the word. Normally, L2 learners know nouns and verbs before they learn adjectives or adverbs.

Using reference materials

My suggestion for learning new words is to first try to add a visual image to the new word and, if you can't find an image (for instance, for an abstract word like *conscience*), find L2 synonyms or L2 definitions that explain the meaning. You can add these definitions and synonyms to your flashcards or notebook. I recommend using the L2 as a reference as much as possible, including L2 dictionaries.

TIP

Novice learners may find using an L2 reference book difficult and even frustrating, so it's okay to start with L2-L1 dictionaries and their translations, and move to a monolingual L2 dictionary or thesaurus as your proficiency level improves.

Looking for cognates

Cognates are similar words (in form and meaning) in your L1 and L2. For example, *television* and *televisión* are cognates in English and Spanish. When the form is similar in the two languages, word acquisition is easier. So, your vocabulary can really grow thanks to cognates.

When I come across a new L2 word, I often try to find a synonym that's a cognate. For example, *speak* in Spanish is *habla*. If you search for synonyms of *speak*, you may find *converse*, which is a cognate of *conversa*. So, I prefer learning *conversa* rather than *habla*, or *converse* rather than *speak*, because *conversa* and *converse* are cognates.

The similarity of some cognates may be clearer in writing than if you just listen to their pronunciation. For example, although the word *Jupiter* is written the same way in Spanish and in English, you may find it difficult to see that the words are cognates based only on their pronunciation.

WARNING

But you need to be careful with what are commonly called *false friends* or *false cognates*. On occasion, some words look very similar in two languages, but they have very different meanings. A couple common examples sometimes occur in my classes: L1 English speakers learning Spanish want to say *embarrassed* but use the word *embarazado/a*, which means *pregnant*. Or L1 Spanish speakers who want to say *constipado* (to have a cold) in English say *constipated*, which has quite a different meaning.

Repeating whatever you can

Do you know the lines of some movies or songs? Do you like repeating them in conversations? If you've never done that, I encourage you to try it. You can really have fun memorizing some movie phrases or songs in your L2 and repeating them out loud, trying to imitate the performer. This strategy of repeating the L2 as it's used by native speakers is an excellent way to start getting used to L2 vocabulary, phrases, and grammar.

TIP

An easy way to learn movie lines is to use captions or subtitles when you're watching movies or TV shows. You can find song lyrics online or read them in your favorite music app. Play with the words, sing them or say them out loud, write them down, and study them. You'll enjoy the process.

You can do the same thing with L2 reading excerpts. Try to memorize what you read, keep it in your memory, and later try to write the excerpt on a piece of paper without looking at what you read. You can also try repeating the sentence out loud. Then, compare what you wrote (or said) to what you read. This helps you focus on specific words, phrases, and forms.

Creating rhymes and playing games

Some L2 learners benefit from creating rhymes or songs with new words. If you're the type of learner who remembers things by creating and memorizing rhymes, try it with your L2 vocabulary. The funnier or more shocking the rhymes are, the easier it will be to remember them.

Feel free to play with your L2 and name everything you see, and if you don't know what something is called, look it up in a bilingual dictionary or ask another speaker, and say it out loud. Write the word down on a flashcard or in your notebook and review it a couple times that day. It's natural for people to rehearse the new words they learn. Sometimes you do it out loud, and other times you may prefer doing it silently, but you're mentally practicing how to use the new word. This is called *language play*.

For instance, imagine how you'd use an L2 word in your everyday activities. I do this all the time. I just envision myself living in the L2 culture and using my L2 in everyday life. I ask myself how I would ask X, Y, and Z, and how I would answer these questions.

Playing vocabulary board games or word games can also help you learn and recall vocabulary words while paying attention to their spelling. You can play Banana-grams, Scrabble, or Upwords, for example, or you can do crossword puzzles. You may also enjoy playing games in the L2 such as Taboo and other word association games.

TIP

Finding crossword puzzles in your L2 may not be easy, but you can create your own crossword puzzles using words you've added to your flashcards or notebook, as well as synonyms, mnemonics, definitions, and more. You can create them at www.puzzlemaker.com. There, you can browse around some other word games (such as word searches) they offer for free.

Engaging with the L2 community

A great vocabulary learning exercise is participating in L2 community events that interest you. While you attend these events, you can observe L2 users, pay attention to their language, and then note new L2 words and expressions in your notebook (or flashcards). Review your notes as often as possible to reflect on the new vocabulary and try using the words in other meaningful and real-life situations.

Considering the Role of Grammar in Your Language Learning

Grammar is the backbone or structure of a language. Although all languages share a universal grammar (UG; see Chapter 2), according to Noam Chomsky's proposal, each language has its own way of following these grammatical principles or set of norms.

Furthermore, when you acquire a language, you follow a certain acquisition order and predetermined developmental stages that cannot be altered, reordered, or edited, although you may pass through certain stages at different rates. See Chapter 5 for details.

Some people argue that explicit grammar instruction may change these universal and ordered processes. Actually, right after you receive grammar instruction and practice the rule with drills, you may produce perfect and grammatically accurate language. But this "perfection" is an illusion that captivates those who insist on the core importance of teaching grammar in language classes. This accurate grammar production right after learning a rule may be

>> **Permanent:** This happens when the grammatical explanation aligns with your current developmental stage or order of acquisition. So, the apparent progress you've made may be permanent, because the rule was learned and practiced in perfect timing with your internal and universal developmental processes.

>> **Temporary:** This happens when the grammatical explanation and practice don't align with your developmental level. So, you may show some temporary progress in your learning, but you'll eventually return to the developmental stage where you belonged before the grammar lesson. In fact, teaching language rules beyond the learner's developmental stage or outside their acquisition order can delay their learning of those rules and even cause a regression or backsliding in their learning.

Extremes are usually not the best option. And that's certainly the case with two extreme theories for teaching grammar: Some researchers believe that language instruction should be based on teaching/learning grammar rules, and others think that no grammar instruction is necessary because learners will acquire grammar by picking up the rules through exposure to comprehensible input. An in-between proposal supports the idea that, in addition to exposure to plenty of comprehensible input, formal grammar instruction can help in the L2 learning process.

My position is that being exposed to rich, comprehensible input should be enough for novice L2 learners, but as your L2 proficiency level grows, you may also benefit from some simple grammatical explanations or conscious learning of the L2 grammar. Other factors to consider are the learner's age and learning style. Younger learners don't benefit from grammar explanations as much as older learners or adults do. Additionally, deductive and analytical learners benefit from grammar explanations. You can find out how certain personality traits affect language learning in Chapter 3.

TIP

If you're a novice learner, don't stress out over learning and memorizing L2 grammar rules from the beginning. Instead, you may want to use your study time to read and be exposed to rich L2 input at your proficiency level, or to review your vocabulary flashcards. If you're the kind of learner that needs to understand the rules behind what you're being exposed to, review the grammatical rules as needed, but don't be frustrated if you don't get a particular rule right away. Start by trying to follow the rule in writing before producing it in your speech. Writing gives you time to consider the rule and monitor its use. Also, keep in mind that you may not be at the appropriate developmental stage or acquisition order in your language learning journey.

Chapter **14**

Considering the Role of Technology

Technology is a fundamental part of life these days, keeping people connected globally and allowing instant communication. It can also serve as an engaging way to support your second language (L2) learning, and an excellent resource for broadening your exposure and understanding of the L2 culture.

In this chapter I introduce you to only a fraction of the language learning applications and online platforms available. While you research the resources in this chapter, pay attention to what's available in your L2 and whether it can enhance your language learning experience.

TIP

Bear in mind that more programs are created daily, and others may disappear or change their URL (website address). You can start organizing your technological learning resources using sites like **Wakalet** (https://wakelet.com/#), **Symbaloo** (www.symbaloo.com/), or **Pearltrees** (www.pearltrees.com/).

Deciding Which Technology to Use in Your Language Learning

You may be wondering whether technology is actually useful for learning a new language. Well, using technology to bolster your L2 learning gives you the option of

>> Accessing authentic and up-to-date resources from anywhere in the world

>> Practicing all four language skills (speaking, listening, reading, and writing)

>> Using all three modes of communication (interpretive, interpersonal, and presentational)

>> Researching and learning about the L2 culture

>> Getting real-time feedback

>> Adapting the resource to your needs (especially if it's powered by artificial intelligence, or AI)

TIP

With all the apps and programs focused on language learning, deciding what to use can be tough. Some questions to bear in mind when you're choosing among your options include the following:

>> How useful is this piece of technology to reach your goal?

>> Is it serving the purpose you need it for?

>> How appropriate is the content for you?

>> How easy to use is the product?

>> Is the price worth the learning value?

REMEMBER

Most second language acquisition (SLA) researchers agree that interaction with other L2 speakers (teachers, tutors, conversation partners, and other learners) is essential in the development of L2 interpersonal communication skills. If you can't find interaction opportunities in your community, you may need to resort to technology to look for tutors, conversation partners, and other learners.

Likewise, technology provides you with opportunities to obtain a deeper understanding of the L2 culture and to develop your intercultural competence, which you can rely on when you interact and communicate with native L2 speakers or teachers.

Furthermore, some students feel less anxious or embarrassed if they make errors using technology than if they do so when interacting with other L2 users in face-to-face situations. Technology may help these students feel more comfortable using the L2, at least in the beginning.

In the rest of this chapter, I introduce you to a broad array of technology-mediated communication apps, courses, and programs to help you with your overall L2 learning experience or with specific skills (speaking, writing, listening, reading, or expanding your vocabulary).

TIP

Don't feel overwhelmed by the sheer number of language learning applications and programs. Before committing and purchasing a program, course, or app, test the free version. This gives you an opportunity to consider its usability, as well as the appropriateness of the content to your proficiency level, learning style, and goals. What works best for you may not fit the needs of someone else. So, select what fulfills *your* needs.

Considering Language Learning Platforms and Courses

The number of language learning platforms is continuously growing and changing. Nowadays, many platforms are AI-powered, which provides the advantage of personalizing your lessons based on your learning style, needs, and patterns. Here are some of the most popular ones in alphabetical order (be sure to check whether the platform you're interested in offers your L2):

>> **Babbel** (www.babbel.com/) gives you diverse learning routes. One important feature is that, through *spaced repetition,* it reintroduces words several times. It offers a wide variety of language resources: live (online) classes, podcasts, games, videos, and the like.

>> **Busuu** (www.busuu.com/en-us) is perfect for language learners who self-study. This AI app personalizes your learning experience with lessons that develop around a specific communicative focus, such as introductions, descriptions, or participating in everyday situations. Busuu offers features to improve your listening, speaking, and writing skills, interactive lessons and games, flashcards, grammar exercises, conversations, live lessons, and L2 native speakers/tutors.

>> **Drops** (https://languagedrops.com/) is a great program for visual learners divided into short 5-minute sessions. It focuses on content comprehension through swiping and tapping, but not typing.

>> **Duolingo** (www.duolingo.com/) is a *gamified* AI platform for language learning. In other words, you can advance and unlock higher levels by completing levels and getting rewards points. Each level allows you to practice specific vocabulary and grammar topics, and to occasionally review previous topics (*spaced repetition*). You can practice your listening, speaking, reading, and writing skills. It's set up to send you daily reminders to use the app.

>> **FluentU** (www.fluentu.com/) focuses on using real-world video and audio to learn new words in multiple contexts. It also includes flashcards and personalizes your quizzes.

>> **Language Transfer** (www.languagetransfer.org/) offers free online language audio courses that focus on explaining grammar and vocabulary in a relaxed way. It uses similarities between your first language (L1) and L2 in your L2 learning (*language transfer*).

>> **Lingoda** (www.lingoda.com/) is an AI-powered platform that personalizes your lessons, keeping track of your learning patterns. It provides opportunities to practice vocabulary, grammar, speaking, listening, and writing activities.

>> **LingoDeer** (www.lingodeer.com/) is an AI app offering online classes that adapts and personalizes your L2 learning into bite-size interactive lessons and games. It helps you learn vocabulary and grammar, and improve your speaking, listening, and writing skills.

>> **Mango Languages** (https://mangolanguages.com/) is a perfect L2 learning system for intuitive learners, who can make their own connections without explicit instruction. Its methodology is based on conversations that reinforce grammar, vocabulary, and culture. Some libraries have subscriptions to this program.

>> **Memrise** (www.memrise.com/en-us/) is an AI language learning platform that adapts to your needs in a gamified setting, using a flashcard approach and spaced repetition. Some features include video clips with native L2 speakers having casual everyday conversations, speech-recognition exercises, adapted review plans (using memory techniques), and grammar lessons.

>> **Mondly** (www.mondly.com/) is a gamified app that has short daily lessons on different topics and real-world situations. It includes a *chatbot* (a computer character that acts like a person) and quizzes.

>> **Pimsleur** (www.pimsleur.com/) is an online platform that focuses on the language learning method developed by linguist Paul Pimsleur. It has 30-minute lessons centered on repetition and common phrases. It also offers readings, a voice recognition feature, flashcards, role-plays, and conversational games, and it connects history and culture. Pimsleur helps you set daily goals and sends you reminders.

» **Rocket Languages** (www.rocketlanguages.com/) is a language app that helps you learn your L2 by using audio lessons, interactive activities, and readings.

» **Rosetta Stone** (www.rosettastone.com/) is an AI-powered language learning app that adapts your learning experience to your needs. It's a more formal L2 learning app than the gamified ones. It focuses on immersive bite-size lessons connecting words to objects and events around you (avoiding translation). It also centers on interactive lessons and activities to enhance your speaking and listening skills so you improve your real-life conversations. It has its own speech recognition system, and you can access tutoring sessions. Check whether your library has a subscription to this program.

Practicing Your Listening and Reading Skills

Listening to and reading your L2 is essential in your language development. In this section, I highlight some online tools you can use to get L2 reading and listening material.

TIP

LingQ (www.lingq.com/en/thefluentshow/) offers a broad array of interpretive resources, giving you access to reading material, such as books and articles (and even emails), and to listening material, such as songs and podcasts, in more than 20 languages.

Audio and video samples

If you want to find authentic samples of people talking in many different languages, you can try **Audio Lingua** (https://audio-lingua.ac-versailles.fr), **FluentU** (www.fluentu.com/), or **Yabla** (www.yabla.com/). Yabla's videos offer subtitles, and you can click on words from the videos to get definitions. It also offers games and activities (like dictation, speaking, and pronunciation). Of course, you can also access L2 audiovisual material on **YouTube** (www.youtube.com/).

Language Reactor (www.languagereactor.com/) is a browser extension that can give you subtitles, translations, and a pop-up dictionary when you're watching Netflix or YouTube, and it can suggest vocabulary to focus on, save it, and highlight it every time it appears. It also has a chatbot with AI.

Radio Garden (https://radio.garden/search) gives you access to live radio programs around the world.

MobileGPT (https://mobile-gpt.io/) can tell you a story in your L2, allowing you to choose the topic and your level of proficiency. You can even ask it to quiz you with comprehension questions afterward!

If you love music and want to enhance your L2 learning through songs or music videos, you may want to use **Spotify** (https://open.spotify.com/) or **Lirica** (www.lirica.io/). The lyrics that accompany the songs in Spotify can help you learn your L2 and practice your pronunciation. Lirica also focuses on music and video lyrics to help you learn vocabulary and grammar.

Podcasts

Coffee Break Languages (https://coffeebreaklanguages.com/) offers, among other features, free podcasts in several languages. You can also purchase language courses through the app.

Duolingo Podcasts (https://podcast.duolingo.com/) are available in a few languages (French, Spanish, and English) and target different cultural topics, movies, and the like. Transcription is provided.

Books, audiobooks, and other reading resources

Beelinguapp (https://beelinguapp.com/) offers access to books and audiobooks, news, and songs in several languages.

Some applications that may be useful when you're reading texts or working with authentic materials include the following:

>> **Fluent** (www.fluent.co/) is a Chrome extension that highlights words in the online text you're reading, and gives you their pronunciation and meaning. Right now, it's available in English, French, German, Italian, Portuguese, and Spanish.

>> **Lingro** (https://lingro.com/) allows you to type a URL into its web viewer and then click on any word on the web page and see its translation. It functions like the Google Translate extension, but you don't need to install it. Furthermore, it keeps track of the words you looked up and can create word lists with those words and even include them in game-like activities.

>> Some AI options that can read text for you are **Copilot** (`https://copilot.microsoft.com/`) for online web pages and PDF text, and **Perplexity** (`www.perplexity.ai/`) for PDF text.

>> **ChatGPT** (`https://openai.com/chatgpt/`) can simplify text that's too complex for you, following the parameters you give this AI tool.

Working on Speaking and Writing

Speaking to proficient and native speakers of your L2 is very important in your language development. If you can't find L2 speakers in your community or travel to a country where your L2 is spoken, technology can help you! You can find online tutors, conversation partners, and *language exchange partners* (someone who wants to learn your language and will teach you theirs in exchange) that may fit your needs. The following sections can help you get started.

TIP

Regardless of whether you meet other L2 users online or face-to-face, make your communicative exchanges more effective and successful in the following ways:

>> Find people who share some of your interests, and try not to hop around from speaker to speaker.

>> Choose topics in advance, considering your proficiency level and the subjects you can discuss, and prepare yourself by learning some of the vocabulary and expressions you think you may need. If you feel like you're running out of topics, you can get ideas at `http://iteslj.org/questions/index.html`.

>> Let the conversation flow and be ready to get a bit sidetracked from your original conversation.

>> Keep your conversations interesting and fun.

>> Comment and expand on the information shared.

>> Have a notebook handy to jot down important vocabulary or expressions you encountered and to journal how the exchange went.

Online tools to find in-person speakers

One ideal situation is finding conversation partners or language exchange partners locally and meeting in person. You may find them at local gatherings, such as festivals, university events, cultural celebrations, library or church events, and the like. But online tools can also help you find people to chat with.

Meetup (www.meetup.com/) helps you find a local language exchange partner so that you can practice in person. Using social media, such as **Facebook** (www.facebook.com/), is another way to find local groups that meet to practice your L2, or L2 speakers who meet to do some activity. If you can't find any local groups, create your own and ask your friends to share information about your group so you can start meeting people.

Conversation and language exchange partners

If you can't find local L2 conversation partners, language exchange partners, or tutors, you can look for them online, although most of these programs aren't free. After you find someone to converse with, you may need to meet them using a video or videoconferencing app such as **Zoom** (www.zoom.com/), **Google Meet** (https://meet.google.com/), **Whereby** (https://whereby.com/), or **WhatsApp** (www.whatsapp.com/).

My favorite conversation partners service is **TalkAbroad** (www.talkabroad.com/). It connects you with trained native speakers from countries around the world via video call, and you can talk about any topic you want to discuss.

If you want to find people who want to exchange language lessons and conversation opportunities (because your L1 is their L2 and vice versa), you can find language exchange partners through the following apps and websites:

>> **HelloTalk** (www.hellotalk.com) is an AI app that connects you with native speakers that seem to be the right exchange partner for you. It offers some built-in learning aids, such as translations, pronunciation, and corrections.

>> **Idyoma** (www.idyoma.com/) provides a safe environment to practice your L2, because the people participating have been verified and you have control over who can connect with you.

>> **Lang-8, Inc** (https://lang-8.jp/en/) offers an app called **HiNative** that connects you and other native speakers around the globe so you can share your knowledge and experience with your language and culture.

>> **The Mixxer** (www.language-exchanges.org) is an app that links people who want to practice their L2 through video calls.

>> **Reddit** (www.redditinc.com/) focuses on finding communities of speakers, and you can find communities interested in less commonly taught languages.

>> **Speaky** (www.speaky.com/) is an app where you can connect directly (without having to schedule a chat beforehand) with other individuals willing to practice your L1 and L2.

>> **Tandem** (https://tandem.net/) connects you to a filtered group of native speakers, and you can communicate via video chat or text. It's AI-powered.

Other options include **Boomalang** (www.boomalang.co/), **Conversifi** (https://conversifi.com/), **My Language Exchange** (www.mylanguageexchange.com/), **italki** (www.italki.com/), **Lingbe** (www.lingbe.com/), and **LinguaMeeting** (www.linguameeting.com/).

Artificial intelligence and virtual reality

Sometimes, you may choose to have conversations created by AI (that is, not with real people). Some creative and helpful conversational AI chatbot tools are **Google Gemini** (https://gemini.google.com/) and **Character.AI** (https://beta.character.ai/).

If you like virtual reality and have the gadgets needed to enjoy it, you may want to try **Immerse** (www.immerse.com/), which is a language immersion platform where you can meet and talk to people from around the world, or **ImmerseMe** (https://immerseme.co/), which is another tool where you can practice and improve your fluency in real-life scenarios.

Written exchanges

If you want to practice writing with a conversation partner, you may want to use an app such as **WhatsApp** (www.whatsapp.com/) or **Voxer** (www.voxer.com/), where you can share written text messages as well as voice messages, images, and the like. Or you can play with your L2 and create a texting-type exchange using **iFake TextMessage** (https://ifaketextmessage.com/). Some of the apps covered in the earlier section "Conversation and language exchange partners," such as Speaky and Tandem, also have options for written exchanges with people who speak your L2.

TIP

Interpersonal communication with other L2 users may also happen *asynchronously* (not in real time, but on a delayed schedule). If you want to communicate with others in a written format in an asynchronous way, you can participate in online forums, post on blogs, send emails, or write social media posts.

Help with pronunciation and fluency

If you want to work on your pronunciation, **Glossika** (https://ai.glossika.com/) allows you to listen to a native L2 speaker, record yourself repeating what they said, and then compare your version to the native speaker's. **Forvo** (https://forvo.com/) is an online dictionary that helps you with pronunciation.

If you want to improve your L2 fluency, you can practice reading aloud. For example, you can add voice-over to a favorite video by reading the script or caption in your L2.

Enhancing Your L2 Vocabulary

As I explain in Chapter 13, L2 vocabulary learning involves figuring out many features of a word, including its use in different communicative situations. When you're creating flashcards or working with vocabulary in general, online dictionaries or **ChatGPT** (https://openai.com/chatgpt/) can help you get the information you may need, such as definitions, translations, synonyms or antonyms, or *collocations* (words that go together, such as *black and white* or *peas in a pod*). Chat-GPT can also use your vocabulary words in phrases, sentences, or stories so you can learn L2 vocabulary in context.

In this section I cover some technological tools you can use to create flashcards and programs that offer exercises and activities to help you practice vocabulary.

Vocabulary lists

Finding some frequency-based vocabulary lists may be one of your first assignments. You can have a look at some premade vocabulary lists in different languages at www.wgtn.ac.nz/lals/resources/paul-nations-resources/vocabulary-lists, or just search online for "word frequency lists in [your L2]" in your favorite search engine.

ChatGPT (https://openai.com/chatgpt/) can create word lists from text you input or vocabulary lists based on certain topics or proficiency levels.

Vocabulary organization

TIP

Vocabulary is learned better when it's organized thematically (for example, in categories like family, food, people, colors, clothing, and so on). You can brainstorm and organize words into topics using apps that give you access to the information from anywhere at any time.

Some technological resources that help you organize your L2 vocabulary are **MindMup** (www.mindmup.com/), **AnswerGarden** (https://answergarden.ch/), **Padlet** (https://padlet.com/), the word cloud generator **Wordart** (https://wordart.com/), **Simple Mind** (https://simplemind.eu/how-to-mind-map/basics/), and **FigJam** (www.figma.com/figjam/).

Flashcards

Vocabulary flashcards are one of the most popular tools for L2 learners. Flashcard apps offer a variety of options, which makes them perfect for learners of any age. Some apps allow you to create your own deck of flashcards, or you can use some of the premade flashcards available in the app.

My favorite flashcard app is **Anki** (https://apps.ankiweb.net/), which lets you include images, audio, and videos in your flashcards, and get frequency lists. You can also set how many words you want to review per day, so you don't feel overwhelmed.

The **Brainscape** flashcard app (www.brainscape.com/) allows you to share your flashcards with other L2 users or mix/shuffle card categories so they don't come up in a specific sequence.

The **Cram** flashcard app (https://www.cram.com/) has several different options. For example, one mode removes the vocabulary you already know from the deck, leaving only the vocabulary you're still working on. Another mode offers spaced repetition of vocabulary words.

Some other flashcard apps include the game-like **Drops** (https://language drops.com/), **DuoCards** (https://duocards.com/en/), **iKnow!** (https://iknow.jp/), **Lingvist** (https://lingvist.com/), which is easy to use, with vocabulary words in sample sentences, **Memrise** (www.memrise.com/en-us/), another easy-to-use app that's available in more than 20 languages, and **Quizlet** (https://quizlet.com/gb), which teachers love to use.

Other vocabulary activities

In the **Clozemaster** app (www.clozemaster.com/) you can practice vocabulary with fill-in-the-blank activities, choosing a word from a series of options. The app offers some adaptability features, such as adjusting the difficulty of the activities to your proficiency level and the rate of the listening activities to your learning needs. You can also access word meanings in its dictionary.

Poodll (https://poodll.com/poodll-languages/plugin-poodll-wordcards/) offers activities such as listen-and-type, choose-the-answer, and type-the-words tasks, as well as speech cards.

AI, such as **ChatGPT** (https://openai.com/chatgpt/), can create almost anything to help you practice your vocabulary. For example, it can create activities targeting specific vocabulary and using different formats, such as matching pairs, multiple choice, odd one out, word rearrangement, fill in the blanks, true-false, or open-ended questions.

You can create your own activities/games, such as word searches and crossword puzzles, using **Puzzlemaker** (https://puzzlemaker.discoveryeducation.com/).

Vocabee (www.vocabee.org/) is a vocabulary game-based learning platform that you can create and adapt to your needs. It's versatile and easy to use.

Interacting with Your L2's Culture

Interacting with the L2 culture in any way enriches your L2 learning experience immensely. Try to learn about the L2 culture by talking to native speakers, researching the culture online, or saving interesting cultural material (like an infographic, an ad, a photo, a video, or a screenshot). In this section I direct you to some websites and apps where you can get access to bits and pieces of your L2 culture. Bookmark any website that interests you or take screenshots of what you like.

Images

Learning about your L2 culture may include observing and analyzing its streets, buildings, food, and the like. You can do that with some of the websites described here:

>> **Google Earth** (https://earth.google.com/web/) is a popular tool you may have already used. You can view and investigate places in countries where your L2 is spoken. For example, you can have a look at a city center, or at the street where a friend lives.

>> **TasteAtlas** (www.tasteatlas.com/) is a great website for exploring the type of food eaten in a certain location.

>> **TheTrueSize** (www.thetruesize.com/) allows you to compare the size of two countries by dragging and dropping one over the other.

>> **WindowSwap** (www.window-swap.com/) gives you a peek into what you can see if you look out a window in another country.

Videos and sounds

The following websites give you access to real or virtual reality (VR) videos:

>> **360Cities** (www.360cities.net/map) offers VR images and videos from around the world.

- » **AirPano** (www.airpano.com/) is an excellent VR project that has 360° high resolution images and videos from many locations around the world.

- » **Audiomapa** (www.audiomapa.org/) allows you to hear the sounds of different areas in the world. Occasionally you also hear people talking, but the goal is to experience the sounds of the location.

- » **City Walks Live** (https://citywalks.live/) is one of my favorite websites, because it shows videos of what you would see if you were walking around several cities across the world.

- » Another great website that takes you to different cities, in this case while driving and listening to the radio and street noises, is **Drive & Listen** (https://driveandlisten.herokuapp.com/).

- » **Webcamtaxi** (www.webcamtaxi.com/en/) shows the views from live webcams around the world. Another webcam site is **EarthCam** (www.earthcam.com/), which focuses mostly on touristy locations.

Of course, YouTube has thousands of videos from around the globe that help you experience the culture of the country/countries where your L2 is spoken. For example, one YouTube channel that provides views into many different countries is **Geography Now** (https://www.youtube.com/c/GeographyNow/playlists).

Arts and culture

You can do virtual expeditions to places around the world and access art exhibits and take cultural field trips using **Google Arts and Culture** (https://artsandculture.google.com/?hl=en and https://artsandculture.google.com/project/expeditions). In another Google link you can find art collections housed in some of the world's finest museums (https://artsandculture.google.com/partner?hl=en).

TIP

I love taking virtual tours of museums around the world. Because of space limitations, I can't list all the museum virtual tour web pages here, but if you type phrases like "virtual tour [museum name]" or "virtual tour museum in [country]" in your online search engine, you may find the museum you're looking for, or another interesting one in a country where your L2 is spoken.

Getting Help

In this section I feature some of the ways in which technology can help you find tutors, dictionaries, and other language guidance.

Tutors

HiNative (https://hinative.com/) is a question-and-answer forum where both humans and AI answer your questions about 113 languages.

Italki (www.italki.com/) not only provides you the option of finding a tutor, but also allows you to participate in group classes. The connection happens through video chat. You can download it onto your phone and use it anytime.

Preply (https://preply.com) and **LanguaTalk** (https://languatalk.com/) are tutoring tools that learners can use in many languages, and you can filter tutors by country, your availability, and even price range. Preply also has a filter for the type of tutor you need (for example, professional, highly rated, native speaker).

Q-Chat (https://quizlet.com/qchat-personal-ai-tutor) is a free AI ChatGPT tutor that works with the library found in the Quizlet app. The questions are personalized to your learning needs (for example, vocabulary, grammar, reading comprehension).

Verbalplanet (www.verbalplanet.com/) offers native language tutors from around the world.

Dictionaries

Two good websites to bookmark are https://smartlinks.org/dictionaries.html, which lists many different monolingual and bilingual dictionaries, among other interesting links, and **WordReference** (www.wordreference.com), which is one of my favorite online dictionaries.

Monolingual dictionaries in 15 different languages can be found online at **TheFreeDictionary** (www.thefreedictionary.com/). **Larousse** (www.larousse.fr/) offers a French monolingual dictionary, as well as a bilingual one (French and Arabic/Chinese/German/English/Italian/Spanish). **Duden** (www.duden.de/) is a monolingual online German dictionary, and the official Spanish dictionary is the one associated with the **Royal Spanish Academy** (www.rae.es/). **Dicio** (www.dicio.com.br/) is a monolingual Portuguese dictionary.

Some online bilingual and multilingual dictionaries include **Bab.la** (https://bab.la/), **Glosbe** (www.glosbe.com), **Langtolang** (www.langtolang.com/), **Linguee** (www.linguee.com/), **Logos** (www.logosdictionary.org/), and **Multitran** (www.multitran.com).

Besides being a bilingual dictionary, **Forvo** (https://forvo.com/) offers pronunciations of words and phrases in several languages: English, French, German, Italian, Japanese, Portuguese, Russian, and Spanish.

TIP

Throughout this book I emphasize the importance of keeping track of vocabulary that's meaningful and useful to you. You can create your own dictionary at **MeaningCloud** (https://tinyurl.com/55ws889x).

Assessing Your Progress

Assessing your progress and celebrating your gains is essential to keep you motivated to continue learning your new language. So, I encourage you to keep track of your progress using some of the apps mentioned here.

>> You can ask **ChatGPT** (https://openai.com/chatgpt/) and other AI tools to give you feedback on any writing samples you produce. ChatGPT can comment on your language choice, your grammar, your style — whatever you need to assess.

>> **Extempore** (https://extemporeapp.com/) is a speaking assessment tool used by many language teachers.

>> **Quizlet** (https://quizlet.com/gb) is a flashcard app that allows you to keep track of your progress so you can monitor how you're progressing in your language learning.

>> **Poodll** (https://poodll.com/poodll-languages/plugin-poodll-readaloud/) can assess your reading speed and accuracy in several languages.

>> **Yask** (https://yask.app/en) is a free app in which native speakers check your pronunciation and writing, and give you feedback.

TIP

I encourage you to keep track of your progress on your language learning path by uploading your work to an e-portfolio, such as **LinguaFolio** (https://linguafolio.uoregon.edu/).

5
The Part of Tens

Chapter **15**

Ten Tips for Starting Your New Language Journey

t's no secret that nowadays everyone expects to see results immediately. You want to know how to do something and to do it well right away. Most of the time, you can quickly figure out the basics of the new skill you're trying to master, but to become an expert or excellent at it, you need time and effort. Practice makes perfect!

Learning a second language (L2) is no different. You can certainly pick up some basics and start communicating in your L2 right away, but you won't sound like a native speaker in just a couple of months. You need time, consistent effort, excellent sources of *input* (L2 samples), active engagement with the language, and patience with uncertainty and errors. In this chapter, I give you some tips to help you get started on the right foot.

Pinpointing Your Motivation

Motivation can move mountains! When you have a strong motivation to learn an L2, you won't mind dedicating time and effort to learning it. So, before you start your L2 journey, think about your motivation. Are you learning an L2 to

>> Communicate/interact with someone important in your life?

>> Be competitive when looking for a job?

>> Vacation in a place where the L2 is spoken?

>> Improve your brain function and decision-making abilities?

>> Challenge yourself?

TIP

Your reason(s) for learning the L2 may be different from other people's. Write down your motivation and put it in the place(s) where you plan to study the L2. If you can find a photo that reminds you of what's driving you to learn the L2, add it to the mix. For example, if your motivation is talking to your significant other (and their acquaintances), place a photo of that person next to your study notes as a reminder of your inspiration. Find out more about motivation in Chapter 11.

Focusing on Learning Vocabulary

Having a broad array of L2 vocabulary that allows you to talk about everyday topics is essential, especially for beginning learners. Search online for a list of high-frequency vocabulary words in your L2. After you find 700–800 of the most frequent vocabulary words in your L2, add to your list any other words that are important for you (or that you'd use in your everyday life). Have a goal of learning the most frequent 2,000 words in your L2 — but don't feel like you must do it all at once!

TIP

You can create a set of vocabulary flashcards or use online flashcard apps. Then, set your learning goals (for example, 20 new words per week). See Chapter 13 for more guidance on building your vocabulary.

Finding Compelling Sources of Input

The most important ingredient you need to enhance your L2 learning experience is lots of quality L2 input. As I explain in Chapters 2 and 8, your L2 input must be

>> **Comprehensible:** You need to understand the input you receive. If you don't comprehend what's being communicated, the input isn't appropriate for you.

>> **+ 1:** The input you receive can go just a little beyond your comprehension level, what linguist Stephen Krashen calls *input + 1,* so that you continue advancing your learning. But you should still understand most of the message, and you should need to compensate only a little to guess the meaning of the message.

>> **Compelling:** The content of your L2 input needs to be interesting and pleasing to you. It should be so compelling that you forget you're getting input in your L2.

>> **Communicative and purposeful:** The input needs to have a communicative purpose, and processing it should require you to accomplish a communicative function.

>> **Varied:** The more varied the input is (with regard to its content and the way you receive it), the more opportunities you have to enlarge your vocabulary and become more familiar with new and already-known sounds, meaning, and grammatical structures. This is especially important for intermediate and advanced learners.

>> **Received in a low-anxiety environment:** The best setting in which to transform the L2 input you receive into *intake* (the L2 you understand and retain) is a relaxed and stress-free environment — what Krashen calls having a *low affective filter.*

TIP

One of the best ways to receive comprehensible sources of linguistic input is through reading. A great advantage of reading is that you can read at your own pace. Start with topics that are compelling to you. For example, if you like cooking, pick up L2 books about cooking and food. That way, some content may be familiar to you, and you'll be able to make intelligent guesses and inferences about vocabulary words you don't know. Find out more about accessing compelling input in Chapter 12.

Playing with the Language

Play is commonly linked to development, growth, and learning. Playing with language is no different. Play around with your L2 and be creative with the words you're learning. Imagine situations and act them out in the L2. Think about what you'd need to say to participate in specific L2 conversations, such as how you'd order your lunch. You can do this in your head, say it aloud, or both. I love playing with my L2 when I'm taking my morning walk.

TIP

Using your smart assistant (Siri or Alexa) can be a fun and creative way to play with your L2. You can change your smart assistant's language setting to your L2 and converse with it. Ask Siri/Alexa about the weather, music, sports, food — any random question. Asking questions and receiving responses makes the conversation seem real, and you can continue the exchange by following up on the responses you get.

Interacting and Negotiating Meaning with Others

Two of the elements needed for successful language learning are receiving comprehensible input (as I mention earlier in this chapter) and interacting with others in your L2. Interacting with others helps you determine if the language you're forming (your *interlanguage*) is adequate and understood by your *interlocutors* (other L2 speakers).

When you have miscommunication issues, you need to negotiate meaning with your interlocutors to solve the breakdown in communication. Interacting and negotiating meaning with others gives you an idea of which aspects of your L2 you know and which parts you need to work on.

Developing strategies to negotiate meaning and request comprehensible input will help you advance in your language learning. Likewise, the feedback you receive from your interlocutors is essential to keep your language learning on track. Look up how to say a few sentences that will improve your interactions, such as *Can you speak more slowly, please? Can you repeat that? Can you give me an example, please?* and *How do you spell it?* You may also want to learn a few phrases to check that you're communicating clearly, such as *Do you understand me?*

TIP

Find a tutor and a conversation partner to enhance your language learning experience. They will help you practice your interpersonal communication skills, correct your pronunciation when it interferes with your communication, and answer your questions about the language or culture. In Chapter 14 I give you some suggestions about how to find language partners locally or online.

Taking Risks and Accepting Errors

REMEMBER

You'll make many errors along your L2 learning journey, as you did when you were acquiring your L1. Some of the most common errors you'll produce involve grammar, word choice, and pronunciation. Be brave, take risks, and use the L2 you have at your disposal (your interlanguage) to communicate with other L2 users to the best of your ability.

Accept that you won't know or understand many things as you begin using your L2 to communicate. Keep in mind that errors are part of the learning process. If your errors interfere with your communication, ask your interlocutors to point them out and correct them for you. Don't stress yourself out trying to understand and say everything perfectly because you may stop enjoying the L2 learning experience. Instead, use your interlanguage to guess the meaning and move on.

Building a Learning Plan and Sticking to It

First, you have to find the strong motivating factor that pushes you to learn a language. Once you have that, you need to set a learning plan, create routines, and stick to them. Consider the best time(s) during the day when you can be focused on learning your L2 and go for it!

TIP

You may want to use the SMART method to set your learning plan and goals. Chapter 12 gives you details.

Immersing Yourself in the Language

Immersion forces you to process L2 input quickly and respond consistently in your L2. This repetition and persistent use of the language may end up making you think in your L2.

The best way to immerse yourself in the language is to visit a country where your L2 is spoken. Better yet, living in a country where your L2 is spoken gives you the opportunity to use all your language skills and learn about the L2 culture first-hand. If you cannot travel to another country, try to immerse yourself in your L2 in as many ways as possible in your community. Use the L2 in your daily life to communicate and interact with other L2 users, and find ways to get lots of quality input every day.

Using Good Learning Materials

TIP

Chapters 13 and 14 provide lots of details on selecting L2 learning materials. Here are a few tips to get started:

>> If you can, take L2 classes in which you learn and review vocabulary and grammar in communication (orally and in writing).

>> Try to find a good textbook that focuses on communication and separates chapters by topic. Check that the textbook uses the L2 throughout and contains a glossary with L1 translations and relevant grammatical information. Make sure grammar rules are explained in your L1 so you understand them well enough to apply them when using the L2. But don't stress out about producing grammatically perfect language in the early stages of the learning process. Focus on communicating ideas.

>> Use bilingual and monolingual dictionaries and a thesaurus to help you with synonyms and antonyms.

>> Look for apps that can help you learn your L2. Select only the one(s) that supplement what you're learning and make sure you don't overuse them. Remember that less is more!

>> Make sure you have access to conversation partners or *language exchange partners* (people who can teach you the L2 in exchange for you teaching them your L1). Also, if possible, find a teacher or tutor that can answer your questions about the L2 and its culture.

Celebrating Your Progress

Evaluate your progress and celebrate your accomplishments, even if they're small. Compare what you were able to do with your L2 a few weeks ago to what you can do now. Tracking your progress motivates you and pushes you to continue learning.

REMEMBER

Celebrate your progress and accomplishments by rewarding yourself with things you enjoy. Cheer yourself on!

Chapter **16**

Ten Areas to Master in Your New Language

Every language has a set of key phrases you need to learn to succeed in everyday conversations and basic communicative interactions. In this chapter, I highlight ten situations in which it's helpful to know those phrases or expressions.

TIP

As you read this chapter, look up the key expressions that you'll use in your second language (L2). You may want to start by using some of the tech resources in Chapter 14. Then, ask a proficient L2 user or native L2 speaker to check your findings and confirm if they're correct and appropriate. Fix the expressions as needed and work on learning them. Keep a notebook handy for your questions and notes.

Familiarizing Yourself with Your L2's Culture

Language and culture are interrelated, as I mention throughout this book. To communicate effectively in another language, you need to keep its culture in mind. So, it's important to learn the cultural and social practices and expectations in your L2. Table 16-1 includes some culture-related topics and questions to consider. I encourage you to find this information online and ask your tutors or native L2 speakers to check the accuracy of your findings. Ask them to give you any extra details you need to be aware of.

TABLE 16-1   ## Having Cultural Awareness in Your L2

Areas Affected	Questions to Consider	Your Notes about Your L2 Culture
Grammar/ language structure	Is there a specific linguistic form to be used with people of different ages and status to show politeness? If so, how is it grammatically accomplished?	
Social norms	Is there a way to show respect or politeness to people you interact with, such as shaking hands, bowing, and the like? If so, how is it done? When do you use these social norms?	
Rituals and traditions	What specific phrases do you use during certain festivities or ceremonies? List the most popular festivities in your L2 culture, and add the greeting that accompanies these festivities. For example, how do you say "Happy birthday" in your L2? Is there a song you need to know?	
Cultural taboos	Are there any cultural practices you should avoid or be careful about using (for example, when someone offers you food or gives you a present)? Are there any topics you shouldn't talk about in public (for example, religion, income, politics)?	
Social distance	What's the polite amount of social distance in your L2 culture? Do people stand close together or far apart?	
Gestures	Are there any gestures you need to be careful about using? Are there any common gestures you should be aware of?	
Other ideas	Check out any other cultural questions you may have (such as attitudes toward women or children, clothing that's considered inappropriate, and the like).	

Greeting People and Saying Farewell

Your answers to some of the questions in Table 16-1, such as whether your L2 has respectful linguistic forms for older people, are important to note as you figure out the appropriate ways to greet or say farewell to others. Start with basic greetings and expressions, such as the ones here, and add more specific ones later:

- **»** Hello.

- **»** Good morning/afternoon/night.

- **»** How are you?

- **»** I am okay, thank you, and you?

- **»** Goodbye.

Understanding and Requesting Basic Information

Requesting basic information and responding to requests for basic information are key tasks you'll perform during your first few communicative exchanges. You can start with the ones here and add more questions and answers as you encounter them.

- **»** What is your name?

- **»** How old are you? (Check whether this is a culturally appropriate question to ask.)

- **»** What do you do? (Check whether this is a culturally appropriate question to ask.)

- **»** What time is it?

- **»** What time is breakfast/lunch/dinner served?

Embracing Conversation Starters and Taking Your Turn

Do some research on typical or common topics used as conversation starters in your L2. Then, find how to start those L2 conversations. For example, many English speakers use the weather as a conversation starter, as in *It's cold/hot today, isn't it?*

Likewise, ask some native L2 speakers how to take turns in a conversation and how to best interrupt a conversation if necessary. Know some phrases like *Let me add . . .* and *Give me a minute to add . . . .*

Knowing Numbers and Letters

TIP

As you may expect, you'll need to use letters and numbers in your L2 in different situations. For example, if you don't understand a certain word someone says while they're speaking, you can ask them to spell it to help you recognize it or look it up in a dictionary. Likewise, if someone doesn't understand what you're trying to say, you can spell it for them. Numbers are key to know when you're shopping, giving someone your cell phone number, asking for directions, and the like.

Thanking People and Saying "You're Welcome"

Make sure you learn very early on how to thank people in your L2. Also, you should be aware of any body language or gestures that are part of thanking people.

Likewise, make sure you learn how to say "You're welcome" to L2 speakers, and find out any cultural practices linked to this language interaction. Reacting appropriately in a thanking situation may demonstrate politeness.

Using Your Manners in a Restaurant

Most likely, if you travel to a country where your L2 is spoken, you'll end up eating at a restaurant. If so, it's very important to know how to order food, the name of your favorite meals or foods, and how to make special requests (for example, related to allergies). You'll also need to know how tips work in that country.

Some basic phrases to ask for what you want at a restaurant and understand what you're being asked include the following:

>> What would you like to eat/drink?

- I would like to eat/drink _____.

- I cannot eat _____. Do you have any meals without _____?

>> Can you bring me the check, please?

>> I am allergic to _____.

>> Where is the restroom?

Saying You're Sorry and Other Niceties

Apologizing in the L2 may involve more than just saying you're sorry. Make sure you research how native L2 speakers apologize, including any cultural practices you may need to be aware of.

In addition, consider the different L2 situations you'll encounter and the need to use niceties such as "Excuse me" and "Pardon." Ask native L2 speakers about the best way to address these situations, or do some online research. For example, what would you need to say in your L2 when you want to get someone's attention, when you're about to enter someone's office, when you bump into someone by accident, and the like.

Discussing Public Transportation and Places

If you travel to a country where your L2 is spoken, you'll probably need to use public transportation. So, look up L2 words for various types of transportation you may use and places you may visit, as well as any other travel-related information that's important for you. Here are some phrases you may need to know:

>> How can I go to _____?

>> Where is the/a _____?

>> Where can I pick up _____?

TIP

Review some words and phrases used for giving directions (*next to, to the right, to the left, straight ahead, north, south, east, west,* and so on) so the answers you get make sense to you.

Asking for Help in an Emergency

REMEMBER

Don't underestimate the importance of alerting someone that you have an emergency or understanding when others have an emergency. The ability to express or understand the need for help can be critical in a life-threatening situation. Here are some expressions you should know in your L2:

>> Help!

>> Be careful!

>> Look to your right/left!

>> Stop!

>> Attention!

>> Watch out!

>> Get out!

>> Come in!

>> Quickly!

>> Call an ambulance, please!

Index

C

caregiver speech, 136
Carroll, John B. (researcher), 45, 46
cartoons, 136
category procedure, 162
ceremonial formulas, 218
Character.AI, 239
ChatGPT, 237, 240, 241, 245
Cheat Sheet, 3
chemical-olfactory mode, 16
child-directed speech, 136
Chomsky. Noam (linguist), 32, 86, 89, 103, 109
City Walks Live (website), 243
clarification request, 140
closure-oriented learner, 53–54, 204
Clozemaster (website), 241
code, 13–14
code-mixing, 85
code-switching, 85
Coffee Break Languages (podcast), 236
cognates, 188, 226–227
Cognitive Ability for Novelty in Acquisition of Language-Foreign test (CANAL-F), 46
cognitive control, 65–66
cognitive decline, delay in, 68–69
cognitive knowledge, 89
cognitive/mental flexibility, 68
collocation, 156
Common European Framework of Reference for Languages (CEFR), 56, 128
communication
  categories, 12–13
  curricular plans and, 127
  defined, 12
  design features. See design features
  interpersonal, 13

interpretive, 12
one-way, 12
origin for the word, 13
overview, 11–12
presentational, 13
problems, 216
standards, 127
two-way, 12
communication chain
  code, 13–14
  context, 14–15
  feedback, 14–15
  interlocutors, 13
  medium, 14
  message, 13
communication skills, 69
communicative approach, 116, 120–125
communicative competence, 31–33, 89
communities, 128
community language, 26–27
comparative charts, 172
comparisons, 127
compensatory strategies, 177–178
competence, communicative, 31–33, 89
compound bilinguals, 29–30, 95
comprehensible input, 110, 112, 132, 133
comprehensible output hypothesis, 38
comprehension, 78–79
comprehension check, 140
conative function, 19
confidence, 49
confirmation feedback, 140
connections, 127
consistency, in language learning, 9–10, 48, 200
content-based instruction, 123–124
content words, 36

context clues, 156
contexts
  defined, 14–15
  instructional settings, 148–150
  naturalistic settings, 147–148
  paying attention to, 173–174
contextualized setting, 173
continuum, 31
contrastive analysis hypothesis (CAH), 47, 108
Converifi (website), 239
conversational formulas, 198–199
conversation starters, 257–258
co-occurrence of features, 34
coordinate bilinguals, 29–30
Cope, Joann, 44
Copilot, 237
core vocabulary, 212
correction, 140
covering strategies, 177–178
Cram (website), 241
creativity, 48, 63
critical period hypothesis (CPH), 40, 96, 104–105
cultural events, 189
cultural perspective, 71
cultural transmission, 17
culture, 127, 242–243, 255–256
Cummins, Jim (researcher/professor), 62
curricular plans, 126–127

D

daily life, language learning in, 9–10
decision-making, 63
deductive learner, 46, 53, 204
Defense Language Aptitude Battery (DLAB), 46
DeKeyser, Robert (researcher), 83
dementia, 68

grammar-transition method, 117–118

greetings, 215–216, 256–257

H

habit formation, 108–109

HelloTalk (website), 238

heritage language, 26–27

HiNative (website), 244

historical linguistics, 23

Hockett, Charles (linguist), 15

home language, 26–27

Horwitz, Elaine, 44

Horwitz, Michael, 44

human communication systems, 17–18

I

Idyoma (website), 238

iFake TextMessage, 239

iKnow! (website), 241

imitation, 108–109

Immerse (website), 239

ImmerseMe (website), 239

immersion, 253

imperatives, 19

implicit feedback, 140

incidental vocabulary learning, 173–174

inclusion, 1

independence, 48

inductive learner, 46, 53, 204

inflections, 17

inhibitory control, 67

initial state, 86

innatism. *See also* L1 acquisition

acquisition-learning hypothesis, 110

affective filter hypothesis, 112

Chomsky's approach, 103–104, 109

comprehensible input hypothesis, 112

critical period hypothesis, 104–105

monitor hypothesis, 111

natural order hypothesis, 111–112

input. *See also* output

aural, sources of, 189

comprehensible, 110, 112, 132, 133

defined, 1, 26, 35, 132

in developing language system, 134–135

differences, 103

early L2 learning, 99–100

frequency of, 134–135

innate language abilities and, 35–37

interlanguage and, 35

L2 learning in instructional settings, 149

L2 learning in naturalistic settings, 148

in language acquisition, 35

in language learning, 39

modified, 136–137

optimal, 133–134

quality linguistic data as, 35

sources of, 135–136, 250–251

written, sources of, 189

instructional settings, 148–150

instrumental motivation, 42, 185–186

intake, 46

integrative motivation, 42, 184–185

intelligences, 49–51

interaction hypothesis, 37

interactionism, 106–107, 113–114

interactions

feedback, 138–142

L2, 175–179

language learning and, 37

learning plan and, 208–209

role of, 138–141

interchangeability, 16

intercultural competence, 70–71, 127

interference, 47, 87

interlanguage, 35, 47, 55, 85, 87, 145, 175, 252

interlocutors, 13, 108, 134, 148, 149

intermediate state, 86–87

interpersonal communication, 13

interpersonal intelligence, 51

interpretation, 64

interpretive communication, 12

intonation, 93

intrapersonal intelligence, 51

intrinsic motivation, 184

introverted learner, 54, 205

intuitive/random (nonlinear) learner, 53, 204

italki (website), 239, 244

J

jargon, 88

K

keyword technique, 170–171, 224–225

kinesthetic/tactile learners, 52, 204

Krashen, Stephen (linguist), 44, 78, 84, 109, 111

L

L1 acquisition. *See also* L2 learning

bilingual, 98

characteristics of, 90–92

Reddit (website), 238
reference books/
    materials, 188, 226
referential function, 18
reflexive function, 19
reflexivity, 18
rehearsal, 170–171
relaxation, 10
repetition, 141, 170–171, 227
repetitive encounters,
    176–177
resourcefulness, 48–49
resources, 10, 236–237
restaurant terms, 217, 258–259
resultative motivation, 43
rhymes, 227–228
Rocket Languages (website), 234
romanization, 153
Rosetta Stone (website), 234
routine, setting, 196–198
Royal Spanish Academy
    (website), 244

S

Sapon, Stanley, 46
schemata, 172
Schmidt, Richard (linguist), 138
Scholastic Aptitude
    Test (SAT), 61
second language, 26, 95, 97, 144
second language acquisition. See
    L2 learning
selective attention, 68
self-correction, 111
self-identity, 8
Selinker, Larry (linguist), 45, 145
semanticity, 16
semantic map, 171, 172, 223
semantics, 22, 94
semantic webs, 221
sensitive period, 40, 96, 105

sensory preferences, 52
sequential (linear)
    learner, 53, 204
sign language, 16
silent period, 89, 91, 121
Simple Mind (website), 240
simplified S-procedure, 162
simultaneous bilinguals, 28
situational formulas, 218
Skinner, B. F., 103
slow-mapping, 207, 213, 225
SMART goals, 192
sociability, 49
social events, 189
social-interactive strategies, 175
sociocultural competence, 32
socio-educational model, 42
socio-emotional
    connection, 71–72
sociolinguistics, 23
spaced repetition, 233, 234
spatial displacement, 17
speaking skills, L2, 162–166
Speaky (website), 238
speech-emergence stage, 79
spoken language, types of, 161
Spotify (website), 236
S procedure, 162
standards. See also
    proficiency levels
    curricular plans and, 126–127
    in Europe, 128
    in the United States, 127–128
strategic competence, 32
stress, 93
stylistic formulas, 218
subordinate bilinguals, 30–31
subordinate clause
    procedure, 162
summaries, 155
Swain, Merrill (linguist), 38, 143

Symbaloo (website), 231
syntax, 21–22, 41, 47, 62, 94

T

tabula rasa, 102
tactile/kinesthetic
    learners, 52, 204
talkabroad.com (website), 189
Tandem (website), 239
task-based learning, 123–124
task-initiation, 64
TasteAtlas (website), 242
teacher talk, 136
teaching methods
    audiolingual method, 119–120
    content-based
        instruction, 123–124
    direct method, 118–119
    grammar-transition
        method, 117–118
    natural approach, 122–123
    overview, 116
    task-based learning,
        123–124
    total physical
        response, 121–122
technology
    artificial intelligence, 239
    audio and video
        samples, 235–236
    benefits of, 232
    books/audiobooks/reading
        resources, 236–237
    choosing, 232–233
    conversation and
        language exchange
        partners, 238–239
    dictionaries, 244
    interaction with L2
        culture, 242–243
    online in-person
        speakers, 237–238

About the Author

Dr. María José Cabrera-Puche earned her PhD in second language acquisition and bilingualism from Rutgers, the State University of New Jersey. Cabrera-Puche is a professor of Spanish, linguistics, and language teaching methods at West Chester University of Pennsylvania (WCU). She coauthored the three existing editions of *Tu mundo*, a Spanish language learning program, and is currently working on its 2026 release. She also coedited *Romance Linguistics 2006: Selected papers from the 36th Linguistic Symposium on Romance Languages (LSRL)*. She has published several articles and book chapters about language learning, language assessment, and the use of technology in the language learning process.

Her background and experience in language learning have been very valuable in her coordination of all lower-level Spanish courses at WCU for more than 15 years, and her preparation of future language teachers. Her love for assessment and assessment practices has also been essential in her role as assessment coordinator in her department for more than a decade, and director of the general education program at her university. Moreover, she is a certified ACTFL ILR OPI tester and assesses the Spanish language proficiency of anyone taking that oral test.

Dedication

To my beloved, supporting, understanding, and encouraging family, Ricardo, Sofía, and Marina, for cheering me up always.

To my mom and late dad (you are always with me) and to my siblings, Pedro and Carmen, for your constant presence and love.

And to my admired *hermanita hormiguita*, Magdalena, for always being there, taking care of me, and teaching me.

Author's Acknowledgments

This book is inspired by those who have experienced or are willing to experience what learning a new language really means, entails, and feels like. I am particularly indebted to all my language students throughout my 25 years of teaching Spanish as a second language, as a foreign language, and as a heritage language and, of course, to my bilingual daughters. Observing their language learning process and progress in action has been enlightening and encouraging for me as a language instructor, researcher, and author, and as a language learner myself.

Publisher's Acknowledgments

Senior Acquisitions Editor: Jennifer Yee

Managing Editor: Murari Mukundan

Development Editor: Georgette Beatty

Copy Editor: Kelly Brillhart

Technical Editor: Magdalena Andrade

Production Editor: Tamilmani Varadharaj

Cover Image: © oneinchpunch/Shutterstock

Take dummies with you everywhere you go!

Whether you are excited about e-books, want more from the web, must have your mobile apps, or are swept up in social media, dummies makes everything easier.

Find us online!

dummies.com

Leverage the power

Dummies is the global leader in the reference category and one of the most trusted and highly regarded brands in the world. No longer just focused on books, customers now have access to the dummies content they need in the format they want. Together we'll craft a solution that engages your customers, stands out from the competition, and helps you meet your goals.

Advertising & Sponsorships

Connect with an engaged audience on a powerful multimedia site, and position your message alongside expert how-to content. Dummies.com is a one-stop shop for free, online information and know-how curated by a team of experts.

- Targeted ads
- Video
- Email Marketing

- Microsites
- Sweepstakes sponsorship

20 **MILLION**
PAGE VIEWS
EVERY SINGLE MONTH

15
MILLION
UNIQUE
VISITORS PER MONTH

43%
OF ALL VISITORS
ACCESS THE SITE
VIA THEIR MOBILE DEVICES

700,000 NEWSLETTER
SUBSCRIPTIONS
TO THE INBOXES OF
300,000 UNIQUE INDIVIDUALS
EVERY WEEK

# of dummies

Custom Publishing

Reach a global audience in any language by creating a solution that will differentiate you from competitors, amplify your message, and encourage customers to make a buying decision.

- Apps
- Books
- eBooks
- Video
- Audio
- Webinars

Brand Licensing & Content

Leverage the strength of the world's most popular reference brand to reach new audiences and channels of distribution.

For more information, visit dummies.com/biz

PERSONAL ENRICHMENT

9781119187790
USA $26.00
CAN $31.99
UK £19.99

9781119179030
USA $21.99
CAN $25.99
UK £16.99

9781119293354
USA $24.99
CAN $29.99
UK £17.99

9781119293347
USA $22.99
CAN $27.99
UK £16.99

9781119310068
USA $22.99
CAN $27.99
UK £16.99

9781119235606
USA $24.99
CAN $29.99
UK £17.99

9781119251163
USA $24.99
CAN $29.99
UK £17.99

9781119235491
USA $26.99
CAN $31.99
UK £19.99

9781119279952
USA $24.99
CAN $29.99
UK £17.99

9781119283133
USA $24.99
CAN $29.99
UK £17.99

9781119287117
USA $24.99
CAN $29.99
UK £16.99

9781119130246
USA $22.99
CAN $27.99
UK £16.99

PROFESSIONAL DEVELOPMENT

9781119311041
USA $24.99
CAN $29.99
UK £17.99

9781119255796
USA $39.99
CAN $47.99
UK £27.99

9781119293439
USA $26.99
CAN $31.99
UK £19.99

9781119281467
USA $26.99
CAN $31.99
UK £19.99

9781119280651
USA $29.99
CAN $35.99
UK £21.99

9781119251132
USA $24.99
CAN $29.99
UK £17.99

9781119310563
USA $34.00
CAN $41.99
UK £24.99

9781119181705
USA $29.99
CAN $35.99
UK £21.99

9781119263593
USA $26.99
CAN $31.99
UK £19.99

9781119257769
USA $29.99
CAN $35.99
UK £21.99

9781119293477
USA $26.99
CAN $31.99
UK £19.99

9781119265313
USA $24.99
CAN $29.99
UK £17.99

9781119239314
USA $29.99
CAN $35.99
UK £21.99

9781119293323
USA $29.99
CAN $35.99
UK £21.99

dummies.com